THE ETHICS OF REFUGEE POLICY

Ethics and Global Politics

Series Editors: Tom Lansford and Patrick Hayden

Since the end of the Cold War, explorations of ethical considerations within global politics and on the development of foreign policy have assumed a growing importance in the fields of politics and international studies. New theories, policies, institutions, and actors are called for to address difficult normative questions arising from the conduct of international affairs in a rapidly changing world. This series provides an exciting new forum for creative research that engages both the theory and practice of contemporary world politics, in light of the challenges and dilemmas of the evolving international order.

Also in the series

Cosmopolitan Global Politics
Patrick Hayden
ISBN 0 7546 4276 3

Understanding Human Rights Violations
New Systematic Studies
Edited by Sabine C. Carey and Steven C. Poe
ISBN 0 7546 4026 4

International Environmental Justice
A North-South Dimension
Ruchi Anand
0 7546 3824 3

In War We Trust
The Bush Doctrine and the Pursuit of Just War
Chris J. Dolan
0 7546 4234 8

Edinburgh University Library

Books may be recalled for return earlier than due date;
if so you will be contacted by e-mail or letter.

Due Date	Due Date	Due Date

The Ethics of Refugee Policy

CHRISTINA BOSWELL
*Migration Research Group, Hamburg Institute of International Economics,
Germany*

ASHGATE

Published by
Ashgate Publishing Limited
Gower House
Croft Road
Aldershot
Hampshire GU11 3HR
England

Ashgate Publishing Company
Suite 420
101 Cherry Street
Burlington, VT 05401-4405
USA

Ashgate website: http://www.ashgate.com

British Library Cataloguing in Publication Data
Boswell, Christina
    The ethics of refugee policy. - (Ethics and global
    politics)
    1.Refugees - Government policy - Moral and ethical aspects
    2.Refugees - Legal status, laws, etc. 3.Liberalism
    I.Title
    325.2'1

Library of Congress Cataloging-in-Publication Data
Boswell, Christina.
    The ethics of refugee policy / by Christina Boswell.
        p. cm. -- (Ethics and global politics)
    Includes bibliographical references and index.
    ISBN 0-7546-4519-3
    1. Refugees--Government policy--Moral and ethical aspects.
I. Title. II. Series.
HV640.B65 2005
174'.936287--dc22

2005021091

ISBN-10: 0 7546 4519 3

Printed and bound in Great Britain by MPG Books Ltd, Bodmin, Cornwall

Contents

Preface

This book brings together two deep interests of mine: political philosophy and refugee policy. The two interests were nurtured in rather different settings. My engagement with political philosophy began as an undergraduate in the early 1990s, and had much to do with the stimulating teaching of Adam Swift and Alan Montefiore at Balliol College, Oxford. Later at the London School of Economics and Political Science (LSE) John Charvet, Erika Benner, Chris Brown, and members of the International Political Theory seminar provided an excellent environment for developing and refining my ideas on liberalism and international relations. I also benefited from feedback from my undergraduate students at LSE, especially in the courses on human rights and international political theory.

The interest in refugee issues emerged during the three intervening years between Oxford and LSE, when I worked on the refugee 'policy scene'. I was very lucky to have the opportunity to work with Denis De Jong at the European Commission, and Maria Siemens, Jeff Crisp, Rachel Reilly, Elizabeth Tan, Asmita Naik and Eric Morris in Geneva. Particularly formative was my year as consultant at the Policy Research Unit at the United Nations High Commission for Refugees (UNHCR), where we had many a lively debate on refugee protection. Indeed, it was the ongoing debate between the 'orthodox' guardians of refugee law and the more 'pragmatist' supporters of the direction espoused by the then High Commissioner, Sadako Ogata, that provided the backdrop for the issues discussed in this book. Probably the deepest impression, though, was left by my eight months working with Rwandan refugees for the UNHCR in Burundi – in many ways an unsettling experience, and one that deeply influenced my thinking on a range of political and ethical issues.

The book itself is based on research carried out at LSE between 1997-2000, in the International Relations Department. Over this period, James Mayall was very supportive of my work, indeed he initially encouraged me to move back from policy research to academia, a step I certainly do not regret making. I owe a special debt to John Charvet, who was a constant source of constructive criticism and ideas – indeed the content of the book should attest to his influence. Chris Brown and Andrew Linklater raised some important questions about the line of argument, which I have sought to address in this book. Other important input came from the late Myron Weiner, B.S. Chimni, Gil Loescher and Brian Barry who offered advice and encouragement in the initial stages of the project; and Maria Lensù, Christian Heine, Alex Colàs, Erika Benner, Jacob Nell, Raj Patel and Jill Boswell, all of whom commented on individual chapters.

Some of the themes dealt with have been rewritten or supplemented, based on research I have subsequently carried out for the Royal Institute of International Affairs, and at the Migration Research Group in Hamburg. For this, I would like to thank the Le Poer Trust and the European Union Sixth Framework Programme

Excellent Grant which helped fund this work. I also owe a debt of gratitude to Thomas Straubhaar, whose institute in Hamburg has provided me with an excellent environment for research. Thanks also to the series editor Tom Lansford, to the anonymous reviewer, and to the editorial team at Ashgate, who did a very professional job.

Finally, both of my parents influenced many of the ideas in this book, albeit in very different and often indirect ways. And Tilman Plehn finally shook me into action to get the work published.

Needless to say, the usual caveat about responsibility for mistakes applies.

Introduction

Since the revival of liberal political philosophy in the 1970s, liberalism has been the target of attack from a range of critics. Communitarians, post-modernists and critical theorists have all taken a swipe at liberalism's assumptions about the self, society and ethics, as well as its supposed 'neutrality' between different conceptions of the good. Many liberal theorists have responded astutely to this critique, acknowledging the historical contingency of liberalism, and re-grounding liberal theory on a 'non-metaphysical' basis.[1]

Yet one set of problems in liberal theory has remained relatively neglected: the question of the practical feasibility of liberal theories of ethics. The problem can be simply stated as follows. If we were to apply the demands of most liberal political theories consistently, they would generate extensive ethical obligations to others. Liberal theories of rights, justice or humanitarianism tend to call for quite far-reaching duties with often radically redistributive implications. And, since liberalism typically has little to say about the ethical relevance of communities or nation-states, it has difficulties justifying the restriction of such obligations to particular groups of people. Liberal theory is in a weak position when it comes to delimiting the scope of justice, rights or humanitarian duties to the national sphere. But once such rights or concepts of justice are applied to international questions of human rights, distributive justice or humanitarian assistance, then liberal theory faces a serious problem of feasibility.

The problem of feasibility appears to take its most acute form in the case of refugee rights. No other issue so sharply crystallises the problem of how to motivate consistent application of liberal ethics, in a context in which the performance of liberal duties appears to enter into direct conflict with individual or collective interests. The refugee issue therefore provides an excellent lens through which to explore the plausibility of liberalism's assumptions about the scope of justice. Indeed, a closer examination of the implications of liberal theory for refugee policy unearths more fundamental problems in liberal assumptions about the nature of ethical agency. A central goal of this book is to explore the nature and implications of this tension in liberal thought.

However, the book is also concerned with a second, more practical, question. When applied to the problem of refugee policy, liberal theories run the risk of over-reaching themselves. They set up expectations about individual and collective ethical agency that cannot be redeemed, at least not under the economic and political conditions prevailing in liberal democratic societies. In this way, liberal thought runs the risk of marginalising itself in policy debates about asylum and refugee protection. By setting up unrealistic and uncompromising expectations about ethical behaviour, it risks relegating itself to the margins of public debate in liberal democratic states. Indeed, the contention of this book is that we need a radical rethink of liberal ethics in order to construct a more ethically feasibly, and descriptively plausible, account of duties to refugees. In this sense, the book can be seen as both a critique of liberal political thought; and an attempt to develop an alternative ethical underpinning of duties to refugees.

The main part of the book is devoted to a detailed examination of different strands in liberal thought, especially right-based theories and the social contract tradition. While the starting-point of the discussion is the question of refugee protection, this critique of liberal universalism has wider resonance for liberal ethics, and especially for a range of issues of international justice: not just the ethics of asylum and refugee policy, but also questions of human rights, international distributive justice, humanitarian assistance and international intervention. It also has implications more generally for liberal theory's conception of moral agency and motivation.

However, the prescriptive focus of the book remains the question of what duties liberal democracies and their citizens owe to refugees who seek protection on their territory. This is for two reasons. First, as already suggested, the issue of refugee protection reveals the tensions of liberal theory in a particularly stark way. Evaluating liberal theories according to their ability to address the problem of refugee protection therefore focuses the discussion in a useful way. Second, the focus on refugee rights is also interesting from a more practical perspective. Debates on asylum and refugee protection have been prominent in European countries for more than a decade, and the political importance of the issue shows no signs of receding. It is therefore timely to analyse some of the sources of confusion in the debate on refugee policy, through the lens of political theory conceptions of refugee rights.

The Crisis in International Refugee Policy

Commitment to refugee protection in Europe has been severely put to the test over the past two decades. Large numbers of people continue to seek protection in western Europe, but these countries have displayed an increasing reluctance to host asylum seekers and refugees. Since 1990, the annual number of asylum applicants to the fifteen European Union states has averaged at around 300,000–400,000.[2] Many more are assumed to be residing illegally in European states, without lodging an application for asylum. And this is just a fraction of the roughly 17 million people displaced worldwide. Indeed, the only reason the number of people seeking protection in Europe is not substantially higher is because European countries have made it increasingly difficult for refugees to reach their territory and lodge an application. Since the late 1980s, European governments and their populations have pushed for more stringent measures to restrict numbers of asylum seekers and refugees, measures which have kept down the number of refugees entering and staying in Europe.

Most commentators characterise the crisis as a conflict between refugee rights and national interests, especially in cases of largescale refugee influx. Assisting large numbers of refugees and asylum seekers is considered to impose a financial, social and political burden on receiving states, running directly counter to their national interest. Financial costs include the administrative expense of processing claims, and the costs of social and welfare assistance for non-economically active asylum seekers or refugees and their families. The presence of large numbers of refugees in host countries is also frequently perceived as imposing social costs, through over-burdening accommodation, schooling or health facilities, or generating tensions between newcomers and resident host populations. Since 11th September 2001, there have also been growing concerns about the possible security impact of immigration and refugee flows.

These problems are compounded by concerns about the state's incapacity to control unwanted flows. The rise in irregular migration and labour, and especially more nefarious forms of migrant smuggling and trafficking, have exacerbated fears about a loss of state control over the entry and stay of asylum seekers and immigrants. Moreover, fears that 'non-genuine' asylum seekers are abusing generous refugee and welfare systems have done much to erode public sympathy for refugees. Under these conditions, where governments or political parties are perceived to be lax in their efforts to restrict asylum, they are likely to pay an electoral penalty. Taking these points together, it becomes less surprising that states have adopted what the United Nations Refugee Agency (UNHCR) has coined an 'exclusionary attitude' towards refugees.[3]

Concerns about the costs of asylum in host countries have led a number of states and commentators to cast doubt on the continued relevance of international legal provisions for protecting the rights of refugees. These provisions oblige states to respect a range of rights and standards for asylum seekers and those with refugee status. The centre-piece of these provisions is the 1951 Geneva Convention on the Status of Refugees. Article 33 of the Convention obliges states not to expel or 'refouler' a refugee 'where his life or freedom would be threatened'. Article 1A defines a refugee as a person who has left his or her country of origin 'owing to a well-founded fear of being persecuted for reasons of race, religion, nationality, membership of a particular social group or political opinion'. The Convention was initially intended to cover European refugees, but in 1967 a special Protocol extended its geographical scope to cover refugees from all over the world.[4] Most liberal states have incorporated these or similar provisions into their constitutions or legislation.[5]

Yet these standards have been steadily eroded since the late 1970s. While most liberal democratic states have retained nominal support for the principles of refugee protection, they have introduced a range of measures to limit the substance and scope of these commitments. These restrictive measures have typically taken three main forms. The first is to limit access to their territory, through imposing visa requirements on the nationals of certain countries, and introducing sanctions for companies or individuals found to be transporting people without the required travel documents. Another practice to limit access to asylum systems has been to send asylum seekers back to what are defined as the 'safe' countries through which they travelled, or from where they originate. A second set of measures has involved deterring potential asylum seekers from travelling to European countries or from applying for asylum, through rendering conditions of stay less attractive. Such measures include cutting welfare benefits, replacing financial support with assistance in kind, or dispersing asylum seekers to different locations. Third, host countries have made it more difficult for asylum seekers to qualify as refugees. One way in of doing this has been to introduce streamlined or accelerated procedures, which tend to be less thorough, or imply limited access to legal assistance or rights of appeal. A second way has been to introduce alternative protection statuses which accord less generous rights, such as 'temporary protection', which encourages subsequent return to the country of origin, rather than integration into the host country. European countries have also narrowed down the criteria qualifying applicants to be recognised as refugees. These measures all have serious implications for refugees seeking protection in Europe: even where they can get access to the territory of these countries and file an application for asylum, refugees are likely to have to put up with harsh living conditions, and – more seriously – very slim prospects for having their case recognised.

Most of those defending refugees and asylum seekers against these restrictionist policies invoke liberal universalist arguments to defend refugee rights. Liberal universalist theories are those that give equal moral weight to the welfare of all individuals, regardless of nationality. Liberal universalism provides an accessible and cogent grounding for theories of duties to non-nationals, and its assumptions about the moral equality of human beings deeply pervade moral and political discourse in liberal democratic societies. It is not surprising, then, that liberal universalist theories have a virtual monopoly on arguments for admitting greater numbers of refugees, and more generally for recognising moral duties beyond borders. Yet despite this apparent facility for justifying refugee rights, this book argues that these theories are ill-equipped to provide an account of the relationship between duties to refugees and duties to fellow nationals. Liberal universalist theories have problems accounting for the significance of membership in particular states or communities. Starting from a premise of the moral equality of all individuals, pure liberal universalism denies the moral relevance of nationality and other characteristics that are not universally shared. And unless liberal theorists can find practical or instrumental arguments for diluting this universal commitment (which many of them attempt to do), they proceed to derive theories of duties to refugees that seem hopelessly unfeasible. Consistent liberal universalist theories produce normative prescriptions that are at best utopian, at worst counter-productive to their own ends. The liberal universalist claim about the moral equality of refugees and nationals of receiving states produces practical norms that seem increasingly out of touch with the current debate on asylum policies in liberal democracies.

The patent unfeasibility of these theories generates a risk that liberal universalist arguments will come to be seen as irrelevant to the refugee policy debate. By advancing such stringent conceptions of duties, liberal universalism may be effectively relegating itself to the margins of political discussion. Such accounts can be too readily dismissed as naive or utopian. And this lack of a robust conceptual basis makes liberal universalist theories more vulnerable to attack from crude forms of nationalism, realism, communitarianism or moral relativism. To be sure, this is not the main reason for the demise of more liberal approaches. Yet the conceptual poverty and unfeasibility of liberal universalism appears to be contributing to the marginalisation of more liberal positions in debates on refugee policy.

The dangers inherent in this tendency are clear: if liberal universalism is seen as irrelevant, there is no alternative political theory that could provide anything like a substitute in terms of the breadth and persistence of its appeal. The marginalisation of liberal universalist arguments would leave the field clear for the defenders of 'national interest', or crude forms of communitarianism. Indeed, this tendency is already discernible in political theory discussions. One response to the inadequacies of liberal universalist theory has been to retreat from any commitment to the moral equality of all human beings, limiting the scope of ethical duties to separate communities or states. Crude forms of communitarian or particularist theories reject both the universalist premises of liberal theories, and their substantive prescriptions about duties to non-nationals.

The aim of the book is not, however, to reject the liberal approach. Rather, it recognises the ethical force of arguments about duties to protect refugees. Thus while I am deeply critical of the liberal universalist failure to recognise the importance of community, it is not my intention to abandon notions of refugee rights. I am broadly sympathetic to the liberal universalist normative agenda of promoting refugee protection in liberal democracies. And I assume that most of those socialised in liberal democratic societies will share some affinity with the liberal universalist inspired grounding of refugee protection (even if they simultaneously acknowledge the ethical significance of community ties or the importance of national interests). Indeed, it is precisely because of this acknowledgement of the ethical force of the commitment to refugee protection that I am keen to salvage liberal universalist prescriptions from their more extreme nationalist and communitarian critics. But I believe that the best hope for rescuing liberal universalism is to significantly modify a number of its underlying assumptions.

The main thrust of the argument is that the short-comings of liberal universalism can be traced to its assumptions about moral agency and motivation. Liberal universalist theories are unable coherently to combine a commitment to the rights of refugees with a recognition of the special importance of ties to local communities. They impose seemingly inordinate ethical demands, claims which are patently unfeasible in the current international context. Moreover, their notion of moral agency as requiring abstraction from self-interest creates a theory of motivation that offers limited practical potential for mobilising commitment to universal rights. Thus rather than targeting the liberal universalist commitment to the concept of universal duties, the book challenges its assumptions about the role of particular ties, interests and values in moral agency. In other words, it does not aim to reject the substance of what these theories prescribe, but rather the grounds on which they prescribe them. The task is to reground liberal norms in a more plausible account of moral agency and motivation.

The critique of liberal concepts of moral motivation and agency is not new. Many theorists have challenged liberal assumptions about the self as somehow able to detach herself from her social context and autonomously choose her own interests and goals; or the moral agent as rationally deliberating on practical action, abstracted from her particular ties and values.[6] Indeed, this was a major strand of the communitarian critique of liberalism that emerged from the late 1970s onwards, largely in response to the popularity of John Rawls' liberal theory of justice. However, few accounts have spelled out how the alternative communitarian account of the self can be combined with a commitment to liberal values. This is a central goal of the book: to fundamentally revise liberal universalist assumptions about moral agency, whilst promoting the normative goal of recognising duties to refugees.

Why a Critique of Liberal Theory?

On first consideration, it may seem somewhat counter-intuitive to attack liberal universalist theories as being in some sense responsible for the current crisis in refugee protection. A more obvious way of defining the problem would be to see it as a conflict between a set of ethical principles and the self-interest of states. Why should we begin to cast doubt on universalist ethical values, just because governments and their electorates appear to be too selfish to respect commitments to refugee protection?

Here it is useful to take a look at the state of the policy debate on refugee issues. The debate on refugee protection has become polarised around two apparently incompatible perspectives. On the one hand, advocates of human rights and refugee protection berate states for restrictive measures and a failure to respect the standards for refugee protection defined in international law. These critics of state practice invoke international refugee law as the ethical standard for evaluating refugee policy, basing their normative prescriptions on universalist theories of individual rights.[7] On the other hand, states tend to draw on notions of national interest to justify restriction. They claim that national economic, strategic and social goals take precedence over duties to refugees. Defence of the national prerogative to restrict refugee influx may be couched in pragmatic, *realpolitik* language, or be defended in terms of the ethical relevance of national ties.

The apparent incompatibility of these two perspectives – the nationalist and the universalist – would suggest that there is a conflict or trade-off between these two sets of interests. Indeed, most academics, human rights lobbyists, government and United Nations (UN) officials share a similar characterisation of the basic problem: a conflict between the rights of refugees and national interests in situations of mass influx.[8] This notion of a conflict assumes that the two sets of considerations are shaped independently of one another. National interests reflect exclusively self-interested domestic concerns, and are shaped by interests and beliefs quite separate from those that define ethical duties. On this account, any coincidence between ethical duty and national interest is contingent on economic and political circumstances. The two sets of considerations may converge in certain periods, as indeed they did in the post-war decades, when the need for additional labour encouraged a more generous stance towards both refugees and economic immigrants. But the current configuration of socio-economic conditions in most industrialised states, so it is argued, has generated a clear conflict between national interests and refugee rights.

It should not be any great surprise that the trade-off characterisation is favoured by those keen to restrict refugee influx. Defence of the national interest is a highly effective strategy for mobilising political support. By extension, those who seek to prioritise refugee rights over the nationalist interest can be labelled as politically naïve, unpatriotic or idealistic. The combination of *realpolitik* and patriotic loyalty is politically extremely effective – so that even where there is no vital political or economic interest at stake, the term can be invoked to cover a broad set of moral and pragmatic arguments. It is partly its lack of clear definition that makes it an effective political tool. Where duties to non-nationals are characterised as in conflict with the national interest, there is a cluster of ill-defined but intuitively persuasive arguments to limit the number of refugees recognised.

Given the political uses of this term, it is all the more surprising that many proponents of universal rights have tended to embrace a similar conception of the relationship between universal duties and national interests. They too share the notion that the 'ethical' stance is in conflict with national interests, but they castigate the national interest as selfish and unethical. Any deviation from the requirements of universal rights reflects the self-serving and power-seeking nature of states. On many universal rights accounts, there is an implicit suspicion about the motives of states, and an idea that political objectives are somehow impure and constraining of humanitarian and human rights goals.[9] But while rejecting the legitimacy of pursuing the national interest over ethical duty, they nonetheless accept the assumed dichotomy between the two.

Now it is certainly not my intention to undermine the aspiration of refugee rights activists to encourage a more generous refugee policy. Indeed, as I have already noted, one of the central aims of the thesis is to find a framework that can do justice to commonly held notions about the ethical force of refugee rights. Nor do I want to question here whether there is a moral case to be made for prioritising the 'national interest' over duties to non-nationals in any given situation. My aim is rather to question whether it is both descriptively accurate, and politically expedient, for proponents of refugee rights to accept a sharp distinction between ethical concerns and national interests. In other words, is it an adequate characterisation of the relationship between the interests of compatriots, and duties to non-nationals? And, if not, is there an alternative way of conceptualising this relationship, that avoids the descriptive and practical shortcomings of this trade-off characterisation?

A large body of literature in international relations has cast doubt on simplistic notions of national interest. Many theorists have rejected the claim that there is a set of 'real' interests that can be derived from a rational assessment of national economic and political considerations. Rather, notions of national interest are shaped by a range of values, beliefs and interests that are not directly determined by rational calculations of narrow domestic interests.[10] One subset of this critique involves a rejection of the assumption of nation-states as separate, bounded units of interest, instead stressing the role of transnational or sub-national interests and ties in shaping political action.[11] While this discussion is of general interest to the question of refugee policy, I am more concerned with a second type of critique that stresses the role of shared values in defining interests. The concern here is not so much linked to the empirical claim that political decisions are shaped by sub- or transnational interests. Rather, the point is that it is misguided to conceive of interests – whether individual, national, sub-national or transnational – as independent of ethical values. Just as it is simplistic to assume that an individual's interests are independent of her values and beliefs, so too is it is misleading to conceive of a national interest that is independent of broader ethical considerations. Commitment to ethical values will create implicit norms and expectations about what constitutes acceptable or desirable behaviour. I do not want to exaggerate the role of such ethical norms in shaping refugee policy. But it would be equally wrong to overlook it, especially on an issue as normatively laden as that of duties to refugees. In short, the notion of a dichotomy or trade-off between refugee rights and national interests seems descriptively simplistic.

Quite apart from the descriptive problems with the trade-off conception, there are also considerable practical risks in embracing this account. I shall mention two of these. First, drawing a distinction between national interests and ethical duty is not a particularly effective strategy for motivating support for a generous refugee policy. If adopting an ethical stance is characterised as in opposition to one's interests – as self-abnegating rather than personally fulfilling – then it is not evident how advocates of refugee rights could motivate support for their cause. Castigating the defenders of national interest as self-centred and calling for a more purist moral approach is likely to be counter-productive, especially in a climate where the claims of liberal universalism appear to be so unfeasible. Again, as we shall see in the thesis, there are parallels here with the moral philosophical distinction between the personal disposition and the requirements of morality. The traditional Kantian distinction between will and moral duty seems to have pervaded the discourse on national interest and universal ethics, bringing with it the associated problems with generating moral motivation.

In addition to this practical problem of encouraging motivation, the trade-off characterisation has a second prescriptive weakness: it limits the scope for defining and evaluating possible alternative solutions to refugee problems. Couching the relationship in terms of refugee rights versus national interests precludes the possibility of defining approaches which could meet the concerns of both nationals and refugees. For want of a better term, the trade-off conception constrains the development of 'positive sum' approaches to refugee problems. The requirements of ethical duty are defined in rigid terms, with any incorporation of national concerns representing a deviation from universalist ethics. Yet recent developments in refugee policy seem to have transcended this trade-off conception. A number of innovative policy approaches have been debated and implemented over the past decade, which do seek to address the concerns of states whilst meeting the needs of refugees. For example, the temporary protection regime for Bosnian refugees established a form of short term asylum which was designed to ensure the safety of refugees for the duration of the conflict, whilst minimising the burden on receiving countries. An increased emphasis on protecting those displaced inside their country of origin and monitoring of refugees after they have repatriated also aims to ensure the human rights of refugees through alternatives to asylum. However, these innovations have been *ad hoc* and for the most part lacking a coherent rationale. Debate on and evaluation of these policies has also suffered from a marked lack of consensus on how to define their success. Trapped in the trade-off characterisation, refugee rights activists often criticise them as a compromise of refugee rights under pressure from states.

These descriptive and practical shortcomings of the trade-off account – the simplistic definition of national interest, the problem of motivation and the lack of framework for designing and evaluating new policies – would imply that the current *impasse* in the policy debate is partly a conceptual problem. While it would be a mistake to underplay the conflicts of interest between states and refugees, the main concern being addressed here is that the current characterisation may be inadequate, and even counterproductive to the normative goals of liberal universalism.

Sources of the Dichotomy Characterisation in Liberal Theory

In this book I will argue that this problem of feasibility can be traced to a fundamental flaw in liberal universalist theories. In a nutshell, this flaw is liberalism's notion of a dichotomy between two sets of considerations: national or community interests on the one hand, and the requirements of universal ethics on the other. I shall argue that this dichotomy surfaces at different levels: in the debate on refugee policy, where it is depicted as a conflict between national interest and refugee rights; and in liberal theory, where it is manifested as a conflict between the special ties and commitments of the individual agent, and the requirements of an ethical, 'impartial' perspective that abstracts from these special ties.

A central assumption here is that the ethical concepts underlying the policy debate really do matter. Shared beliefs and values significantly influence how we define refugee rights, national interests, and the range of possible policy responses to refugees. Put another way, the refugee problematic could be conceptualised in a number of different ways. It is these different *conceptions* of duties to refugees that are the focus of this book. The aim is to find a way of conceptualising the current set of empirical conditions in a way that avoids the shortcomings of liberal universalism, whilst retaining its general normative prescriptions regarding duties to refugees. The emphasis is on examining the scope for changing conceptions of what duties we owe to refugees. The book aims to address a current policy dilemma through a conceptual theoretical analysis that seeks to alter the way people understand this configuration of empirical conditions.

What sorts of criteria would a more adequate conception of duties to refugees need to fulfil? If liberal universalist theories are deemed inadequate, we should be clear about why they are deficient, and what sorts of conditions such an alternative account will need to meet. I have already stated that one concern is to find a more realistic grounding for a commitment to refugee protection, and that I have serious doubts that liberal theories are the best candidates for doing this. In considering different theories for grounding this commitment, then, one criterion for appraising the various candidates will clearly have to be how well they capture this commitment. Here it is useful to draw on Rawls' notion of 'reflective equilibrium'. Reflective equilibrium involves testing 'our considered moral judgements' against different conceptions of ethics or justice, to see which theories best fit these judgements. Reflective equilibrium is 'reached after a person has weighed various proposed conceptions and he has either revised his judgements to accord with one of them or held fast to his initial convictions (and the corresponding conception)'.[12] The process of revision is not necessarily one way: Mackie usefully characterises it as a process of adjusting either or both our judgements and some set of principles 'until the most satisfactory coherent compromise is reached'.[13] The Rawlsian model is a good starting-point for evaluating different ethical theories. Indeed, the process of matching different conceptions with one's considered convictions seems to be a good method for ensuring that one finds a theory consistent with one's first order commitment – in my case the ethical force of refugee rights. Rawls' method also puts a premium on conceptual coherence, another important condition for an adequate theory. So I shall follow the Rawlsian model in adopting these two criteria for evaluating different theories: those of normative desirability, and conceptual coherence.

There is a third criterion I shall include, which concerns the practical feasibility of the conception. It was suggested earlier on that questions of feasibility have an important bearing on the adequacy of a theory. This is not simply because an unfeasible theory is of little practical use. More seriously, I would argue that unfeasible moral or political goals may actually be counter-productive. As I suggested earlier in the discussion of liberal theories of universal rights, stringent conceptions of duty may seem impossible to realise, rendering them irrelevant to practical debate. This is not to say that fundamental normative goals should be abandoned simply because they are not considered feasible. But it does imply that where a theory is unable to show how people are or could be motivated to respect its requirements, we should consider it as deficient, at least for practical purposes.

In summary, an adequate conception of duties to refugees should meet three criteria: normative desirability, internal coherence, and practical feasibility. These criteria will be applied to evaluate different theories of duties to refugees.

Outline of the Argument

The book begins by introducing the problem of refugee protection, tracing the emergence of the conflict between refugee rights and national interests in European political thought. Chapter One examines the emergence of liberal notions of duties to refugees, and their codification in the post Second World War refugee regime. The Chapter describes the origins and evolution of more restrictive political and social thought on refugees, especially the emergence of notions of nationalism in European states. It shows how empirical conditions temporarily sustained liberal universalist conceptions in the 1950s and 1960s, but their absence now creates a serious problem of feasibility.

I then devote three chapters to setting out and critiquing the underpinnings of notions of refugee rights in liberal universalist theory. Chapter Two examines liberal universalism and the problem of feasibility. It shows how both utilitarian liberal theories and right-based conceptions impose overly stringent duties when applied to a range of international distributive issues. This in turn reflects their implausible assumptions about moral agency and motivation. In Chapter Three, I show how attempts to incorporate some commitment to community ties into theories of universal duties meanwhile produce incoherent, hybrid theories. Chapter Four considers whether social contract theories might be better equipped to provide an adequate account of duties to refugees. *Prima facie*, social contract theory appears to be a good candidate for solving the problem of motivation, as it explicitly ties its political theory to consent: it requires that contractors be predisposed to accept its norms. However, social contract theories either are designed for application to bounded communities, thus excluding refugees, or they produce unfeasible conceptions of international justice that raise similar or even more problematic questions about motivation.

Chapter Five locates the origins in these shortcomings of liberal universalism in liberal assumptions about the role of reason in moral agency and motivation. It suggests that it is far more plausible to explain moral agency drawing on a modified Humean account, which locates motivation in the emotive disposition of agents, rather than their capacity for reason. Chapter Six develops the implications of this account for refugee rights, drawing on the work of Charles Taylor. It proposes an ethics that accords a privileged status to liberal rights, but denies the foundational claims of most universalist accounts. It combines a communitarian account of the self with a recognition of the fundamental importance of liberal universalist values, at least to members of liberal democracies. It shows how this non-metaphysical account can provide a basis for motivating commitment to liberal rights, based on the affirmation of shared liberal values.

In the final chapter, I draw out the practical implications of this account, showing how this alternative theoretical grounding of liberalism could help mobilise support for a more liberal agenda. How could European states, political parties and refugee and human rights lobby groups better mobilise support for refugee rights?

Before embarking on the analysis, I should briefly introduce a couple of caveats. The first concerns my use of the term 'refugees'. By taking the refugee policy problem as the starting-point of the analysis, I am implicitly accepting the existing legal definition of 'refugee'. As we saw, refugees are defined in international law as those who have fled their country 'owing to a well-founded fear of being persecuted for reasons of race, religion, nationality, membership of a particular social group or political opinion'.[14] In practice, many states also offer various forms of protection and asylum to those fleeing more generalised violence and armed conflict.[15] Many commentators have questioned the relevance of this category, arguing that those fleeing poverty or natural disasters are as much in need of asylum as those fleeing violence and persecution. And I would agree that the distinction between these cases has little ethical relevance. The reason for retaining the narrower definition of refugee is political rather than ethical. In the current restrictionist climate, even those who meet the existing international legal definition are not guaranteed asylum. The continued respect for existing provisions on refugee rights is far from assured, let alone the acceptance of far greater numbers of forced economic migrants. Thus it only makes sense to broach the question of extending the legal definition to cover forced migrants if the already controversial recognition of this narrower category is assured.

A second consequence of accepting this legal definition is that it implies that a number of those not recognised by host countries as refugees may nonetheless meet the criteria for recognition established in the Geneva Convention. Thus when discussing duties to refugees, the category 'refugee' should be understand to incorporate many of those asylum seekers, rejected asylum applicants, or irregular migrants who are not in practice recognised as refugees, but who – according to the principles of the Geneva Convention – should be entitled to such a status. In other words, the discussion of duties to refugees employs a definition of refugees that is recognised in international refugee law, but is not necessarily respected in the practice of host countries.

My second caveat is about the scope of this book. Having said something about the ground I shall cover in this book, I should say something about what the book will *not* do. The bulk of the book is devoted to a discussion of ethics, often at a rather abstract level of argumentation. As I have stressed, the refugee problematic unearths quite deep-seated tensions in liberal theory, which, I believe, need to be addressed before we can begin to have a more coherent debate about the precise content and scope of duties to refugees. The book hopes to provide a basis for conducting such a debate. But it does not offer hard and fast answers to questions of precisely what duties we owe to refugees, or how to balance refugee rights against national interests. As I hope it will become clear, such debates are, and should be, located within particular traditions of ethical thought and political discourse. My aim is to offer a different way of understanding the sources of such ethical obligations, one which can help make sense of the often conflicting claims we face in deliberating on responses to refugees.

Notes

[1] John Rawls, *Political Liberalism* (New York, 1993).

[2] This refers to the fifteen states who were already members of the European Union before the accession of a new wave of members on 1 May 2004. More detailed figures on asylum can be found in: United Nations High Commissioner for Refugees, *Asylum Levels and Trends: Europe and Non-European Industrialized Countries, 2003* (Geneva, 2004).

[3] UNHCR, *The State of the World's Refugees: A Humanitarian Agenda* (Oxford, 1997), p. 264.

[4] *Convention Relating to the Status of Refugees*, Geneva 28 July 1951 (Geneva, 1995).

[5] Guy S. Goodwin-Gill, *The Refugee in International Law* (Oxford, 1996).

[6] For contemporary critiques of liberal ontology, see Michael Sandel, *Liberalism and the Limits of Justice* (Cambridge, 1982); and Charles Taylor, *Sources of the Self* (1989).

[7] See, for example, Jens Vedsted Hansen, 'Non-Admission Policies and the Right to Protection: Refugees' Choice versus States' Exclusion', in Frances Nicholson and Patrick Twomey (eds), *Refugee Rights and Realities* (Cambridge, 1999), pp. 269–88; Reinhard Marx, 'Non-Refoulement, Access to Procedures, and Responsibility for Determining Refugee Claims', *International Journal of Refugee Law*, 7:3 (1995): 383–406; Arthur C. Helton, 'What is Refugee Protection?', *International Journal of Refugee Law*, Special Issue (1990): 119–29.

[8] For an overview of this debate, see Christina Boswell, 'The Conflict between Refugee Rights and national Interests', *Refugee Survey Quarterly*, 18:2: 64–84.

[9] For example, the liberal theorist Brian Barry writes about a 'celebration of selfishness' in UK and US foreign policy – see Barry, 'Can States be Moral?', in Robert J. Myers (ed.), *International Ethics in the Nuclear Age* (Lanham, 1987), p. 106.

[10] For a useful collection of these critiques, see Robert O. Keohane (ed.), *Neorealism and its Critics* (New York, 1986).

[11] For a selection of contributions that can be loosely grouped under this category, see Bruce Burton, *World Society* (Cambridge, 1972); Robert O. Keohane and Joseph S. Nye, *Power and Interdependence* (Boston, 1977); Stephen D. Krasner, *Defending the National Interest* (Princeton, 1978).

[12] John Rawls, *A Theory of Justice* (Oxford, 1972), p. 48.

[13] J. L. Mackie, *Ethics: Inventing Right and Wrong* (London, 1985), p. 105.

[14] Article 1 (A.2), *Convention Relating to the Status of Refugees.*

[15] See, for example, James C. Hathaway, *The Law of Refugee Status* (Toronto and Vancouver, 1991), pp. 19–20; and Goodwin-Gill, *The Refugee in International law*, pp. 21–6.

Chapter One

The Origins of the Crisis in Refugee Policy

It was suggested in the last chapter that the current impasse in the refugee policy debate is partly attributable to political theory conceptions of the relationship between universal liberal ethics and particular interests and ties. Liberal universalist notions of the split between interests and ethical duty risk rendering conceptions of refugee rights unfeasible. Not only do liberal notions of universal duties seem overly stringent in the current political context. But by juxtaposing them with notions of interests, liberal theory makes it difficult to see how people could be motivated to comply with these ethical demands. But while I have argued that the perception of a crisis in refugee policy is a relatively recent phenomenon, notions of both universal rights, and of supposedly conflicting particularist theories, have a long history in political thought. So the question arises as to why this conception of conflict between refugee rights and national interests did not emerge before. Why, in other words, it was not evident that consistent practical application of universal rights would imply unfeasible obligations to non-nationals.

To answer this question, it is necessary to trace the emergence of this notion of a conflict between refugee rights and national interests, and how the conceptions of this conflict have shaped responses to refugee influx.

The Origins of the Conflict in Political Thought

Development of Political Thought and the Refugee Problem

Contemporary theorists draw on two main sets of values to justify refugee rights and the defence of national interests. The first set comprises what I have referred to as universalist theories, which include various conceptions of human rights, international justice or universal duties. Most of these theories can also be characterised as liberal in the broad sense, and it is a liberal variant of universalism that explicitly underlies international human rights and refugee law. Proponents of refugee rights therefore tend to draw on liberal conceptions of universal rights and international justice to justify their claims. The second set of theories rejects the universalist premises of these liberal theories, taking as their starting point the local or particular – usually community or nation. Such particularist accounts place duties to fellow nationals above obligations to other groups. This second category includes an eclectic range of theories, including romanticist and communitarian accounts of the moral relevance of special ties and community practices, and realist theories of international politics that defend national interests on more pragmatic grounds.

Now while both categories of ideas have a long history in western thought, there are two main reasons why the current conception of a conflict between universalism and particularism in the context of refugee policy has only recently emerged. First, as I shall argue later, earlier theories in both the universalist and particularist categories did not have a clearly developed conception of the sorts of practical implications of their theories for duties to non-nationals that have now emerged. Liberal theories of rights, although from early on grounded in some conception of the shared characteristics of humans, were only gradually extended in scope to apply to individuals of all races. And even once they were extended in principle, for a variety of reasons, liberal political theories rarely recognised positive duties to assist individuals in other states. Neither did earlier forms of particularist and nationalist theories clarify the now familiar notion of the national prerogative of controlling immigration until fairly recently. Here the change in political thought reflects the evolution of the system of sovereign states and the rise of nationalism in the nineteenth century, as well as the development of notions of community.

But the emergence of a conception of conflict between refugee rights and national interests was also clearly affected by a second major factor: the changing nature of refugee flows and conditions in receiving countries. While conceptions of duties to non-nationals were shaped by prevalent ideas in moral and political thought, empirical events have in turn revealed tensions or shortcomings in political theory conceptions. Thus while notions of universal rights and particularism may from the outset have differed in their philosophical foundations and practical implications, the conflict between the two in the matter of refugee policy has only emerged as the refugee problem itself has escalated. During periods in which immigration and refugee flows were not considered to be problematic, the question of duties to refugees and its conflict with national interests simply did not arise.

This account of the role of political thought and empirical events in producing the current conception of conflict between refugee rights and national interests does of course make a number of assumptions about the relation between ideas and historical events. Political and moral ideas provide a framework within which people evaluate and the desirability and feasibility of different actions and goals. And changes in empirical conditions can influence these ideas, through drawing attention to their conceptual deficiencies or practical shortcomings. In the case at hand, changes in the nature and scale of refugee movements influenced ideas about duties to refugees in two ways. The refugee crises of the twentieth century seemed to highlight the incompatibility of two different strands of political thought, i.e. nationalist and liberal universalist; and it implied the practical unfeasibility of realising universalist duties.

The Evolution of Conceptions of Universal Rights

The notion of individual rights can be traced back to the concept of *ius* in early Roman law. *Ius* originally denoted objective right – that which was good or fair – and only acquired its subjective form in mediaeval natural law theories. In the twelfth century, natural lawyers asserted that property, or *dominium*, was a *ius*, thus implying a subjective claim that generated requirements on the part of others. The definition of *ius* was subsequently extended in the early fifteenth century to denote a faculty or ability, hence the possibility of talking about a natural *ius* to freedom.[1] Over the next two centuries, discussions of the nature and scope of such a *ius* often revolved around questions of duties to other peoples. Spanish colonisation of America at the turn of the fifteenth century sparked a theological debate about the natural rights of slaves, with the Dominican Vitoria famously asserting that natural liberty could not be exchanged at any price except life itself.[2] Religious wars and the Ottoman threat also influenced the emergence of theories of *ius gentium* in this period, notably Grotius' theory of rights which denied a natural duty to obey the sovereign (although he retracted this by denying a right of resistance in practice). Grotius' theory is also striking in its assertion of a right to intervene on behalf of the natural rights of subjects of other sovereigns, although again, this did not generate a practical right for subjects to rebel against their own rulers.[3]

The mediaeval and renaissance emphasis on the law of peoples shifted in the seventeenth and eighteenth centuries to a preoccupation with questions of national politics and the role of the state. The classical social contract theorists focused on the problems of political legitimacy and the property rights and civil liberties of citizens. Hobbes' social contract theory contained many elements of a recognisably modern theory of rights. Rights were grounded in the natural capacities of man, and thus the good was equated with individual interest. His state of nature depicted men as naturally equal in power and reason, and this equality provided moral and pragmatic grounds for their equal participation in the contract. Locke's more recognisably modern liberal theory also stressed the equal capacity of individuals, although individual rights were derived from duties to God, rather than grounded in human interests. Nonetheless, these rights were also in the interests of human beings and knowable by reason, thus in a sense opening the possibility for a secular theory of rights. Locke also took the significant step of asserting a greater right to resistance, making the sovereign's authority conditional on his respecting the rights of subjects.

These classical theories already contained many of the central elements of modern liberal theories of rights: men in the state of nature have equal natural rights, and they are equal participants in the social contract. The claim that men had a natural interest in securing certain rights, and that they would recognise these interests through the exercise of reason, later became the explicit grounding for theories of the rights of man and subsequently human rights. Yet in light of the emergence of such individualist and universalist accounts of individual rights by the eighteenth century, it is all the more striking that these theories were not perceived to have explicit implications for duties to nationals of other countries. If it was accepted that rights were the natural attributes of all men, in retrospect it might appear odd that classical theorists did not construct theories of universal duties, especially given the extensive treatment of such issues in earlier natural law theories.

We can clarify this disparity between contemporary and classical treatment of the question by categorising the differences along two axes: the question of the *scope* of rights and the duties they generated; and that of the *content* of individual rights. This conceptual scheme will help indicate the types of historical explanations that might account for the relatively recent emergence of notions of duties to non-nationals (although I will not elaborate such an account here).

On the question of the scope of duties to non-nationals, one can distinguish three different senses in which the category of right-holders was restricted. First, despite the presumed equality of men in the state of nature, the scope of political rights was limited in classical contract theories. Women were not equally capable of reason, nor, in most theories, were those from non-civilised cultures, although it is not always clear if this is due to natural inferiority or a lack of development. Hence slavery was morally acceptable, at least until the emergence of the anti-slavery movement in the nineteenth century. These limitations in scope were echoed in the American and French declarations on the late eighteenth century, and went largely unchallenged at the national level until political mobilisation of the working classes and women's movement in the nineteenth and early twentieth centuries.

Closely linked to the question of the moral subjects of rights was the issue of the level of development required to justify exercising natural rights. Thus many liberal theorists who believed in the natural equality of men (and even of women) argued for limiting the scope of legal rights of non-civilised cultures. Some of the most progressive nineteenth century British liberals argued that colonisation was beneficial to inferior peoples, who would benefit from the spread of civilisation. And Mill denied that there was a duty to intervene to protect the rights of subjects of other states, on the grounds that only peoples who were sufficiently mobilised to fight for their own rights were capable of exercising autonomy.

The third sense in which the scope of rights was restricted concerns the preoccupation with political questions within the state. Liberal political theory from the seventeenth century onwards was dominated by domestic concerns, such as the problem of political obligation, and how to maximise national prosperity. Rights were primarily instruments for ensuring the right balance of freedom and state interference. Moreover, the often precarious relations between European states in this period meant that questions of duties to non-nationals became to a large extent irrelevant. Insofar as the international sphere was characterised by insecurity, the central problem of international political theory remained that of regulating conflict between states rather than ensuring the rights of all individuals. The apparent disparity between universalist justifications for theories of individual rights at the national level, and the lack of such rights in relations between states, reflected the perceived salience of the problem of conflict between states. This concern is clearly present in the (limited) writings of social contract theorists on international politics, with Hobbes, Rousseau and Kant more or less converging in their conclusion about the unfeasibility or undesirability of a global social contract.

The second axis of change in concepts of duties to non-nationals concerns the *substance* of rights. The eighteenth and nineteenth century emphasis on negative liberty was predominantly geared towards limiting the role of the state.[4] Rights were used as tools for generating duties of forbearance, not obligations to assist individuals. The rights of non-nationals, where they were acknowledged at all, would therefore be best realised by a domestic contract between rulers and ruled. Yet the emphasis on 'negative' liberty was clearly not common to all political and moral thought: there were other important strands in western thought that invoked a range of different values and objectives, and which also served to influenced liberal theories. Many of these other conceptions were integrated into liberal theories, enabling them to broaden out and encompass a greater range of conditions for human flourishing. So it should be stressed that while this emphasis on negative liberty and property rights was an important strand in eighteenth and nineteenth century politics, the development of liberal political thought was also profoundly influenced by a number of other conceptions of universal duty.

Among these influential strands in political and moral thought were Christian notions of charity and obligation, ideas which were central to the tradition of natural law and explicitly influenced the work of social contract theorists such as Locke, Rousseau and Kant.[5] Also missing from this narrow conception are a variety of teleological moral and political theories, which found early articulation in ancient Greek philosophy and later influenced ideas about 'positive freedom' and human flourishing in the thought of Rousseau, Hegel and Marx. Again, many of these theories influenced the development of liberal theories of rights. Another more teleological strand can be found in eighteenth century theories of moral sentiment and later utilitarian theories. These diverse notions of duties, benevolence and the good life influenced liberal as well as particularist theories, but in many cases their moral prescriptions were not until recently codified in the language of individual rights. Notions of duty and benevolence were often relegated to the private sphere of charitable institutions or the church, or couched in terms of social goals rather than individual rights. The same applied to notions of duties to non-nationals, which were associated with Christian duty or charity rather than duties generated by universal rights.

Nonetheless, theories of rights did eventually take on board a far wider conception of the conditions for individual freedom or flourishing. Liberal thought was profoundly influenced by changing conceptions of the role and functions of the state in the nineteenth century. These conceptions were in turn influenced by the demands of a politically mobilised working class, and the articulation of more radical notions of emancipation and equality. Again, while these social and economic claims were not initially couched in the language of rights, they were integrally bound up with aspirations to freedom. The New Liberalism of the late nineteenth and early twentieth centuries, and what one writer terms the 'Keynesian moment' in the history of liberal thought represented an important shift in notions of the material preconditions for the genuine exercise of autonomy. Once the link between socio-economic equality and liberty had been made in this way, it was a short conceptual step to asserting universal rights to subsistence, shelter, education, healthcare and so on. Most contemporary liberal theories now advocate some combination of negative and positive freedom, although they strike the balance between social justice and legal freedoms in different ways. As I shall argue, it is partly this extension of the substance of rights that has rendered the demands of universal justice so difficult to meet.

Nationalism and the National Interest

While conceptions of the scope and substance of liberal rights were being extended from the eighteenth century onwards, notions of nationalism were also becoming more prevalent from the late eighteenth century onwards. The rise of nationalism and theories of the moral relevance of the nation-state was closely bound up with the processes of state consolidation and democratisation in Europe. These empirical factors also had a direct impact on the phenomenon of refugees: state consolidation and nationalism both generated large numbers of refugees; and encouraged restrictions on their entry in countries of refuge. In examining the emergence of theories of nationalism and the national interest and their impact on notions of duties to refugees, we therefore need to examine two sets of processes. First, the process of state formation and its relation to notions of nationalism. And second, the impact of these empirical developments and political ideas on refugees and asylum.

Central to understanding the emergence of moral and political theories of nationalism was the consolidation of a number of European nation-states from the fifteenth century onwards, notably Spain, France, England and Holland. A combination of industrial development, demographic changes and international conflict led to the gradual centralisation and rationalisation of the state's control over a clearly demarcated territory and the population within it.[6] This process was characterised by the growth of centralised administrative structures to implement policies of taxation, law and order, military recruitment and education. These nations were able to achieve military and economic power in the sixteenth and seventeenth centuries, and set an example to other aspiring nation-states.

The consolidation of the nation-state was often aided by, and in turn encouraged the development of, notions of national identity. The centralisation of administration and education and the imposition of a national language encouraged the emergence or strengthening of a shared national culture and identity. The development of such a sense of shared characteristics and common purpose was essential in order to ensure loyalty to the sovereign, raise taxes and mobilise soldiers for war. The moral and political relevance of such a sense of patriotism was articulated by Rousseau in the eighteenth century in his concept of the 'general will' which transcended the aggregate individual interests of citizens. This more idealised concept of nationality was given impetus by the French revolution, which identified national self-determination with democratic popular resistance against monarchical rule. While the French conception of nationality was essentially liberal and had a civic conception of membership, the idea of popular national resistance was given a more particularist slant by subsequent theories and political movements. Rousseau's notion of general will was expanded in nineteenth century romantic thought, notably in Herder's conception of *Volk*, and his expressivist theory of language. National liberation and unification movements, as well as political élites seeking legitimacy, found it useful to highlight the distinctive linguistic or ethnic characteristics of nationalities in order to mobilise support for existing or aspiring states. The identification of ethnic or linguistic characteristics with state-building was to be a major cause of refugee flows from the late nineteenth century onwards, as we shall see in the next section.

But the growing importance of the nation-state and nationalism also had profound implications for the treatment of refugees. As the state's jurisdiction over its population and territory was consolidated, the criteria of membership and thus the distinction between citizens and non-citizens became more important. And the increasing democratisation of nation-states, part product of the need for popular support for state consolidation, lent a new significance to citizenship. Not only did the state guarantee security, it was also to become the guarantor of civil and political rights, and increasingly of social welfare. The perceived social and economic benefits of citizenship would encourage a reluctance on the part of citizens to share finite resources with non-nationals, especially in times of unemployment and depression. Although the rights accrued to citizens in democratic states were grounded on a characteristically universalist conception of equal rights, they nonetheless had the effect of reinforcing the significance of national membership. Hence it was not only explicitly particularist or exclusivist conceptions of nationalism that generated hostility to non-nationals. While liberal conceptions of citizenship did not generate the types of persecution and expulsions of ethnic minorities that occurred in states attached to a particularist conception of nationality, nonetheless encouraged a reluctance to extend the benefits of membership to non-citizens. Nationalism in both the French republican and the romantic organicist traditions influenced the nature and scale of refugee flows, as well as national responses to influx in the twentieth century.[7]

Finally, it is worth considering the role of international politics in solidifying national loyalties and narrow conceptions of national interests. The political use of nationalist sentiment was not limited to securing support for self-determination or state consolidation. It had helped mobilise support for Napoleon's expansionist policy, and was subsequently important for enlisting popular support for empire building and the imperial conflicts of the late nineteenth and early twentieth centuries. The combination of patriotic zeal and the racist theories invoked to justify imperialist practices lent an even more exclusionary aspect to nationalism.

The rising inter-state tensions around this period, which climaxed in 1914, also reinforced notions about the priority of national interest over transnational cultural ties, free trade or duties to non-nationals.

The 'realist' theories of international relations that emerged in the 1930s and 1940s emphasised the primarily self-interested behaviour of states, and identified 'national interests' with the search for power in international politics.[8] This conception of national interest, and especially its later forms in neo-realist theories, assumed that states define their interests independently of their moral values, and that the objective of states was to promote the interests of those already within their jurisdiction. Unlike the communitarian or romanticist accounts of nationalism, the realist account was ostensibly descriptive rather than normative. And as such, it was in principle compatible with liberal universalist political theories. Many liberals still accept these realist descriptive claims about the nature of national interest, whilst diverging from realists' practical prescriptions. On this account, the gap between 'ideal theory' and the current state of international politics can be explained by the regrettable selfishness of states. And once again this produces a conception of national interest and universal duties as having separate sources – the one self-interested, the other ethical, and both defined independently of one another.

Universal Rights, National Interests and Responses to Refugee Influx

Refugees Before World War One

How did these potentially conflicting conceptions of universal duties and national interests influence the treatment of refugees in the twentieth century? Refugee flows – at least as they are conceived in current definitions – began to occur in Europe from around the end of the fifteenth century. There had been substantial movements of people before then, but most instances of religious persecution in the Middle Ages were localised and sporadic cases, which did not give rise to mass movement. In the late fifteenth and early sixteenth centuries, religious conflict in Europe and the growing power of nation-states led to more widespread and systematic persecution of religious groups.[9] The first major movement of this kind was the expulsion of Jews from Spain in 1492. Further forced displacement in Western Europe followed the Reformation, the French Wars of Religion and the Thirty Years' War. From the 1550s onwards, England began to serve as a place of refugee for displaced Protestants from the Spanish Netherlands, and French Huguenots. When the Edict of Nantes was revoked in 1685, a further 200,000 Huguenots fled to England, indeed, the term *refugié* was first coined to denote this group. It was subsequently adopted in English as 'refugee', and by 1796 the Encyclopaedia Britannica noted that it had been 'extended to all such as leave their country in times of distress.'[10]

Most victims of religious persecution had little problem finding asylum. European states were generally apprehensive about population shortages, and were more interested in restricting emigration from their territory than preventing influx. By the second half of the seventeenth century, a number of English economists were asserting the economic importance of a large labour force, which was seen as a means of improving the balance of trade and thus national wealth. The debate on immigration over the next century revolved around questions of population and national prosperity, and the right of Europeans to settle in colonial territories.[11] There was some debate in the 1700s about whether to restrict the entry of a wave of Palatine refugees, with some concerned that they would take jobs from the English. But there was a perceived economic interest in accepting them, as well as a Christian duty to help fellow Protestants. Daniel Defoe, writing about the Protestant refugees from Germany, talked about 'the People of *England*, who liberally and with open Hearts and Hands contribute to the Subsistance of their distressed *Protestant* Brethren'.[12]

Concern about population shortages were assuaged by the dramatic increase in population from the second half of the eighteenth century. European states for the first time began to encourage emigration to North America and the colonies, and by the 1820s most countries had removed existing restrictions. Yet despite some concerns about over-population, the absorption of refugees did not pose a significant problem for most of the nineteenth century. Refugees usually arrived in small numbers, tended to be fairly affluent, and so were not considered to be a burden on receiving countries. In the first half of the century, many political exiles found refuge in European cities, including Polish, Russian, Spanish, Portuguese, Italian and German dissidents. By the 1850s, London was an important centre for European exiles, and there appeared to be genuine popular sentiment against restricting the entry of refugees, and for allowing them freedom to pursue political activities in exile as long as they respected English law.[13] The Liberal Prime Minister Lord Palmerston is cited as referring in around 1860 to:

> that law of hospitality by which we have invariably been guided with regard to foreigners seeking asylum in this country. Any foreigner, whatever his nation, whatever his political creed, whatever his political offences against his Government...may find in these realms a safe and secure asylum as long as he obeys the law of the land.[14]

Here a Liberal politician is articulating a clear notion of impartial treatment of refugees, rather than special treatment for Christians or Protestants. The notion of duties to refugees was taking on a more secular tone, although it was still not couched as a universal right.

This liberal attitude was more difficult to sustain in the last third of the century, when the rise of nationalism and anti-Semitism was both a cause of largescale movements, and heightened intolerance of refugee influx in receiving countries. From the 1880s onwards, there was a steady and largescale flow of Jews escaping persecution in Russia and East Europe. Most of these were accepted by the United

States – around 2.25 million people between 1881 and 1914 – but significant numbers settled in Western European countries, including some 120,000 in Britain.[15] In the 1880s, the United States, Canada and Australia began to impose restrictions on entry, and this had important repercussions for Europe, generating concern about the diminishing possibilities for emigration to the New World. At the same time, concerns at the continuing flow of East European Jews into West Europe, rising unemployment after 1901 and anti-Semitism in receiving countries brought the issue of immigration control to the fore.[16] In 1904 a Conservative government introduced the first restriction of immigration through an Aliens Bill, designed to exclude 'undesirable and destitute aliens'.[17] There was considerable opposition to the bill from the Liberal Party, partly because of its implicit anti-Semitism, partly because it was seen as constituting an attack on political asylum. Liberal opposition succeeded in amending the 1905 Act, which contained safeguards for refugees, i.e. those who could prove they were 'seeking admission to this country solely to avoid prosecution or punishment on religious or political grounds, or for an offence of a political characters, or persecution involving danger to life and limb'.[18] Entry was further restricted with the introduction of passport controls in 1914. The rise of nationalist feeling, domestic economic and social unrest, and concerns about the insecure international climate generated the first wave of immigration restrictions.

Refugee Flows in the Inter-War Years and World War Two

The inter-war years saw a significant increase in the number of refugees, most of whom were fleeing religious and nationalist based persecution, and fascist regimes. Most refugees in the 1920s were casualties of the processes of state formation and consolidation. The disintegration of the Hapsburg, Romanov and Ottoman Empires was accelerated by the war and the peace treaties of 1919-21. Conflict in the Balkans had already precipitated the 'unmixing' of hundreds of thousands of Muslims and Christians, and the Turkish massacre of Armenians in 1915 had led to the flight of around 350,000.[19] In 1913 a population exchange agreement between Bulgaria and Turkey had led to a transfer of roughly 50,000 from each side. After the 1918 Peace Treaties, the unmixing of nationalities was seen as a necessary, albeit regrettable, means of consolidating the newly independent states.[20] The nationalising process in central and east Europe led to the displacement of millions of ethnic and national minorities from Poland, Russia, the Ukraine, Hungary and Czechoslovakia. Population exchanges were also generally accepted as a means of preventing conflict, with agreements for exchanges between Turkey, and – respectively – Bulgaria and Greece, resulting in the mainly coerced movement of almost two million people. Many of the minorities who did not move were made stateless. Romanian citizenship law of 1924, for example, made 100,000 Jews inside Russia stateless (check), and the Soviet Union stripped almost one million Russians of citizenship in the early 1920s.[21]

While there was no recognition of international legal duties to assist these refugees, the 1920s did see the first international cooperation to address refugee policies. The League of Nations established a High Commissioner on Behalf of the League in 1921 'to coordinate the action of governments and private organisations for the relief of Russian refugees, to regulate the legal status of a large class of persons who had been rendered stateless, and to assist them to find permanent homes and work'.[22] The High Commissioner's services were extended in 1924 to cover Armenian refugees. The High Commissioner was successful in finding homes for most of these refugees, mainly because of labour shortages in Europe, and partly also because of the wide range of approaches used, including creating employment opportunities, and generally linking of assistance to measures to promote European economic development.

However, international cooperation was seen as a provisional arrangement to address the temporary refugee problems caused by the upheaval of World War One and the creation of new states. The refugees under the High Commissioner's mandate were defined on the basis of territory, nationality or religion, rather than on a more abstract and generally applicable definition of 'refugee'. There was no conception of universal refugee rights underlying international cooperation. Moreover, assistance to refugees was explicitly political, rather than humanitarian: methods such as population exchange sought to address security concerns as much as humanitarian needs, and many of the resettlement programmes were explicitly tailored to the labour requirements of receiving states. Unlike the current UN framework, inter-war arrangements were not even nominally founded on recognition of the universal rights of refugees.

Cooperation to address refugee flows was largely paralysed in the 1930s, with economic depression in Europe and America, and unstable international relations. There were largescale movements from fascist regimes in Italy, Spain and Germany. Up to one million Italians were expelled by Mussolini, and around half a million Spanish Republicans fled to France. By the second half of the decade, there was considerable concern at the prospect of mass influx of German refugees into West European states. The flight of Jews from Germany began as a small but steady flow in the early 1930s, increasing dramatically as Nazi anti-Semitic policies became more stringent in 1938. However, economic and political concerns were also motivating restrictive policies in this period. European receiving states faced economic depression in the 1930s, and France in particular had already absorbed large numbers of refugees from Spain and Italy. Already in 1933, the British Home Office was using a far less liberal rhetoric than in the past. As one official put it: 'We do not...admit that there is a 'right of asylum'; but when we have to decide whether a particular refugee is to be given admission to this country, we have to base our decision ... on whether it is in the public interest that he be admitted'.[23] The 'national interest' prevailed over – as yet ill-defined – duties to refugees.

As the persecution of Jews intensified and the plight of refugees from Germany and Austria became more apparent to European states, public opinion in many countries called for the relaxation of restrictions on Jewish immigration. Simpson wrote in 1939 that the Dutch were 'deeply stirred by the intensified persecution of German Jews in November 1938, and the Government were strongly urged to relax restrictions.'[24] In Britain, too, heavy pressure on the government led to the establishment of a special cabinet commission to streamline procedures for receiving and assisting Jewish refugees.[25] But with the onset of war in 1939, restrictions on emigration made it more difficult to flee Nazi persecution. Around 350,000 refugees had managed to escape Nazi persecution before the war broke out, but between 1939–41 only 71,500 managed to flee Germany and Austria.[26]

World War Two precipitated huge refugee flows, with an estimated 30 million people displaced in Europe over the course of the war. The largest movements of refugees in Europe occurred in the last stages of the war, as millions of people were displaced by intensive fighting and aerial bombardments in 1944–5. In 1943 the Western Allies established the UN Relief and Rehabilitation Administration (UNRRA) to provide relief and assist repatriation. Between 1943–6, UNRRA repatriated around fourteen million people in Europe. But around one million 'unrepatriables' remained, most of whom were Soviet citizens who refused to return to the USSR. Again, while this period was marked by the movement of large numbers of refugees, the problem was characterised as the result of temporary conflict and upheaval in Europe. Once these displaced people had been repatriated, it was hoped that refugee flows would largely dry up, and there would be no further need for international mechanisms.

The inter-war years, then, had been characterised by largescale refugee flows, mainly resulting from nation-state formation in the 1920s and fascism in the 1930s. The Christian and liberal notions that had influenced responses to refugees in the nineteenth century proved difficult to sustain in the face of economic depression and international security concerns. But as yet, no clear-cut conceptions of refugee rights had been codified, and so the notion of a conflict between refugee rights and national interests was still not conceptualised in the way it is today. However, in the post-World War Two era there was a discernible shift from refugee definitions based on group characteristics to a more general definition based on violation of individual rights. In particular, Cold War politics had a huge impact on the design and evolution of the post-war international refugee regime, producing an individual right-based conception of refugees and an emphasis on resettlement as the favoured response to refugee flows.

Refugee Rights Since World War Two

The shift towards a right-based and resettlement oriented approach first emerged in the context of discussions over the constitution of the new International Refugee Organisation (IRO), established to take over responsibility from the provisional UNRRA. In the negotiations over its mandate in 1946, there was a sharp division between communist countries and the West over whether it should assume responsibility for the million 'unrepatriables' from the communist bloc. The Soviet

Union was concerned that the IRO would block the repatriation of these 'traitors, quislings, and war criminals', and use them as a source of recruitment for spies.[27] The predominant Western view was that repatriation must be a voluntary decision eventually prevailed, and the Soviet Union refused to join IRO.

The IRO succeeded in resettling most of the remaining UNRRA caseload. There were substantial labour shortages in Europe, the Americas and Australia, and a clear political incentive to accept those fleeing communist regimes. However, there were growing concerns on the part of the United States (US) about the international expansion of the IRO's activities in the late 1940s. Indian partition, the Palestinian conflict and the Korean War all produced large refugee flows, generating fears that refugee flows would not be limited to East–West movements. In 1950, the Statute of the current United Nations High Commissioner for Refugees (UNHCR) was accepted. The UNHCR had a limited mandate, and its influence was constrained by the refusal of both the US and the Soviet Union to join. Nonetheless, its definition of refugee and the goals of international cooperation to deal with refugees still shapes international refugee policy. similar definition was adopted in the subsequent Convention on the Status of Refugees, drafted in Geneva in 1951. As we saw in the last chapter, the Convention defined refugees as those who are outside their country 'owing to a well-founded fear of being persecuted for reasons of race, religion, nationality, membership of a particular social group or political opinion'.[28] Those party to Convention were obliged not to expel or send refugees back to countries where their 'life or liberty' would be at risk, thereby establishing the right to *non-refoulement* (Article 33 of the Convention). The definition of refugee was clearly based on a universalist theory of human rights, although – as has subsequently been argued – with a bias towards civil and political rights rather than economic, social and cultural ones.

At the time of drafting, there was already some anxiety on the part of states about the potential scope of duties it imposed. As the French delegate argued: 'The right of asylum rested on moral and humanitarian grounds which were freely recognised by receiving countries, but which had certain essential limitations.' In particular, there was considerable debate over the applicability of the right to *non-refoulement* to large groups, with France, the Netherlands, Italy and Germany all arguing that the terms of the Convention should apply to individuals rather than mass influx. Indeed, the Dutch delegate 'wished to have it placed on record that the Conference was in agreement with the interpretation, that the possibility of mass migration across frontiers or of attempted mass migrations was not covered by Article 33'.[29] Nonetheless, the Convention sets no restrictions on the right to *non-refoulement* based on national interest, other than the extreme case in which a refugee may be expelled 'on grounds of national security or public interest', and even in this case the refugee has the right to appeal.[30]

The concerns voiced by some states in the course of these negotiations may have seemed rather exaggerated in the 1950s. The Convention included no right to asylum or nationality, and restricted its provisions to refugees who had become homeless before 1 January 1951. The decision whether or not to include non-

European refugees also remained a prerogative of governments. Yet regardless of the initial intentions of its members, the geographical and temporal scope of the Convention was subsequently expanded. Already from 1957 onwards, the mandate of the High Commissioner was being extended to cover refugee problems in developing countries, including the refugees generated by independence struggles and post-independence civil conflicts.[31] Faced with the *de facto* expansion of international involvement in refugee problems, it was only logical that the right-based definition of refugees be extended to cover refugees from all countries. The provisions of the Convention were given global application by a 1967 Protocol. Indeed, in many states the definition of refugee was also broadened to include those fleeing generalised violence and armed conflict, and more recently gender-based persecution.

The expansion of the scope of refugee law was not perceived as particularly problematic in the 1950s and 1960s, which were dominated by East–West flows. The first major refugee flow was a result of the 1956 Hungarian Revolution, when 200,000 refugees were in need of resettlement. A similar number fled Czechoslovakia after the Soviet invasion. But restrictions on emigration from the Soviet block for the most part kept the numbers of refugees limited, and the continued demand for labour raised no perceived conflict with national interest. Both of these factors, and the ideological symbolism of refugee flows from the East, led to a strong preference for resettlement. The repatriation emphasis of the inter-war years was replaced with what has now been characterised as an 'exile bias',[32] as well as a reluctance to consider ways of addressing the causes of refugee flows. There was little if any discussion of the typically pre-war concern with the range of 'solutions' to refugee problems. UNHCR's role was seen as essentially palliative, its task being to address the symptoms of conflict and human rights abuse rather than their causes.

The terms of the 1951 Convention and the focus on resettlement began to create problems in the 1970s. Since the mid-sixties, there had been concerns about racial tension in the UK, and of societies being 'saturated' with immigrants. The 1973 oil crisis and ensuing recession also led to a decline in the demand for labour, and by the late 1970s all industrialised receiving states had introduced legislation that largely halted immigration flows. With restricted possibilities for immigration, many people from developing countries turned to the remaining routes for entry into industrialised states: family reunification, illegal immigration and asylum. By the 1980s, European asylum systems were overwhelmed with applications, generating the 'asylum crisis' described in the previous chapter.

Faced with large numbers of asylum seekers they had little obvious economic or political incentive to accept, industrialised states found their international legal obligations difficult to fulfil. Two rather different but related problems emerged. One was the administrative and legal difficulty of sorting through large numbers of cases to sift out *bona fide* from what are now termed 'bogus' or 'non-genuine' applicants. This triggered a series of policy measures to reduce access of 'economic migrants' to the asylum procedure, 'streamline' the procedures for determining status, and enforce the return of asylum seekers whose claims were rejected. The focus was on distinguishing between genuine refugees and economic migrants.

What is of more concern to this thesis is the second problem of how to respond to large numbers of *bona fide* refugees, in other words those whose claims *did* meet the criteria for Convention status. The increase in refugee flows to industrialised countries presented a serious challenge to international refugee policy, one that went beyond questions of administrative efficiency and enforcement of restrictionist migration policy. Even if asylum procedures could be reformed to sort through genuine cases quickly and reliably, it is certain that there would still be too many Convention refugees – or at least many more than liberal democracies would be willing to take at present. The feasibility of the 1951 Convention had been contingent on small-scale flows and a willingness of governments to receive refugees. While these flows remained limited and there was a demand of labour in industrialised countries, these provisions were interpreted generously, with states usually granting a wide range of social and political rights and often permanent residence. But by the 1980s the generosity of these provisions and the 'exile bias' became a problematic model for responding to mass influx. For the first time, the universal duties embodied in the Convention seemed clearly to conflict with national interests in restricting immigration.

The perceived conflict between refugee rights and national interests was exacerbated with the end of the Cold War. Most refugees were fleeing persecution and human rights abuse in communist countries, and the West was only too pleased to demonstrate the superiority of the capitalist system through welcoming these victims of oppression. But by 1989, accepting refugees from the East no longer served this symbolic ideological function. This interest had given way to concerns about potential mass influx from eastern Europe and the Soviet Union once emigration restrictions were eased.

Over the same period, there was an alarming increase in illegal immigration, which raised serious concerns about migration control. The rise in irregular movement, entry and stay was in large part a product of increased restrictions on legal possibilities for entry and residence. With the halting of labour migration programmes and the increased restriction of asylum systems, increasing numbers of people sought to reach European countries through illegal border crossing (through smuggling or forged documents). Others entered legally on tourist or business visas and illegally overstayed, often finding work on the black labour market, or delaying deportation through applying for asylum. As border controls became stricter, there was a rise in organised smuggling networks, which assisted would-be migrants in travelling to western Europe, often through highly dangerous routes. Still more nefarious was the practice of trafficking in migrants, which involved assisting people to move and subsequently subjecting them to forced labour, typically prostitution. Many of these routes passed via Central Europe or the Western Balkans, taking advantage of more lax border controls after 1989, as well as the break-down of police and control structures in countries undergoing transition or ethnic conflict. The rise in illegal migration, smuggling and trafficking added to perceptions that migration and asylum flows were becoming unmanageable, that host countries were being flooded with an uncontrollable flux of migrants.

Finally, the prevalence of ethnic conflict in Africa, the former Soviet Confederation of Independent States (CIS) and the former Yugoslavia created largescale movements of refugees to western Europe. The refugee flows caused by conflict in Bosnia and Herzegovina, which ran into hundreds of thousands, dealt a final blow to confidence in existing arrangements, with refugee law seemingly imposing unfeasible requirements.

The refugee crisis that began to emerge in the 1970s sharply focused the notion of a conflict between universal rights and national interests. The theories of universal duties that underpinned the post-World War Two international refugee regime had evolved over centuries, from natural law theories in the sixteenth century, through the Enlightenment and nineteenth century liberalism. But prior to this century, the applicability of liberal universalist theories of rights to refugee issues had never seriously been put to the test. The increase in refugee flows in Europe from the end of the nineteenth century onwards implicitly challenged the feasibility of universalism as the basis for determining asylum policies. But the conflict between liberal universalism and notions of national interest most clearly emerged in the second half of the twentieth century, when the universalist implications of liberal rights were given substance in international refugee law. The liberal universalist conception of refugee rights embodied in the Geneva Convention was seen as feasible in the context of the Cold War and economic growth. But with changes in the nature and scale of refugee flows, and economic and social tensions in receiving countries, these international obligations seemed to impose overly stringent demands. And the nationalist ideas and narrow definitions of the 'national interest' that had been influencing immigration restriction since the 1900s seemed to be incompatible with universal duties.

Reconsidering Liberal Universalist Conceptions of Duties to Refugees

This perceived conflict between refugee rights and national interests has raised serious questions about the feasibility and, in some quarters, the desirability of recognising universal duties to refugees. So what, then, are the prospects for rescuing liberal universalist conceptions from this critique, and encouraging a less restrictionist policy to refugees?

Liberal universalist theories are now caught in a difficult position. Having successfully codified a conception of universal rights in international refugee law, there is a risk that this conception will become increasingly marginalised because of its perceived conflict with national interests. To many, it no longer seems feasible to expect states to perform duties that run so directly counter to their political and economic interests. This problem of the feasibility of realising refugee rights is partly a product of the liberal universalist notion of a split between universalist ethical duty and self-interest. Liberal universalists have tended to assume a separation between the spheres of impartial ethics and interests, a separation that is also reflected in the liberal universalist conception of rights framed in the current international refugee regime. Existing provisions on refugee rights are thus premised on the notion that states should and will be motivated to adhere to their international obligations from liberal or humanitarian principles, rather than because it is in the national interest.

These requirements of refugee law seemed feasible in the 1950s and 1960s, when recognising refugee rights appeared to coincide with national interests. This meant that the problem of feasibility did not arise, and there was no real need to question whether states were motivated to respect refugee rights out of moral duty or self interest. However, since the 1970s there has been a growing perception of the economic and social costs of refugees, and hence a perception that these international obligations conflict with the national interest. Many consider that it now seems unrealistic for states to respect their international obligations on refugee rights: the only motivation to do so would be moral, a question of pure ethical principle, rather than through any interest the state may have. And this is the source of the current problem of feasibility for liberal universalist theories. Not only are ethical considerations viewed as separate from political and economic interests, as they were in the 1950s and 1960s. They are now perceived as being directly in conflict with them, and the only reason to respect refugee rights seems to be a purely altruistic – some would say utopian – commitment to moral principle.

There are two possibilities for overcoming this perceived conflict and avoiding the marginalisation of liberal universalist conceptions of refugee rights. One would be a change in the empirical conditions that have prompted states to see refugees as a threat to national interests. Such a shift could create a coincidence between current conceptions of national interests and duties to refugees. I have already given my reasons for not pursuing this sort of empirical analysis. My focus is on the potential for changing conceptions of the relationship between refugee rights and national interests. This second possibility for resolving the perceived conflict between refugee rights and national interests involves rejecting the liberal universalist (and realist) assumption of a split between duty and interests. The claims is that conceptions of ethical duty can shape national interests, so that it is simplistic to assume any clear separation of the two.

The task of the next two chapters is to examine current universalist conceptions, and to suggest the origins of this problem of marginalisation. Using the criteria outlined in the introduction – normative desirability, practical feasibility, and internal coherence – it will critically evaluate the main variants of different liberal theories in turn.

Notes

1   Richard Tuck, *Natural Rights Theories: Their Origin and Development* (Cambridge, 1979), p. 8.
2   F. de Vitoria, 'De Indis', in A. Pageden (ed.), *Vitoria: Political Writings* (Cambridge, 1991).
3   Hugo Grotius, *Grotius on the Rights of War and Peace*, trans. William Whewell (Cambridge, 1953).
4   J.W. Gough, *The Social Contract: A Critical Study of its Development* (Oxford, 1936).
5   Charles Taylor, *Sources of the Self: The Making of Modern Identity* (Harvard, 1989), pp. 361–6.
6   For accounts of the early history of nation-state formation, see Hagen Schulze, *States, Nations and Nationalism: From the Middle Ages to the Present* (Oxford, 1996); and Charles Tilly, *The Formation of National States in Western Europe* (Princeton, 1975).
7   Michael Mann, 'A Political Theory of Nationalism and its Excesses' in Sukumar Perival (ed.), *Notions of Nationalism* (Budapest, 1995), pp. 180–200; and 'The Dark Side of Democracy: The Modern Tradition of Ethnic Cleansing', *New Left Review*, 235 (1999): 18–45. Rogers Brubaker, *Citizenship and Nationhood in France and Germany* (Cambridge, 1992).
8   Hans Joachim Morgenthau, *Politics Among Nations: The Struggle for Power and Peace* (New York, 1954).
9   Daniel Statt, *Foreigners and Englishmen: The Controversy over Immigration and Population, 1660–1760* (Newark, 1995), pp. 25–6.
10 Cited in Michael Marrus, *The Unwanted: European Refugees in the 20th Century* (New York, 1985), p. 8.
11 Statt, pp. 43–51.
12 Daniel Defoe, *A Brief History of the Poor Palatine Refugees, Lately Arriv'd in England* (London, 1709), p. 9.
13 Marrus, pp. 18–19.
14 Cited in Statt, p. 89.
15 Sarah Collinson, *Europe and International Migration* (London, 1994), p. 34
16 James Walvin, *Passage to Britain: Immigration in British History and Politics* (Harmondsworth, 1984), pp. 63–4.
17 Cites in John A. Garward, *The English and Immigraiton, 1880–1910* (Oxford, 1971), p. 46.
18 Garward, pp. 46 and 88.
19 For figures, see Collinson p. 36.
20 Mann, 'The Dark Side of Democracy', p. 65.
21 Marrus, p. 174.
22 Cited in John George Stoessinger, *The Refugee and the World Community* (Minneapolis, 1956), pp. 15–16
23 Cited in Marrus, p. 150.
24 Sir John Hope Simpson, *Refugees: A Review of the Situation since September 1938*(Oxford, 1939), p. 78.
25 Ibid, p. 69.
26 Marrus, p. 205.
27 Stoessinger, p. 66.

28 Article 1A, *Convention Relating to the Status of Refugees*, Geneva 28 July 1951 (Geneva, 1995).

29 Paul Weis, *The Refugee Convention, 1951: The Travaux Preparatoires Analyzed* (Cambridge, 1994), p. 335.

30 *Convention*, Article 32 (1). There are other grounds for the exclusion of a refugee from the terms of the Convention, but they are not directly related to the national interest – see Article 1 (f).

31 Leon Gordenker, *Refugees in International Politics* (London, 1987), and Cecilia Runstrom-Ruin, *Beyond Europe: The Globalization of Refugee Aid* (Lund, 1993), pp. 22–3.

32 See Gervaise Coles, 'Approaching the Refugee Problem Today', in Gil Loescher and Laila Monahan (eds), *Refugees and International Relations* (Oxford, 1990), pp. 373–410.

Chapter Two

Liberal Universalism and the Problem of Feasibility

Most legal and ethical arguments for extending duties to refugees derive their justification from some form of liberal universalist theory. International refugee law is grounded in a conception of universal rights, and proponents of a more generous asylum policy tend to invoke notions of universal duties to defend their claims. It therefore makes sense to start our discussion of conceptions of duties to refugees with an examination of liberal universalist theories. Why do they appear inadequate for mounting a robust defence of refugee rights?

Refugees and Liberal Political Theory

Categorising Liberal Universalist Theories

A universalist moral or political theory is one that gives equal weight to the interests or well-being of all human beings. Thus whatever the theory's conception of the good or the conditions for human well-being, it will start from the premise that every individual has an equal moral claim to this good and/or the means for pursuing it. Universalist theories are based on an assumption of the moral equality of human beings. This implies that the morally relevant characteristics of human beings are those which are universally shared, for example the capacity for reason, or interest in maximising pleasure. A radical or 'thick' universalist theory will assume that the only morally relevant features of human beings are those that are universal. The theory will give equal consideration to the interests of each individual, regardless of their particular characteristics, ties, or other non-universal features.

Universalism, as noted in Chapter One, should be contrasted to communitarian or 'particularist' theories, which hold that the proper subject matter of morality is specific groups or communities rather than all people *qua* human beings. Such special moral claims may be grounded in scepticism as to the possibility of establishing a universally accepted system of ethical values, or more radical moral relativism. This may provide an argument for limiting the scope of moral duties to the relevant sphere of shared ethical values. Alternatively, particularism may be based on a theory of morality that holds that certain groups or individuals have a greater moral claim by virtue of their relationship to the moral agent. For example, family members may have a special moral claim even if the conditions for their well-being are universally shared. Their interests may generate special duties on the part of particular agents (in this case other family members), despite the fact that these interests may be common to all human beings.

While universalist theories all give equal weight to the claims of individuals, they differ on the question of which universal characteristics give rise to claims to equal treatment. Broadly speaking, liberal theories are characterised by the importance they attach to liberty. Thus the relevant shared characteristics in liberal theory will be the individual's interest in freedom or the conditions for realising freedom. But beyond this loose definition of liberal universalism, there is considerable divergence between different theories.

First, there is an important distinction to be made between deontological and consequentilaist theories. Deontological theories hold that the morally relevant characteristic of human beings is their rationality, or capacity for autonomy. The purpose of political theory is to ensure the equal distribution of freedom to enable individuals to exercise these capacities. The equal distribution of freedom is usually ensured through a system of rights, which enable individuals to realise individual freedom. The guarantee of the relevant rights over-rides other goods, for example the pursuit of social goals or maximisation of pleasure.

There are two main types of deontological theories. First, there are those that derive and justify rights and theories of justice through consent. These are better known as social contract theories, which aim to secure individual autonomy through a procedure which enables individuals to select terms for regulating their interaction. Most social contract theories have traditionally been designed to construct rules for a given group of people or society, typically for separate states. In this sense they are less straightforwardly universalist, as many (but not all) of them see their object as to secure compliance with rules to regulate the interaction of given communities or states. The focus on the domestic social contract raises a number of issues distinct from the discussion of purer forms of right-based universalism, and will be examined in Chapter Four. The second type of deontological theory comprises those theories that derive rights from a specific conception of interests and needs. This second variety of right-based universalist theories take as their starting point a more elaborate account of the conditions for freedom or well-being, rather than a procedure for selecting principles. This second form of deontological theory will be discussed later in this chapter.

Consequentialist theories, by contrast, are not aiming to create the conditions for people to realise autonomy. Rather, they are concerned with end-states: whether people end up being happy, or fulfilled, or meeting their needs. The most important form of consequentialism is utilitarianism. Unlike right-based theories, utilitarian theories consider the morally relevant characteristic of humans to be their interest in happiness, pleasure or some other conception of well-being. Utilitarianism holds that the rightness of wrongness of an act or rule depends on its effect on the welfare of all human beings. Welfare in this context can be defined in a number of ways. Bentham defined it in a narrow sense, as pleasure and the absence of pain, while Mill famously distinguished between 'higher' and 'lower' pleasures, according a privileged status to intellectual well-being over sensual pleasures.[1] Some recent utilitarians have broadened it to encompass more general conceptions of well-being, including notions of the 'good' that are at least partially independent of their contribution to pleasure and the absence of pain.[2] The emphasis on utility, however defined, does raise a number of issues about what counts as a legitimate interest, need or desire. In particular, it will make a significant difference to the theory whether utility is measured according to subjective, perceived well-being, or defined on the basis of some external standard. I shall return to this distinction later in the discussion.

Two main elements distinguish utilitarian theories from deontological theories. The first is their consequentialist structure. They evaluate acts according to their effect on the well-being of people, rather than on the grounds of any intrinsic value of the act or principle in question. Their central concern is to promote the greatest good for all people: they do not attribute moral significance to the typically deontological concern with integrity or intentions. Secondly, utilitarian theories do not accord any intrinsic value to individual freedom. Liberty is valued insofar as it is instrumental to well-being or happiness, but is not an end in itself. Nonetheless, most utilitarians argue that liberty is an essential component or precondition for well-being, and thus defend a robust conception of liberty on utilitarian grounds. Utilitarian theories may therefore be classified as "liberal" in a broad sense, and it is to these liberal utilitarian theories that I now turn.

Maximising Utility

Utilitarianism might initially appear to provide a good basis for characterising duties to refugees. Indeed, a number of theorists have employed utilitarian theory to construct accounts of duties to non-nationals.[3] The universalist premises of utilitarian theories mean that they attach no special moral relevance to nationality, over and beyond duties to humanity in general. A utilitarian theory of duties to non-nationals would give equal consideration to the interests of all. Any recognition of special duties would have to be justified on instrumental grounds – as the best means of realising universal utility. As the utilitarian theorist Goodin points out, on this account the 'duties that states (or, more precisely their officials) have *vis-à-vis* their own citizens are not in any deep sense special. At root they are merely the general duties that everyone has toward everyone else worldwide'.[4]

Utility and the Problem of Subjective Preferences

The first major hurdle for a utilitarian theory is the problem of how to define utility. Classical utilitarians defined utility as a subjective state experienced by individuals. On this account, utility denoted the individual's happiness, or pleasure and the absence of pain. The level of happiness or pleasure experienced by the individual provided the main criterion for assessing the rightness of acts and evaluating rules and goods. The *quantity* of utiles (units of happiness) experienced was, according to this form of classical utilitarianism, the sole basis for such evaluations. Thus the goal of any act or policy would be to maximise the utility of all people, including non-nationals.

One central problem with this classical account is that it fails to make any qualitative distinctions between the sorts of goods that may contribute to utility. As Mill was to point out, the account allows for no distinction between different sorts of pleasure. Thus there is no scope for prioritising more enriching experiences over, for example, instant gratification of the senses, except on the grounds of the *quantity* of pleasure derived. So a contented slave could be said to derive as much utility as an angst-ridden philosopher who enjoyed a far higher level of autonomy and intellectual satisfaction. This will clearly not do for a conception of duties to refugees. It would fail to make the relevant qualitative distinction between different types of pleasure or pain. For example, it could not adequately capture the qualitative distinction between the subjective state of a refugee who had been able to escape persecution but felt lonely and disoriented in his country of asylum; and one who had been imprisoned in his country, but continued to enjoy the friendship of fellow inmates. Both may derive the same level of utility – or the second may derive even more – but many would value the freedom of the refugee over the pleasure felt by the prisoner. The classical concept of utility seems too crude a measurement for evaluating the desirability of different states.

Mill's solution was to introduce a qualitative distinction between higher and lower pleasures, while maintaining that these different types of pleasure all fell within the same category of 'utility'. He thus qualified the purely quantitative account of pleasure provided by classical utilitarians, but without abandoning utility as the sole and ultimate standard of evaluation. Mill's justification for this qualitative distinction is extremely weak. It is difficult to see how one can defend a *qualitative* distinction between different types of pleasure, solely on the grounds that higher pleasures produce a greater *quantity* of utility. In other words, Mill seems to be implicitly accepting the existence of a standard of evaluation which is independent of the criterion of pleasure. What he refers to as the heterogeneity of pleasure surely reflects an acknowledgement of a plurality of values. The 'intrinsic superiority' of higher pleasures such as academic study over, say, eating chocolate is based on the value attached to intellectual achievement, knowledge, or independence of thought. And the superiority of seeking asylum over imprisonment is based on the intrinsic value attached to liberty. In addition to pleasure, then, one might want to introduce additional criteria for assessing the value of different goods. Such criteria might include the contribution of acts or goods to the development of virtues (for example intellectual excellence, compassion or creativity); or the intrinsic value of exercising certain capacities (autonomy, reason or moral integrity). Even if one accepts Mill's argument that those who have experienced higher and lower pleasures will tend to prefer the former – and this is a highly dubious empirical claim – it is far from clear that this preference is based solely on the contribution to utility. Rather, it would imply that utility is not the sole standard of evaluation. In short, the concept of subjective utility will not suffice on its own.

There is a second problem with the subjective account. In addition to the problem of qualitative distinctions, relying on subjective states may produce extremely unpalatable patterns of distribution. Certain people might have very expensive or demanding tastes, and require a greater amount of a particular good to achieve the same level of utility. An especially difficult case for the utilitarian is that of how to deal with those with morally objectionable preferences. For example a racist person's utility might be increased through the restriction of asylum. If duties to refugees are determined on the basis of the equal consideration of individual preferences, then these racist attitudes would be factored into the equation of utility distribution. If the strength of racist feeling were sufficiently high, then the loss of utility resulting from taking in refugees might provide grounds for restricting influx. Yet most liberal theorists would not accept racist attitudes as a morally acceptable ground for limiting refugee influx. While they may in fact influence government policies on restriction, liberals would not consider such views to constitute moral grounds for justifying a particular distribution. In other words, some preferences would not generally be considered as providing morally legitimate grounds for claiming goods or preferring certain states of affairs. Accepting such attitudes as a basis for distributing utility would produce a pattern of distribution that would seem to contradict the universalist principles on which utilitarian theory is based.[5]

In conclusion, not only does the exclusive reliance on the standard of utility deny the existence of other values. It also potentially legitimises morally dubious preferences. The only acceptable route for utilitarians seems to be to introduce a broader conception of utility, which embraces a plurality of values that contribute to human well-being. And, moreover, to define well-being on the basis of certain external, non-subjective criteria. Indeed, many utilitarians have argued that the problems raised by relying on subjective utility justifies the introduction of objective criteria for measuring welfare.[6] Thus utility should be defined in terms of objectively definable goods, such as wealth, healthcare, accommodation, security, and so on. Utilitarian theories based purely on the notion of the individual's subjective happiness seem to be untenable. And this represents the first of a number of retreats from utility towards some theory of rights.

Distributing Utility: Aggregate Maximisation and Equality

Once the question of *what* to distribute has been settled, the issue arises of *how* to distribute these goods. The two most famous distributional principles are the maximising or 'aggregating' principle, and the egalitarian principle. Let us consider the maximising principle first, often termed the 'aggregate utility' principle. According to this principle, the ultimate goal of any action or policy is to maximise the total amount of utility or welfare. This aggregate utility principle has been widely criticised as failing to be sensitive to the distribution of utility between individuals.[7] If what matters is the maximisation of total aggregate utility, then this goal may be achieved through profoundly unequal patterns of distribution. For example, one person's interests might be legitimately sacrificed for the sake of a smaller increase in the well-being of a large number of people. The possibility of such sacrifice raises familiar objections to utilitarianism, notably its conflict with widespread intuitions about justice. As Rawls puts it, on a utilitarian account 'there is no reason in principle why the greater gains of some should not compensate for the lesser losses of others; or more importantly, why the violation of the liberty of a few might not be made right by the greater good shared by many'.[8]

The case against this extreme form of aggregate utility is now widely accepted, and most contemporary utilitarian theories have defended some alternative principle for distributing utility. The most obvious alternative is to embrace an egalitarian principle of distribution. Egalitarian theories aim to achieve equal utility for all, giving equal consideration to the welfare of each individual. One can find an example of this type of average utility approach in the work of Peter Singer, who advocates a principle of equal consideration. In his discussion of the distribution of welfare, he argues that this principle of equality 'acts like a pair of scales', which 'favour the side where the interest is stronger or where several interests combine to outweigh a smaller number of similar interests'.[9] In other words, the distribution of goods is determined on the basis of an evaluation of relative interests. The distributive principle should give precedence to more pressing concerns over less fundamental interests. It would also mean that the claims of those with less of the good in question are given priority over those with a greater quantity of the good. The principle of equal consideration would therefore necessitate a redistribution of goods until the interests of all parties are equally met, thus achieving a balance of equal consideration.

Singer applies this principle of equal consideration to the question of refugees.[10] He argues that since the concern to escape from persecution is clearly more pressing than the concerns of those in receiving countries to limit admission, there are grounds for a considerable extension of duties to refugees. Where there is a conflict between the interests of refugees and rich receiving states, the latter should be expected to make greater sacrifices of welfare than they currently do. The utility gained for the refugee by avoiding torture or death will be far greater than the utility sacrificed by receiving countries through a rise in taxes, or living in a more densely populated country.

However, Singer is aware that the scales model of equal consideration could imply substantial loss of utility for receiving countries. A generous entry policy would be likely to encourage far more people to emigrate from poorer countries, potentially leading to mass influx into richer states. This could jeopardise the more fundamental interests of receiving countries. On the principle of equal consideration, restrictions on entry would only be justified in cases where the sacrifice of individuals in the receiving state outweighed the benefits derived by refugees. But this might lead to a situation in which the utility of both refugees and receiving states is scaled down to a significantly lower level. Rather than increasing the welfare of refugees, the principle of equal consideration might imply a decline in the welfare of receiving states until it was equal to that of the refugee sending state. Singer acknowledges that this would be problematic when he writes,

> Since the interests of the refugees in resettlement in a more prosperous country will always be greater than the conflicting interests of the residents of those countries, it would seem that the principle of equal consideration of interests points to a world in which all countries continue to accept refugees until they are reduced to the same standard of poverty and overcrowding as the third world countries from which the refugee are seeking to flee.[11]

Not only does this conception of duties to refugees seem to be totally unfeasible, it also leads to what Joseph Raz has termed a problem of 'wastage'.[12] Singer's scales model fails to distinguish between policies that equalise utility by *withdrawing* a good or entitlement; and those that ensure an equal distribution through granting this good to those who do not have it. In the former case, the principle of equal consideration would cause wastage of utility. Where equality of utility is the main goal, it may result in a substantial decline in the utility of each person. In this sense, it would conflict with the goal of utility maximisation. As Barry puts it, 'the principle of equal utility, if interpreted strictly, would require us to say that a situation of equally shared misery was morally preferable to a situation in which everyone was very happy but some were more so than others'.[13]

The best way of avoiding these distributional problems would be to introduce a threshold of welfare or utility, below which individuals should not morally be required to fall. This is the approach implicitly adopted by Singer to respond to the problem of wastage. He argues that there are certain grounds on which it would be justifiable to restrict influx prior to the point at which the welfare of receiving countries was scaled down to that of refugees. For example, where there is a threat of irreparable damage to the environment, or a serious danger to security, 'the balance of interests would have swung against a further increased in the intake of refugees'.[14]

This is a reasonable condition, but it is not one that Singer can easily incorporate into his scales model. The scales model assumes that goods should be maximised, consistent with their equal distribution. Loosely stated, the goal is to achieve the greatest possible amount of utility for each person. But the introduction of the notion of a threshold implies that the goods in question have other characteristics not captured by this distributive principle. First, it implies – as we have seen – that there is a minimum level of welfare, below which individuals should not be expected to fall, even if this means that others remain even worse off. This means that there is a minimum acceptable quantity of the good, and that ensuring the minimum amount for some could take precedence over ensuring equal distribution for all at a level beneath this minimum. So the distributive principle becomes more complex than that of simply maximising utility consistent with its equal distribution. A second feature of goods not recognised by the scales model is what Raz has termed 'satiability'. Raz argues that maximising principles such as the one advanced by Singer are not sufficiently nuanced to capture the notion that most claims to utility or welfare are satiable. In other words, they are demands that can be met by a given level of distribution. Any allocation of utility above this level becomes unnecessary, or at least a less urgent concern. Satiable goods are also 'diminishing', in that the more of the good a person has, the weaker the reason to give her more of this good.[15]

According to Raz, '[t]he ideals at the foundation of morality and politics are all diminishing and satiable principles'.[16] Certainly, the sorts of goods at stake in the conflict between refugee rights and national interests would seem to be satiable and diminishing. These would include interests of refugees in securing physical security and material welfare, and the interests of receiving goods such as a healthy natural environment, or a tolerant society. These are not goods that it would make sense to maximise indefinitely. For example, the interest in physical security or living in a tolerant society involve goods that will be satiated at a certain level. Such satiable goods allow one to define a level of needs, or threshold of welfare, below which individuals or groups should not be expected fall. And the notion of satiability enables one to distinguish between priority cases, where individuals are lacking even the most basic needs, and cases where basic needs are satisfied and thus of less urgent concern. This notion of satiation departs from utility maximising principles, introducing a layer of needs. But it is a concept that is simply not captured by utilitarian models based on equality and/or maximising principles. In fact, this is true not just of Singer's theory, but of all such utilitarian accounts.

To summarise the argument so far, utilitarian theories face a number of problems that point strongly to the need for a conception of rights. Firstly, theories that rely on subjective states have problems defining utility, and can lead to morally unacceptable patterns of distribution, necessitating the introduction of some external or objective criteria for measuring welfare. Secondly, utilitarian theories have difficulties with distributive principles. Those theories based on an aggregate maximising principle will be insufficiently sensitive to questions of distribution. Utilitarians have attempted to avoid this problem through adopting a principle of average utility maximisation. However, this averaging principle creates its own problems. Strict equality may call for distributions that simply scale down the average utility, rather than tolerating some inequality at a higher level of utility for all. The discussion will now consider whether alternative accounts of utilitarian theory can avoid these problems.

Alleviating Suffering

Before turning to right-based theories, it is worth examining a second variety of utilitarian theory that appears to avoid these problems. Rather than seeking to maximise utility, such theories have the (apparently) more modest goal of alleviating suffering. One of the more sophisticated theories of this kind is provided by Goodin. Goodin's theory of universal duties avoids many of the shortcomings of utility maximising theories. He defends a consequentialist theory of duties to non-nationals that is defined on the basis of an objective criterion of well-being – the concept of vulnerability. He argues that individuals have a duty to protect and assist those who are dependent on them or vulnerable to their actions and choices. The theory is universalist, in that it denies the intrinsic significance of special duties to compatriots. Non-nationals and refugees in principle have an equal claim to be protected and assisted. As he writes, 'the state's special responsibility to its own citizens is, at root, derived from the same considerations that underlies its general duty to the refugee.' As such, 'it would be wrong for any state to press the claims of its own citizens strongly, to the disadvantage of those who have no advocate in the system', i.e. refugees.[17]

Protecting the Vulnerable

The notion of vulnerability seems to overcome the two central problems with the theories discussed in the last section: the need for thresholds, and the problem of relying on subjective preferences. First, the vulnerability principle is not an exclusively maximising principle, in that it does not aim at an unlimited increase in utility. Nor does it aim to maximise total utility at the expense of equal distribution. Rather, it has the more negative aim of avoiding harm and suffering. The notion of avoiding harm clearly assumes a threshold of welfare below which individuals should not be expected to fall. Where they are below this level, other agents are morally required to assist or protect them in order to attain the acceptable threshold of well-being. In the case of refugees, one might define the threshold as including protection from physical threats, assistance to meet material needs, or some other list of conditions linked to the 1951 Convention definition of refugee. Since the principle is based on a threshold concept rather than a scales model, it would not justify redistribution which involved denying these goods to those who already enjoyed them, for the sake of achieving the goal of equality.

Secondly, the vulnerability thesis is less susceptible to the problem of subjective preferences. The conditions necessary for avoiding harm and suffering would be objectively definable, and would apply equally to all human beings. They would be based on a conception of universally shared human needs, and thus the quantity required for each individual would not vary significantly (or at least not on morally arbitrary grounds). Thus the problem of inter-personal comparison would not arise.

However, there are a number of rather different problems with Goodin's account. The first difficulty is that of how it responds to the problem of feasibility. If all individuals are morally obliged to protect and assist others, then there seems to be no limit to the moral demands of the vulnerability thesis. It would imply the obligation to extend protection and assistance to all those below the relevant threshold, thus imposing potentially limitless duties on moral agents. In terms of refugee policy, the vulnerability thesis would deny the relevance of special duties to compatriots, and thus advocate a far more generous refugee policy. Goodin attempts to avoid the problem of feasibility by arguing that there are instrumental or pragmatic grounds for dividing responsibility for protection, on the basis of an agent's relation to other individuals.

> On balance, persons relatively near to us in space and in time probably *will* be rather more vulnerable to us. Their interests are more likely to be affected more heavily by our actions and choices than are the interests of persons more distant; and our nearer neighbours in space and time are more likely to be depending on us, more or less exclusively, for assistance and protection.[18]

The notion of allocation based on vulnerability, then, provides the justification for a moral division of labour on instrumental grounds. Goodin argues that a moral agent has special duties to those who stand in a particular relation to her. 'What is crucial, in my view, is that others are depending on us. They are particularly vulnerable to our actions and choices. That, I argue, is the true source of all the standard special responsibilities that we so readily acknowledge'.[19] On this account, the moral agent has a special responsibility to people who are currently dependent on her support, thus presumably limiting the scope of moral duty to manageable proportions.

Yet it is difficult to see how one can sustain a distinction between actual and potential dependency. Why should a moral agent have a duty to assist those currently dependent on her, but not to extend protection and assistance to all those who might benefit from it? The distinction between actual and potential dependants seems to rest on some implicit notion of the instrumental benefits of division of labour. Such instrumental arguments for dividing universal duties – as will be seen in the next chapter – tend to be based on some argument about why an agent will be better qualified to assist or protect those nearer to her. For example, one could justify a division of labour on the grounds that people with close geographic or cultural ties would have better information about people's needs, or could be more efficient in supplying their needs. I may have a better understanding of the needs of people from my tribe or neighbourhood, or may be better located geographically to deliver food to people living near to me.

Now while some of these arguments may justify a division of labour on instrumental grounds, Goodin's account does not seem to provide a very convincing defence of such an arrangement. The criterion of actual dependency does not seem to be a legitimate ground for allocating responsibility. It may potentially be far more effective for a particular agent to perform duties to a given group of people who are not currently dependent on her. For example, she may have a particular talent for conflict mediation or be especially motivated to help lepers in Calcutta. Even though they are not actually vulnerable to her actions, there would be strong utilitarian grounds for her to carry out duties of assistance to these leprosy sufferers or attempt to resolve conflict between two ethnic groups. Conversely, one could imagine a group of people living in extreme poverty on a desert island, with no particular ties to other peoples. In this case their welfare would not be directly dependent on the actions of any specific agents, and thus there would be no obvious candidates for assisting them.[20] The division of responsibility according to actual dependence does not seem to be justifiable on utilitarian grounds. It will not be the most effective means of meeting needs, and will thus fail to promote universal welfare.

Quite apart from the dubious justification of the division of moral labour, there is also a significant practical problem with the thesis. As has been argued, the relation in which an agent stands to her dependants is not permanently fixed. If the vulnerability thesis were to provide a universal principle for the distribution of responsibility, then it would presumably lead people to alter their relations so that they could derive increased benefit from agents. If one person or state is in a good position to extend protection and assistance to others, then it is likely to encourage more people to enter into a relationship of dependency on this state. This would clearly be the case with refugee policy. On Goodin's account, a state would have special responsibility for those who are claiming asylum at their borders or in their territory. Since these people are especially vulnerable to the actions of receiving states, this would generate special duties on the part of the state to accept them. But this would presumably encourage much larger numbers of people to travel to the state in question so that they too would be in a similar dependency relation. Thus Goodin's argument for division of labour is practically unworkable, as well as ethically unjustifiable.

Vulnerability and Dependency

There is a second problem with the potential consequences of adopting the vulnerability thesis, and this is common to all utilitarian theories that employ a notion of harm avoidance, or what I shall term the negative conditions for basic well-being. One of the virtues of the vulnerability thesis, as we saw, was its ability to define objective conditions for avoiding harm that were equally valid for all human beings. Yet defining the theory's end or *telos* as avoidance of harm and protection of the vulnerable provides only a partial conception of well-being. The classical utilitarians – problematic as their theories were – did at least have a conception of well-being which incorporated happiness as well as the absence of pain. And the provision of such a positive conception is vital for a consequentialist theory. After all, these theories evaluate acts according to the desirability of their consequences. So without a full account of desired consequences, one can only have a limited assessment of the desirability of the act.

The absence of a fuller conception of flourishing would not be so problematic if securing these minimum conditions were a pre-condition for achieving positive well-being. But the difficulty for the vulnerability thesis is that achieving its goals detracts from and even undermines the search for human flourishing. If one limits the political goal to the avoidance of harm, then there is a risk that this will limit scope for seeking more satisfactory solutions that address the causes of vulnerability, and achieve a fuller form of human flourishing. Relieving distress and protecting the vulnerable would encourage dependency on short-term assistance, which would detract from the longer term goal of addressing the conditions that gave rise to dependency, and also limit the development of autonomy.

We can illustrate this point by considering the implications of the dependency thesis in the area of refugee policy. A reliance on immediate assistance and protection would risk encouraging dependency on external aid, to the neglect of actions to address the causes of refugee flows. In particular, a greater dependency would undermine the longer-term capacity to improve conditions in sending countries. The provision of assistance would therefore fail to address the causes of vulnerability, and may well even be counter-productive to this goal. Indeed, concerns about an exclusive emphasis on relieving symptoms prompted a shift of emphasis in the early 1980s towards measures to address the 'root causes' of refugee flows.[21] The root cause approach advocated forms of redistribution and the promotion of human rights in sending countries, through measures such as debt relief, trade liberalisation and foreign direct investment. Although this was largely motivated by the desire to limit refugee flows and thus relieve the burden on receiving countries, it was also seen as a means of improving the situation in sending countries as an end in itself. Measures to empower those in areas of potential emigration was seen as ethically preferable to providing assistance and protection once people were forced to flee.

Likewise, at the level of political theory, the problems of relying on a notion of vulnerability have generated criticism from justice theorists. Barry, for example, has argued that theories of justice are far better placed than notions of humanity to achieve a fair distribution of resources. The principle of humanity sets a limited task of relieving suffering where it occurs. By contrast, justice provides guidance on the best procedures and mechanisms for ensuring a fair distribution of resources. In Barry's words, 'humanity is a question of doing good; justice is a question of power'.[22] The just distribution of resources provides the means of empowering people, and hence can both address the causes of vulnerability, and provide the conditions for autonomy. Such a conception justice would involve the distribution of rights, rather than the distribution of goods that immediately relieve vulnerability.

This notion of autonomy implies commitment to a more positive conception of human flourishing, one that is central to liberal political thought. Yet it is a conception that is not adequately captured by utilitarian theories. As I have tried to show, conceptions of the negative conditions for basic well-being, such as Goodin's vulnerability thesis, provide only a partial account of the goal of political and moral action. The notion of avoiding suffering is not only insufficient as a *telos*, it also potentially undermines the achievement of more positive goals, through encouraging dependency on outside assistance. On the other hand, we should also recall that utilitarian theories that do try to incorporate a thicker conception of flourishing have problems defining and distributing the goods necessary for individual well-being. The more complex the conditions for human flourishing, the more problematic it becomes to ensure the fair distribution of these conditions. In particular, where individual autonomy is central to the conception of flourishing, as it is on the liberal account, then the utilitiarian account is ill-equipped to ensure proper distribution. What all of this points to is the need to introduce objective entitlements or goods that enable individuals to realise these goods – in short, a theory of rights.

Utilitarian theories do not after all appear to be very good candidates for characterising the relationship between refugee rights and national interests. The arguments against utilitarian accounts in this section have been various, and it is worth briefly recapitulating the main steps of the critique. First, theories based on subjective preferences or conceptions of welfare failed to produce morally acceptable patterns of distribution. As a conception of duties to refugees, the utility-maximising, subjective preference model would lead to morally unacceptable patterns of distribution. Moreover, the emphasis on utility maximisation failed to take into account notions of satiation and diminishing returns, implying the need for some notion of threshold. Many critics of utility maximising theories therefore point to the superiority of right-based theories in ensuring adequate distribution.

Having dismissed utility maximising accounts, the discussion considered whether Goodin's vulnerability thesis could avoid these two problems. He introduced a satiable and diminishing conception of welfare based on external criteria. However, the theory encountered a different set of shortcomings. The first problem of the grounds for dividing labour was specific to his theory, and it is also a problem that recurs in different forms in right-based theories. So it was relevant to the critique of Goodin's account, but did not imply that we should reject all negative utilitarian accounts. The second problem, however, was common to all such theories. It was the point that the focus on avoidance of suffering would be likely to encourage further dependency on assistance, thereby increasing the problem of feasibility. And dependency on the provision of immediate assistance and protection might lead to a neglect of the causes of vulnerability.

Utilitarian theories seem to face a choice between a positive conception of utility that faces insurmountable problems of distribution; and a negative conception that undermines the achievement of human flourishing. Again, the preferable alternative seems to be a theory of justice that distributes the means for achieving autonomy and self-sufficiency. So I shall now turn to an examination of right-based theories.

Right-based Universalism

Deontological or right-based theories may derive and justify rights from a number of different assumptions about the nature of human beings. Typically, liberal theories derive rights from a conception of the individual as having an interest in freedom. This interest justifies imposing duties on others to respect one's freedom. Since all people have a common interest in freedom, there is an equal right to such freedom, and hence duties should be imposed so as to ensure the equal distribution of this right.

In a now classic article, the liberal philosopher H.J.L. Hart argued that all rights derive from the basic right to freedom.[23] On this account, the assertion of any right presupposes a commitment to a fundamental right to freedom. This attempt to trace all rights back to a basic right to freedom does, however, have the effect of excluding a large body of liberal rights theories that do not ground all rights in the individual's interest in freedom. For example, it would exclude need-based theories, which hold that rights are grounded in other basic interests, such as the need for subsistence and physical security.[24] Since I want to consider this second class of theories as potential candidates for a conception of duties to refugees, I shall adopt a broader definition of rights. A rights can be understood as an interest of an individual that is important enough to generate requirements of action on the part of others. According to Raz's definition, 'X has a right if and only if X can have rights, and other things being equal, an aspect of X's well-being (his interest) is a sufficient reason for holding some other person(s) to be under a duty'.[25] The notion that there is some such set of universal rights and that these rights are the fundamental principles of morality seems to accord with the prevalent human rights framework.

Right-based universalism has certain *prima facie* advantages as a candidate for reconciling refugee rights and national interests. As with utilitarianism, since nationality has no intrinsic moral relevance, the interests of compatriots are accorded no special weight. Conflicts of interest between refugees and receiving countries can be resolved on the basis of a common scale of value, with each person's interests accorded equal weight. Duties to compatriots would have no special quality or strength over and above duties to the rest of humanity. Let us consider in more detail how well equipped such theories are for the task at hand.

Universal Rights and the Problem of Feasibility

As with utilitarian theories, right-based universalist theories hold that the only morally relevant features of individuals are those which are common to human beings in general. An individual's nationality will therefore not affect the weight accorded to her moral claims. This implies that where certain universal rights are considered fundamental to well-being, each individual should have an equal right to live in a state where these rights can be enjoyed. From this equal right to enjoyment of universal rights, one can derive a universal right to move. If there is a disparity in the quality of universal rights between states, and a person's fundamental rights are not being guaranteed in her home country, she has a right to move to a country where her rights will be better protected. The right to relocate may be understood as derivative of fundamental universal rights. Equally, the fact of being a member of a particular state does not in principle affect the nature and strength of duties to compatriots. Duties to refugees are just as binding as duties to compatriots. While there may be good arguments for dividing up responsibility for enforcing these duties on the basis of a system of separate states, thereby generating a system of special duties between compatriots, such special duties would be justified in an instrumental rather than an intrinsic sense. They would be justified on grounds of efficiency, for example because of proximity or mutual dependence or local knowledge. But these instrumental arguments for a division of labour would be likely to prescribe the extension of duties to those seeking asylum in one's state, since the receiving states would be well placed to provide practical assistance.

On the right-based universalist account, then, there would be no good justification – either intrinsic or instrumental – for privileging the rights of fellow nationals over non-nationals. Indeed, the existence of inequalities between states in terms of the enjoyment of universal rights would imply a duty to admit refugees. The receiving society has no moral justification for restricting influx, except where admission will infringe the universal rights of its nationals to an equivalent or greater degree than the infringement of the universal rights of non-nationals which results from non-admission. As one right-based universalist argues:

> On this view, the collective interest of a receiving society could not be weighed against the individual's right to move, in the sense that the interests of an economy, a culture or a theory of the nation could not be advanced against the right. Only infringement of recognised individual human rights could justify exclusion.[26]

As with the utilitarian universalist accounts considered in the previous section, the most glaring problem with this account is the question of feasibility. States' refugee policies do not remotely approximate to this universalist theory of ethics, nor do states appear to recognise such duties as morally binding. Right-based universalist theories tend to respond to this problem of feasibility in two ways. First, some acknowledge the gap between existing practice and the requirements of universalist rights, defining the problem as a lack of moral motivation. On this account, individuals and their political leaders are simply too selfish to perform the required ethical duties to refugees. In terms of individual nationals of the receiving state, the lack of moral motivation would be characterised as a conflict between duty and self-interest, in which the latter prevails. At the group level, it may be defined as a conflict between universal rights and national interests, in which domestic strategic and economic concerns override duties to non-nationals.

I already raised doubts about the practical implications of this account in the Introduction. Explaining the gap between current practice and the requirements of universal ethics as a problem of motivation is not problematic simply because it produces an unfeasible theory. More seriously, it is potentially counterproductive to its own objectives. Where a theory defines the requirements of morality at an unattainable level, non-compliance with these standards can produce an outcome which is further from the desired goal than the successful realisation of less demanding, or 'second best' moral rules. The possible effects of non-compliance therefore need to be taken seriously. If people are simply not motivated to comply with the relevant moral rules, it suggests the need for a more critical evaluation of the assumptions being made about moral motivation.

Instrumental Justifications for Restriction

The second response of right-based universalist theories to the problem of feasibility is to introduce a series of instrumental arguments for justifying restrictive approaches towards asylum seekers and refugees. This is a common route for universalist right-based theorists, many of whom argue that there are universalist liberal grounds for limiting the equal distribution of rights to refugees in practice. For example, the maintenance of law and order may be a precondition for guaranteeing the right to freedom from arbitrary killing. Likewise, a degree of social stability will be required for the effective functioning of social institutions, again a necessary condition for the protection of universal rights. Such preconditions for individual rights could override equal distribution of rights, as indeed Dummet argues this when she admits that the goal of national security could trump the right to immigrate.[27]

This limited claim about the need to preserve national security is fairly uncontroversial. Indeed, it would be rather paradoxical to argue on universalist grounds for the erosion of the conditions necessary for the realisation of universal rights. Yet the goal of ensuring national security would not provide grounds for a significant restriction of influx. It would still commit liberal receiving states to admitting far higher levels of refugees than at present – possibly millions. So the introduction of the goal of national security as a precondition for the effective exercise of universal rights would not solve the problem of feasibility.

Other liberal universalists have provided more extensive instrumental grounds for justifying restriction, incorporating a wider list of goods or goals which may be considered pre-conditional for the enjoyment of universal rights. A number of liberal political theorists writing on the subject of immigration argue that a range of public goods is necessary for the nurturing of liberal values and institutions. These may be concrete procedural or institutional arrangements, such as the rule of law, due process and a democratic constitution, or more abstract concepts such as the values of tolerance and fairness. Ackerman, for example, argues that citizens must be willing and able to engage in a liberal dialogue, which justifies restriction of immigration 'to protect the ongoing process of liberal conversation'.[28] In similar vein, Matthew Gibney recently suggested that restriction can be justified to preserve the trust and solidarity necessary for sustaining the social state: states should accept 'as many refugees as they can without undermining the provision of collective or public goods amongst their members'.[29]

Yet as the list of requirements gets longer and more complex, it becomes increasingly difficult to evaluate the respective demands of universal rights, and the goods necessary for the longer term enjoyment of these rights. There seems to be a wide margin of variation in assessments of the preconditions for the preservation of universal rights in liberal states. Liberal universalist instrumental arguments could be used to justify a range of immigration policies, from almost open borders to extreme restriction. As Nardin observes, 'liberal egalitarianism sometimes looks like little more than a vehicle for whatever opinions happen currently to be in favour in democratic societies'.[30]

The possibility of defending highly restrictionist policies on such seemingly nebulous instrumental grounds does raise doubts about the adequacy of the right-based model. It seems to create a high level of indeterminacy. The impact of the admission of non-nationals on the goods that are preconditional for the exercise of rights is at best uncertain. Liberal rights theorists would insist that this grey area of indeterminacy could be cleared up – at least in principle – by an assessment of the empirical preconditions for the exercise of rights. The problem of indeterminacy is simply a reflection of the complexity of evaluating exactly how the goods in question will contribute to the enjoyment of rights. In short, a right-based universalist may argue that indeterminacy is not a sufficient reason for abandoning right-based universalism as a framework for refugee policy.

However, the grey area of indeterminacy does beg a number of questions. On the universalist right-based model, as we saw, the problem of indeterminacy allows for a range of justifiable stances on refugee policy. Disagreement over policy revolves around questions of which public goods are necessary for securing universal rights in receiving states and for exporting these rights to other countries, and the extent to which influx of refugees may undermine these goods. Yet it is patently false that disagreements of this kind account for the spectrum of policy positions on admission, or even that they are characteristic of the current policy debate. Those advocating more restrictionist policies tend to do so on domestic-centric grounds, rather than on the basis of tenuous arguments about the longer term protection of universal rights. Such arguments do not start from an impartial, universalist perspective, but particularist considerations, often premised on the moral relevance of nationality.

Right-based universalism would deny the legitimacy of such considerations in designing refugee policy. Particularism is simply a 'rationalization of selfishness'.[31] Yet in many cases, their instrumental arguments for restriction arrive at suspiciously similar conclusions to those of particularists. It would be difficult to dispute that a certain minimum of security is necessary for realising the basic rights

of fellow nationals to subsistence and physical security, and civil liberties. But it is far from evident that the right to housing benefit or use of public parks could trump the right of a non-national to freedom from torture. At any rate, this prioritisation of the rights of compatriots could not be justified on universalist grounds. To put it bluntly, the instrumental arguments for protecting liberal institutions appear somewhat disingenuous – they seem to be excuses for smuggling in a commitment to special ties and the protection of particular ways of life. It is not my intention to deny that such particularist values may be worthwhile. The point is rather that they cannot be justified on purely universalist grounds.

There is a further reason for incorporating at least some form of particularism. Thus far, it has been argued that the grey area of indeterminacy in evaluating the competing interests of refugees and receiving states may disguise a commitment to particularism. Some account of the significance of particular ties and projects, and their relation to moral motivation, will be vital if the universalist perspective is to provide an adequate theory of duties to refugees and to compatriots. Yet there is also a case for incorporating some notion of particularism on the basis of the diversity of values. As was noted in the previous section, a number of liberal theories justify restriction to protect a complex bundle of rights and goods in the receiving state. On a universalist account, the value of these goods and rights is wholly derivative of universal rights. Yet if one considers the sheer diversity of the sorts of goods and rights which are valued in different states, it seems implausible to claim that their value is derived from their contribution to the same set of universal rights. Even if all societies do share an interest in enjoyment of these rights, these rights do not necessarily exhaust that society's conception of ethically relevant rights, goals and goods, or – to put it another way – of the conditions for well-being.

The need for a layer of additional or supplementary rights and goods, combined with a recognition of the diversity of such rights and goods in different societies, is a powerful argument for introducing some degree of particularism into universalist theory. It is at least *prima facie* plausible that such considerations could co-exist with recognition of certain universal duties, including duties towards refugees. One possible objection is that incorporating particularist considerations may legitimise a more restrictive refugee policy. Recognising the moral relevance of (some) special duties is hardly the most promising route for motivating a sense of duty towards refugees. Yet the force of particularist concerns in motivating action cannot be overlooked, and may be integral to understanding the moral relevance of special ties and values. Moreover, as suggested earlier, the requirements of universalist ethics are so demanding that it may be preferable to legitimise some degree of particularism under certain specified criteria, rather than retain standards of morality which are likely to be disregarded. The danger of excessively high standards is that lapses or lack of motivation are indiscriminately unethical: the model does not allow for degrees or prioritisation of different forms of immorality. Incorporating a theory of legitimate particularism will at least allow for a more nuanced evaluation of the various types of non-ethical (particularist) actions. The next chapter will consider whether the types of 'thin' universalism produced by such a theory could be good candidates for the task.

Conclusion

This chapter considered two forms of liberal universalism: utilitarianism and right-based theories. Having categorised different theories in the first section, the second and third sections of the chapter considered the shortcomings of two distinct variants of utilitarianism. The first account relied on a concept of utility that raised problems with measurement of well-being, and with its distribution between individuals. These difficulties suggested the need for a conception of well-being that was objectively definable and measurable, and that included a notion of thresholds of basic welfare. Goodin's vulnerability thesis addressed both these needs, but raised additional problems of its own. Its partial, negative account of welfare had potentially damaging consequences for autonomy, and suggested the need for a concept of justice.

I went on to discuss whether a theory of universal rights could provide a better account of duties to refugees. It was argued that these theories provided a better substantive conception of duties to refugees, thus meeting the criterion of normative desirability. However, these theories failed on the criterion of practical feasibility. There were two possible responses to the problem of feasibility. First, right-based theorists could define the gap between moral duty and practice as a problem of motivation. Initial doubts were raised about the practical implications of this approach, although a more detailed analysis of the assumptions about moral motivation and agency was deferred until later in the thesis. The second response was to justify restriction on instrumental grounds. Yet neither was this approach satisfactory – it seemed to represent a tacit defence of special ties.

It was suggested in conclusion that universalists may provide a better conception of the relationship between duties to non-nationals and compatriots by incorporating a (limited) commitment to particularism. Such theories of thin universalism are considered in the next chapter.

Notes

[1] John Stuart Mill, *On Liberty and Other Essays Utilitarianism* (Oxford, 1991), pp. 139-43.

[2] A notable example is Amartya Sen. See 'Plural Utility', in John Elster and John E. Roemer (eds), *Interpersonal Comparisons of Well-being* (Cambridge, 1991), pp. 78-88.

[3] Robert E. Goodin, *Protecting the Vulnerable: A Reanalysis of our Social Responsibilities* (Chicago 1985); and Goodin, 'What is So Special About Our Fellow Countrymen?', *Ethics*, 98:4 (1988): 663–86; Peter Singer, *Practical Ethics* (Cambridge, 1979); Anthony Ellis, 'Utilitarianism and International Ethics', in Terry Nardin and David R. Mapel (eds), *Traditions of International Ethics* (Cambridge, 1992), pp. 158-79.

[4] Goodin, 'What is So Special', p. 681.

[5] See, for example, Ronald Dworkin on the problem of racist attitudes, in *Taking Rights Seriously* (Guildford, 1996), p. 235.

[6] John Elster and John E. Roemer (eds), *Inter-Personal Comparisons of Well-Being* (Cambridge, 1992).

[7] Critiques include John Rawls, *A Theory of Justice* (Oxford, 1972), p. 26; Bernard Williams, 'A Critique of Utilitarianism', in J.J.C. Smart and Bernard Williams (eds), *Utilitarianism: For and Against* (Cambridge, 1993), pp. 77-150.

[8] Rawls, *Theory of Justice*, p. 26.

[9] Singer, *Practical Ethics*, p. 22.

[10] Peter and Renata Singer, 'The Ethics of Refugee Policy', in Mark Gibney (ed.), *Open Borders? Closed Societies? The Ethical and Political Issues* (New York, 1989), pp. 111-30; and Singer, *Practical Ethics*, especially the chapter on 'Insiders and Outsiders', pp. 247-63.

[11] Singer, 'Insiders and Outsiders', p. 261.

[12] Joseph Raz, *The Morality of Freedom* (Oxford, 1988), p. 227.

[13] Brian Barry, *Theories of Justice* (Berkeley, LA, 1989), p. 79.

[14] Singer, 'Insiders and Outsiders', p. 262.

[15] An example of a satiable and diminishing good is that of human needs, which might be captured by the principle that everyone's needs should be met. This good is satiable, in that the needs in question can be met, and it is diminishing in that the closer a person is to having these needs met, the less she will benefit from a further increase in the relevant good. Conversely, as Raz writes, 'the further one is from the point of satiation the stronger is one's right to the benefit conferred by the principle.' Raz, p. 236-7.

[16] Ibid., p. 241.

[17] Goodin, 'What is So Special', pp. 684-5.

[18] Goodin, *Protecting the Vulnerable*, p. 21.

[19] Ibid., p. 11.

[20] See Onora O'Neill's discussion of the scope of moral duties in: *Towards Justice and Virtue: A Constructive Account of Practical Reasoning* (Cambridge, 1996), pp. 100-6

[21] Christina Boswell, 'The External Dimension of Justice and Home Affairs' *International Affairs*, 79:3 (2003): 619-38.

[22] Brian Barry, 'Humanity and Justice in a Global Context', in Brian Barry (ed.), *Liberty and Justice: Essays in Political Theory* (Oxford, 1991), p. 245.

[23] H.J.L. Hart, 'Are There Any Natural Rights?', in A. Quinto (ed.), *Political Philosophy* (Oxford, 1967), pp. 53-66.

[24] See, for example, Henry Shue, *Basic Rights: Subsistence, Affluence and U.S. Foreign Policy* (New Jersey, 1980). The definition also excludes religious accounts, such as John Locke's grounding of rights in duties to God, although this omission is of less concern, as the discussion is focusing on modern western, secular theories.

[25] Raz, *The Morality of Freedom*, p. 166. Raz himself rejects right-based theories.

[26] Anne Dummett, 'The Transnational Migration of People Seen from within a Natural Law Perspective', in Brian Barry and Robert E. Goodin (eds), *Free Movement: Ethical Issues in the Transnational Migration of People and of Money* (Hemel Hempstead, 1992), p. 177.

[27] Dummett, p. 177.

[28] Bruce Ackerman, *Social Justice in the Liberal State* (New Haven, Conn, 1980), p. 95.

[29] Matthew Gibney, *The Ethics and Politics of Asylum: Liberal Democracy and the Response to Refugees* (Cambridge, 2004), p. 84.

30 Terry Nardin, 'Alternative Ethical Perspectives on Transnational Migration', in Brian Barry and Robert E. Goodin, *Free Movement: Essays in the Transnational migration of People and of Money* (Hemel Hempstead, 1992), pp. 268-9.

31 Andrew Belsey, 'World Poverty, Justice and Equality', in Robin Attfield and Barry Wilkins (eds), *International Justice and the Third World* (London: Routledge), p. 41.

Chapter Three

Thin Universalism and the Problem of Internal Coherence

There have been a number of attempts to reconcile universalism with recognition of the moral relevance of duties to compatriots. This chapter will discuss two main approaches to the question. The first approach takes as its starting point a commitment to ensuring basic rights, which trump non-basic rights and goals where they conflict. By keeping the list of universal rights to a few very basic requirements, such theories hope to limit the scope of universal duties to manageable proportions, and to allow for the value of special duties. The second type of account, dealt with in section two, starts from a particularist perspective, and attempts to show that this is compatible with a commitment to at least some universal duties. The particularist approach explicitly defends the value of special ties and interests, but argues that attachment to these goods still leaves room for performing duties to non-nationals. Both of these approaches thus offer some means of combining universalist and particularist duties.

In the discussion that follows, it is important to bear in mind the rationale for incorporating particularist considerations into universalist theories. Pure universalism encountered a problem of practical feasibility: it was unable to show how people could be motivated to respect the requirements of universal ethics. It also faced a second problem with accounting for the diversity of rights, goals and goods that are valued in different communities. *Prima facie,* thin universalist theories seem to avoid both problems because they allow for a layer of particularist values, thereby both limiting the stringency of the requirements of ethics, and allowing for cultural diversity. Most importantly for the current discussion, they attempt to address the practical problem of motivation by restricting the content of universal duties.

Basic Rights Theories

Theories of basic rights limit universal rights to a restricted list of core, or essential claims. As one theorist writes, they offer 'a relatively narrow and manageable focus' for duties to non-nationals, and thus do not seem to create the problems of feasibility discussed in the last chapter.[1] And since they do not claim to cover all aspects of well-being, they allow for a degree of cultural diversity in the definition of non-basic rights and goals. This section will consider whether theories of basic rights can provide an adequate conception of duties to refugees.

Basic Rights and Motivation

Basic rights are usually taken to mean rights which are in some sense essential for well-being or action.[2] According to these theories, basic rights do not exhaust the conditions for human well-being. Nor is the enjoyment of basic rights necessarily more rewarding or worthwhile than the enjoyment of non-basic rights or goods. The point is rather that such rights are conditions for the exercise of all other rights and goods. As Alan Gewirth argues, basic rights 'have as their objects the essential preconditions of action, such as life, physical integrity, mental equilibrium'.[3] These rights are an essential prerequisite for human action. Where basic rights conflict with non-basic rights, the former should be given priority: 'Basic rights must be fulfilled before other rights'.[4] A similar theory is advanced by Shue, who holds that the enjoyment of the basic rights to physical security and subsistence 'is essential to the enjoyment of all other rights'.[5] Shue's theory is especially worth pursuing, as he deals explicitly with questions of duties to non-nationals, so in the discussion that follows I shall focus on his account. However, the criticisms I level at his theory apply to other theories of basic rights, including that of Gewirth.

Shue does not explicitly incorporate particularist values into his theory of basic rights, but the structure of his theory is (at least superficially) compatible with a form of thin universalism which allows for the intrinsic value of particularist rights and goals. Shue's list of basic rights is limited to the right to subsistence and physical security.[6] He calls these rights 'inherent necessities' – their enjoyment is an essential component of the realisation of other rights. Shue argues that these universal basic rights generate duties that should trump the enjoyment of non-basic rights and goods. 'One is required to sacrifice, as necessary, anything but one's basic rights in order to honor the basic rights of others'.[7] Shue's theory of basic rights is clearly intended to cover duties to non-nationals, indeed part of his book on the subject is devoted to a discussion of United States foreign policy. He does not consider that realisation of universal basic rights will raise a serious problem of feasibility: since the list of basic rights is so restricted, it will be unlikely to impose overly stringent duties.

Yet even on the basis of his minimalist list of rights, the problem of motivation remains. Ensuring the enjoyment of the rights to subsistence and physical security would require an enormous investment of resources by wealthy states in developing countries. It would require not only radical redistribution of wealth, but also intervention or stringent enforcement mechanisms to ensure the relevant political and economic changes in a number of states. The question of motivation is even more problematic in the case of refugee influx. Refugees have by definition fled actual or threatened human rights violations, and a refusal to admit them may be tantamount to failure to carry out a duty generated by basic rights. So simply scaling down the list of universal rights to a bare minimum may not bring us any closer to finding a practically feasible and normatively desirable candidate for characterising duties to refugees: even basic rights theories may encounter problems in motivating action consistent with their ethical requirements.

One response to the problem of motivation mentioned in Chapter Two was to introduce an instrumental justification for dividing responsibility for ensuring rights. In the discussion on utilitarianism, I considered Goodin's theory for dividing responsibility. While this instrumental defence was difficult to sustain, I did not rule out the possibility of justifying a division of labour on other instrumental grounds. It is worth considering whether basic rights theorists could overcome the problem of motivation by invoking alternative arguments for a division of labour.

Shue's suggestion for a division of labour in realising duties to refugees revolves around the role of institutions. He argues that the 'burdensome' duties of any one individual should be limited through institutional arrangements.[8] Shue distinguishes between negative duties not to infringe the rights of others, and positive duties which require the expenditure of resources to ensure that others enjoy their rights. While negative duties are universal, these more burdensome positive duties can and should be divided up between duty bearers. He argues that '[o]ne cannot have substantial positive duties toward everyone, even if everyone has basic rights. The positive duties of any one individual must be limited'.[9] The best means of parcelling out these positive duties is through organisations and institutions which can both perform duties more efficiently, and also provide an important 'psychological buffer' to avoid needless anguish and guilt when individuals are unable to perform all the duties that seem to be required of them. The performance of duties through institutional arrangements generates indirect 'duties to create, maintain, and enhance institutions that directly fulfill rights'.[10]

The first point to make about this account is that it is not clear what sorts of duties fall on individuals in the absence of the appropriate institutional arrangements. Shue does not specify whether or not performance of duties is strictly conditional on the effective functioning of the relevant institutions. If institutional mechanisms for co-ordinating duties fail for any reason, it is not clear on Shue's account whether individuals are obliged to fill the gaps and ensure full coverage of rights, or whether the absence of institutional arrangements effectively lets them off the hook. In the former case, the absence or breakdown of institutional arrangements would imply that individuals had positive duties to ensure the basic rights of others. For example, if there were no institutional provision for assisting refugees once they had arrived in one's country, individuals would be morally bound to meet the basic rights of refugees by providing them with food, shelter and physical protection. Alternatively, in the second case, the claim would be that individual duties were conditional on the existence of effective institutions. Where such institutions did not exist, individuals would have no obligation to assist refugees.

It is highly doubtful that Shue would commit himself to this second claim that duties were contingent on the existence of institutional arrangements. This would be tantamount to arguing that the division of labour was valued solely for its ability to limit individuals' duties, rather than because it was the best means of realising the basic rights of those in need. It would imply a limited commitment to realising basic rights, which does not seem consistent with Shue's robust moral defence of the universal scope of these rights, and their status as trumping other rights and goods where they conflict. Yet if Shue accepts the alternative claim that institutions are simply the best means of realising basic rights, then the failure of these arrangements would mean that individuals faced potentially unlimited positive duties to guarantee basic rights. And in this case, the problem of motivation would remain.

Of course, it could be argued that the failure of institutional arrangements would generate a duty to establish relevant public provisions, or to strengthen those that already exist. Yet even assuming this were feasible, there is a second major problem with Shue's argument. Institutions may render the performance of duties more efficient or simple, and may thus limit the 'burden' of performing positive duties in many case. But they will not significantly limit the requirements of universal duties in cases involving the division of finite resources. In the context of refugee policy, there are already a number of institutions at national, regional (European Union) and global levels which perform these duties on behalf of individuals. Yet they have certainly not provided a neat solution to the problem of individual motivation to perform duties. This is to a large extent because the duties generated by refugee rights cannot be neatly sectioned off for performance by designated institutions. Refugee influx could potentially affect the lives of citizens of receiving societies at many different levels. Delegating responsibility to institutions for ensuring the welfare and security of refugees will not serve to alleviate nationals of the receiving society of their duties to refugees.

This attempt to divide responsibility for performing duties generated by refugee rights seems to circumvent the problem of motivation. The duties generated by basic rights simply are immensely demanding in the context of refugee influx. This implies that many of the descriptive and prescriptive problems attributed to right-based universalism in the last section equally apply to thin universalist theories of basic rights.

Basic Rights and Well-being

The second criticism of basic rights theories revolves around their grounds for prioritising certain rights over other values and goods.

As we have seen, basic rights theorists argue that these rights represent the necessary conditions for the enjoyment of all other rights and goods. For example, I may not be in a position to appreciate a right to higher education or running water in my home if I am severely malnourished, or in constant danger of being shot by armed gangs. This distinction between basic rights and non-basic rights and goods seems to be an effective way of recognising cultural diversity whilst retaining duties to respect the basic rights of those from different cultures.

Yet the notion of basic rights as preconditional to the enjoyment of other rights and goods becomes problematic in cases where rights conflict. If basic rights are to be trumps in cases of conflict with non-basic rights, then the implication is that basic rights are in some sense more fundamental to well-being than other rights and goods. Shue argues that while basic rights are 'inherent necessities' of well-being, they are not necessarily of special intrinsic value: 'rights are basic only if enjoyment of them is essential to the enjoyment of all other rights, irrespective of whether their enjoyment is also valuable in itself'.[11] For example, the right to education may be 'much greater and richer – more distinctively human – than merely gong through life without ever being assaulted'.[12] This implies that the relationship between basic and non-basic rights is more complex than that of straightforward hierarchy. Basic rights may be the *sine qua non* for the (long term) enjoyment of other rights or goods, but their actual enjoyment is not necessarily of intrinsic value, or at least is less intrinsically valuable than the enjoyment of non-basic rights.

However, theories prioritising basic rights seem to assume that the supplementary rights and goods that are supposedly made possible by the realisation of basic rights will in fact simultaneously or subsequently by realised in the society in question. In other words, basic rights may in themselves have little intrinsic value, but they are necessary for laying the foundations for the enjoyment of a further set of intrinsically fulfilling goods and rights. The value of basic rights lies in their role in enabling the realisation of other rights. Basic rights theorists would presumably acknowledge that a life in which basic rights were realised but no other rights or goods were realisable would not be fulfilling. Yet this creates problems where there is a conflict between the enjoyment of basic and non-basic rights. If one is forced to choose between the two, it is not evident that basic rights will be valued over non-basic ones. For example, a person may prefer to relinquish the right to physical safety, in order to retain the self respect and fulfilment derived from, say, practising her religion, or expressing her political convictions, or having a homosexual relationship. In a more extreme scenario, one could imagine a society in which all but the most basic rights have been forsaken to secure the basic rights of others. In this case, life without non-basic rights and cultural enrichment may simply not be worth living. Many if not all people would choose to risk physical insecurity and subsistence in order to enjoy at least some non-basic rights and goods. This could be the case even if immediate enjoyment of non-basic rights at the expense of basic rights would be life threatening or undermine the possibilities for enjoying any rights or goods in the long term.

The issue of the prioritisation of basic rights is more evidently problematic in cases where the individual's rights conflict with the basic rights of others. Under these circumstances, Shue argues that the individual should forego all non-basic rights and goods if they conflict with the basic rights of others. Where basic rights come into conflict with supplementary or particularist rights, goals and goods, basic rights must be trumps. This involves sacrificing, in ascending order of importance, preference satisfaction, cultural enrichment, and non-basic rights.[13]

This raises the question as to whether rights and goods essential to one's well-being – but are not 'basic' in Shue's sense – should be sacrificed for the sake of more hollow and less intrinsically valuable basic rights. There seems to be little point in retaining basic rights and giving up all other rights and goods, if the former are valued only as instrumental to enjoyment of the latter.

Shue avoids confronting this problem by asserting that 'in fact it is most unlikely that anyone would need to sacrifice anything other than preferences, to which one has no right of satisfaction and which are of no cultural value, in order to honor everyone's basic rights'.[14] Yet the possibility of such sacrifices is not so unlikely in the context of mass influx. The rights of refugees in such cases could plausibly conflict with, for example, access to welfare benefits and employment; or with more abstract public goods such as living in a tolerant and liberal society. In some cases, it is not unimaginable that an individual would choose to forego basic rights in order to secure non-basic rights or goods.

The point here is not so much that of whether this level of sacrifice is justified, but rather it concerns the criteria for distinguishing and prioritising different rights. It is not being denied that refugee rights may justifiably require immense sacrifices on the part of the receiving country. Rather, the point is that Shue's hierarchy may not be an appropriate prioritisation of the goods and rights that we would be willing to renounce, and the order in which we would wish to renounce them. Shue's account assumes that rights that are preconditional to the enjoyment of non-basic rights should not be traded in for non-basic rights, even though the value of these basic rights may be purely instrumental. This may well be a useful prioritisation for the purposes of foreign aid or intervention. In these cases, promoting the enjoyment of basic rights by non-nationals may not directly conflict with the rights of citizens in the donor country. Moreover, the focus on basic rights allows for national or local autonomy in designing institutions and policies that embody the values of the particular society. As such, the basic rights model is able to define duties towards non-nationals in a precise and practically useful way, which nonetheless respects the diversity of particularist values and institutions in different societies. Yet the case of refugee influx reveals the inadequacy of this prioritisation in cases of extreme conflict between the rights and interests of nationals and non-nationals.

Donnelly makes a similar point in his critique of basic rights. He considers a number of attempts to produce an ultimate list of core writes, but argues that they all 'share a common and fatal problem':

> They could all be fully enjoyed, and still people could be left living anomic, degraded lives, unable to speak their minds, to choose their religion, to become involved in politics, to have a reasonable chance of finding a job, to get an education, to associate with whom they choose, and so forth.[15]

Donnelly's point is that basic rights cannot be separated from the wider list of human rights that all should enjoy. He argues for a more exhaustive list of universal rights that would incorporate all the rights necessary to 'protect human dignity'.[16] Yet this alternative to basics rights theories simply takes us back to the types of thick universalist theory criticised in the previous chapter. Basic rights theories may be committed to an untenable hierarchy of rights; but more comprehensive theories of rights encounter the old problems of motivation and cultural diversity. So the answer cannot be to supplement the list of basic rights, as Donnelly proposes.

An alternative response to the criticism of basic rights theories is to deny the possibility of laying down rigid norms about the priority of basic rights at all. Rather than supplement the list, this approach would involve the rejection of any absolute prioritisation of moral claims. Bernard Williams puts this point cogently, arguing that an individual's projects may be so integral to his existence that life without them would be meaningless and not worth living.[17] If these projects conflict with the requirements of universalist ethics – in our case with the basic rights of refugees – it may not be reasonable or desirable for people to give up the source of meaning in their lives for the sake of others. 'There can come a point at which it is quite unreasonable for a man to give up, in the name of the impartial good ordering of the world of moral agents, something which is a condition of his having any interest in being around in that world at all'.[18] Williams' point is that it may not be reasonable to demand that basic rights trump non-basic rights or goods if the latter are more critical to well-being. This would imply that there could be legitimate space for personal projects or special ties that are not ethical in the universalist sense, but are nonetheless essential to the individual's well-being.

Whether or not this is a reasonable demand which would be compatible with any form of thin right-based universalism will be considered in the next section. It will be argued that this kind of thin universalism is unconvincing, partly because of its reluctance to abandon the separation of the impartial and self-interested perspectives.

Particularism and Basic Rights

Basic rights theories, as we have seen, fail to overcome the problem of motivation, and have problems justifying a rigid hierarchy of rights in cases of conflict. An alternative approach to combining universalist and particularist claims is to start from particularist premises, and then show how such a position could be combined with commitment to at least some universal rights. I shall consider two varieties of this argument. The first defends a communitarian conception of moral duty, but argues that such an approach could nonetheless accommodate basic rights. The second variety claims that there is a legitimate sphere of self-interest that should be protected from encroachment by the demands of universal ethics.

Miller and Basic Rights

In his discussion of the 'ethics of nationality', David Miller attempts to find 'some compromise view' that combines a commitment to particularist and universalist ethics.[19] Having rejected universalist attempts to incorporate particularist considerations, he suggests that it would be more productive to start from the other direction, incorporating universal duties into a particularist ethical theory. His attempt to do so clearly illustrates the problem with such approaches, and will thus provide us with a good exemplar of this sort of argument.

Miller starts from a particularist perspective which accords intrinsic value to special relations between members of families, communities and nation-states. He rejects 'the view that the subject matter of ethics is persons considered merely as such, independent of all local connections and relations.' Instead, he adopts 'a second view of ethical agency in which the subject is seen as already deeply embedded in social relationships. Here the subject is partly defined by its relationship and the various rights, obligations and so forth that go along with these, so these commitments themselves form a basic element of personality'.[20] Such particular relationships and characteristics create special duties, which are not reducible to or derivative of general duties to human beings. Special duties may be generated at a variety of levels, for example between family members, ethnic groups, or compatriots.

While asserting the ethical relevance of such ties, Miller is reluctant to embrace fully-fledged particularism, and deny the existence of any duties to humanity at large. 'There are generic conditions for living a decent life which can be expressed in terms of rights to bodily integrity, personal freedom, a minimum level of resources, and so forth. We have obligations to respect these rights in others that derive simply from our common humanity.' These rights may 'include rights to provision, for example in cases where a natural shortage of resources means that people will starve or suffer bodily injury if others do not provide for them'.[21] This basic rights thesis establishes a form of thin universalism which, according to Miller, is consistent with his particularist perspective. He 'can see no reason why those who hold particularist views should not also endorse such a list of basic rights'.[22] The assumption seems to be that a commitment to particularist or special duties leaves space for the performance of universal duties that are grounded in basic rights. The two sets of duty are, nonetheless, grounded in distinct types of justification, which, as Miller acknowledges, represent 'two competing accounts of the structure of ethical thought'.[23]

This combination of different ethical commitments raises the question as to which approach should have priority when the demands of the two perspectives conflict. And here Miller's argument is ambiguous. Miller argues at one point that basic rights should be over-ridden if they prove too costly to respect. If intervention to uphold the basic rights of those in other countries conflicts with duties to compatriots, it is not necessarily the case that basic rights should trump special duties. He qualifies this slightly by allowing that obligations generated by very basic rights – for example the obligation to protect people from death by starvation – should probably not be trumped by less basic special obligations, but again, 'provided the cost of protecting these rights is relatively small'.[24] The implication is that where protecting basic rights implies more than a 'relatively small' cost, special duties should trump basic rights. This seems to reflect a fundamental misunderstanding of the moral implications of a commitment to a theory of universal rights. If Miller really believes that we have universal obligations to ensure the conditions for the basic well-being of others, then he cannot waive this duty where it conflicts with special duties. The theory of basic rights he endorses claims that the enjoyment of basic rights is in an important sense core or fundamental to the individual's interests: they are the precondition or necessary requirement for the enjoyment of all other rights.

Now I did of course challenge this type of rigid hierarchy in the previous section, suggesting that attempts to lay down a definitive prioritisation of rights were difficult to sustain in cases of conflict with other rights and goods. But the way to overcome this problem is to reject absolutist lists of basic rights *tout court.* The shortcomings of basic rights theories will not be avoided simply by defending a parallel commitment to particularist ethics. Indeed, the combination of a particularist ethical theory with a commitment to basic rights will produce even greater problems at both theoretical and practical levels.

On the level of theory, I observed in the last chapter that particularist and universalist theories rely on very different assumptions about the validity of moral claims. Universalist theories hold that certain rights or duties are universally valid, and hence applicable across all cultures. Their validity is not contingent on historical or cultural conditions, but is grounded in the essential and universally shared characteristics of human beings. By contrast, the particularist theory espoused by Miller sees moral claims as derived from the shared values of particular communities. How, then, can the two commitments be incorporated into the same moral theory? One possibility is to conceive of the conception of universal rights as a moral belief that is particular to specific communities. A commitment to the universal scope of rights could be defended on particularist grounds if the community in question were committed to a substantive conception of universal rights. In this case, members of that community would shared a commitment to duties to non-nationals. But the commitment would be contingent on intersubjective values, rather than grounded in the objective characteristics of human beings. Miller rejects this justification for basic rights, instead grounding them in a universalist account of the 'generic conditions for leading a decent life'.[25] This justification is clearly at odds with his central account of the source of moral values.

The confusion here is more than theoretical: it has practical implications in cases of conflict between universal rights and particular ties. We have seen that universalist defences of basic rights claim that these rights trump other rights and goods. And indeed they must defend such a hierarchy if they are to be consistent in their reasoning. A basic rights theory would be incoherent if it did not involve a claim that such rights should have priority over non-universalist considerations. Yet consistent commitment to basic rights, as we have seen, could potentially generate substantial duties in the case of refugee influx, thus conflicting with particularist goods and special duties to compatriots. Given Miller's commitment to the ethical relevance of nationality, he would surely be reluctant to accept the consequences of basic rights theories of particularist values. Miller cannot be both universalist and particularist in equal measure – he must choose which claim should have priority. If particularist considerations trump universal rights, then he cannot consistently defend a commitment to basic rights. And if basic rights override particularist considerations, then we are once again confronted with the problems of motivation and hierarchies discussed in the previous section.

Miller appears to believe that he can avoid this practical conflict between the requirements of universal rights and special ties. And he bases his argument on two rather problematic claims: an empirical claim that such conflicts would not in fact arise, or at least that they would not be serious; and an ethical argument that limits duties to intervene to assist non-nationals.

Now we have already seen that the first argument fails in the case of refugees. Contrary to what Miller claims, the case of duties to refugees could generate a serious conflict between basic rights and duties to fellow nationals. The second argument takes a rather different tack, and it is worth considering the problems it raises.

Miller argues that his commitment to the ethical significance of nationality also generates a moral justification for not intervening to realise the rights of nationals of other countries. As he writes, 'if we want to take nationality seriously, then we must also accept that positive obligations to protect basic rights (e.g. to relieve hunger) fall in the first place on co-nationals, so that outsiders would have strong obligations in this respect only where it was strictly impossible for the rights to be protected within the national community'.[26] In this form, the argument for the special duties of fellow nationals is fairly weak: there would still be a duty to intervene if it was 'strictly impossible' for the relevant state to realise the rights of its nationals (however this condition may be interpreted). But Miller goes on to make a stronger claim, effectively relinquishing responsibility for realising the basic rights of others, even where they cannot be met by the other state.

> If bad policies or vested interest in nation A mean that some of its citizens go needy, then, if nation C decides that its own welfare requirements mean that it cannot afford to give much (or anything) to the needy in A, it has not directly violated their rights; at most, it has permitted them to be violated, and in the circumstances this may be justifiable.[27]

In effect, then, the relevance of nationality trumps the duty to intervene. And in this case, Miller would be committed to claiming the priority of particularist over universal basic rights. Yet once again his stance is ambiguous, and at other parts in the argument he seems to retreat from this conclusion. While his defence of nonintervention seems to be based on a claim about the moral relevance of nationality and the responsibilities of governments towards their citizens, he also criticises the liberal commitment to self-determination. As he puts it, 'Why make a fetish of self-government if your basic rights will be better protected by outsiders?'[28] Rather surprisingly given his commitment to communitarian ethics, he suggests that advocates of self-government 'ought to take seriously the case for benevolent imperialism'.[29]

While I have dwelt at some length on the inconsistencies in Miller's account, the purpose of this critique was not simply to highlight the problems with one theorist's account. The point was rather to shed light on the problems inherent in any such combined approach. Miller's failure to take a clear line on the problem of conflict between particularism and universalism, and his inconsistent prescriptions on the question of intervention, reflect the basic theoretical and practical tension between a commitment to particularist and universalism. Theories of basic rights as trumps fail; but so too do theories that attempt to combine particularist and universalist ethics without according clear priority to either. We should now turn to a third variant of thin universalism, which limits the requirements of universal ethics. Examining the reasons for the failure of this third account will elucidate a deeper problem that is common to all thin universalist theories: the assumed dichotomy between the sources and moral demands of universal and particular duties.

The Limits of Ethical Obligation

A number of writers have argued for the legitimisation of a sphere of self-interest, which limits the requirements of universal ethics. Such theories assert that the agent should be free to pursue a range of personal goals without being constrained by the requirements of ethical duty. These arguments for limiting moral obligation, which I shall consider in this section, do not defend personal or particularist claims on moral grounds (as, for example, Miller's argument did), but on grounds of self-interest or pragmatism. The claim is that it is unreasonable to expect people to act in accordance with the requirements of morality on all occasions, as such unlimited duties would lead to an inordinate sacrifice of self-interest. Such arguments are usually based on an acknowledgement of the stringent demands of morality and the problem of motivation. They argue that universal ethical theories – whether utilitarian or right-based – do not adequately reflect the nature of persons.[30] Just as I suggested in Chapter One, these theories claim that consistent application of universalist ethics can present unrealistic demands. And the remedies proposed by these theories is to justify the imposition of a range of limitations on these demands. In this respect, they would seem to be good candidates for addressing the problem of motivation encountered.

A good example of such an argument is provided in the work of James S. Fishkin.[31] Fishkin argues that the 'difficulty in consistently applying this principle [the requirements of impartial ethics] is that we would be led, step by step, to sacrifices of *heroic* proportions'.[32] It is therefore reasonable to establish limits to the level of sacrifice demanded of universalist morality. More specifically, the universalist conception of ethics fails to allow sufficient scope for two main types of particularist or what Fishkin terms 'agent-centred' claims. The first is special duties to particular groups, such as one's family or country, and personal projects. The conflict between such particularist claims and universal duties was considered in the discussion of Miller's account, where I criticised attempts to combine these with a theory of basic rights. But Fishkin concentrates on a second type of agent-centred claim, which seeks to justify imposing limits on the demands of morality, providing scope for the legitimate pursuit of personal goals and interests.

Under this second category of agent-centred claims, Fishkin makes a further distinction between two types of limits on moral demands. Firstly, the 'cut-off for heroism' limits the level of sacrifice demanded of any individual. According to this notion, there are certain levels of sacrifice that should not be morally required of people. And secondly, the 'robust sphere of indifference' prevents moral requirements from pervading every aspect of daily life, allowing 'a substantial proportion' of our actions to fall 'within the zone of indifference or permissibly free choice'.[33] As Fishkin observes, these devices justify the abandonment of the type of equal weighting for everyone's interests that is defended by universalist theories. On this non-universalist account, the individual is not required to consider the interests of all from an impartial perspective. Indeed, these limitations on moral duty 'appear to give extra weight to the interests of particular persons ... compared to the interests of everyone considered impartially'.[34]

Fishkin does not argue that one should ignore the demands of ethics altogether: he is not advocating that people behave in a wholly egoistic way. Rather, he advances what Kagan has termed a 'moderate' position,[35] defending a limited commitment to ethical duty. Yet this intermediate stance between pure egoism and ethical universalism creates problems for the account. By refusing to embrace either a purely universalist ethical or a purely egoistic account, Fishkin is unable to provide well-founded criteria for determining when these limits should be imposed. We can elucidate this problem by considering two main weaknesses of the moderate position.

The first problem relates to the criteria for balancing conflicting considerations. On the moderate account, as Kagan points out, the agent is permitted to give more weight to her own interests than to the interests of others. Considerations linked to securing the agent's own happiness, or realising her rights, count for more in her moral decisions than the happiness or rights of others. The question arises as to the grounds on which such extra weighting is permitted. And there are two possible answers to this question: on egoistic, or on ethical grounds. The first type of egoistic justification is clearly problematic for Fishkin's theory. While he argues for limitations on universal duty, Fishkin does not want to deny his commitment to (at least some) moral duties. His aim is simply to ensure that they are limited to manageable proportions. Yet if he imposes limitations on egoistic grounds, then it is difficult to see how he can be committed to any moral duties beyond those which people are already willing to perform. If the argument for limiting duty is that people's motivation is limited, this implies that moral duty is being defined on the basis of existing motivation. And in this case, morality becomes a legitimisation of existing interests, and there is no reason to encourage people to extend duties beyond their present scope. In the case of refugees, this would imply either retaining the present level of restriction, regardless of the plight of future possible refugees; or it may even imply diminishing current levels, if public opinion feels that existing duties seriously conflict with their self-interest.

Perhaps it could be contended that people do in fact recognise some moral duties, and that basing a definition of ethics on existing motivation will still enable one to retain a commitment to a (limited) ethical theory. Thus most people do accept at least limited duties to a certain number of refugees. But even this limited moral commitment will be undermined by an egoistic-based account of the limits of morality. If people believe that they can legitimately curtail duties if it is not in their interests to perform them, then there seems to be little to stop them from ratcheting down current obligations. The notion of a moral 'ought' would lose its force: morality would no longer set out norms and standards to which individuals should aspire. And in this case, even the limited duties to which they are currently committed could be discarded on egoistic grounds. If morality really is an elaboration of self-interest, then it is hard to see how Fishkin can retain any commitment to even limited universalism. While Fishkin clearly does not intend such a whole-scale abandonment of ethics, this seems to be the implication of an attempt to limit duty on self-interested grounds. Once egoism is defined as trumping the claims of universal ethics, there seem to be no grounds for constraining the priority of egoism over duty.

The alternative route for Fishkin would be to justify the limitation of universal duty on ethical grounds. He could offer a particularist or an instrumental universalist argument for limiting the demands of universalist morality. Thus rather than defining the personal sphere as self-interested, he could define it as a sphere of particularist values, or as a means of meeting universalist demands. On either account, the balance between universalist and particularist duties would be determined by evaluating different moral claims and the best means for realising them, rather than through defence of the self-interested sphere. Now I have already suggested that arguments for allowing particularist considerations to trump basic universal rights lead to incoherence. As we saw in the discussion of Miller's theory, the structure and justification of basic rights theories preclude the possibility that other ethical claims may legitimately trump its requirements. One cannot retain a consistent thin universalist position whilst allowing its requirements to be over-ridden by special duties. So the particularist justification for limiting universalist duties fails. The other route open to Fishkin is an instrumental argument for the division of responsibility for securing universal rights. Again, I shall not rehearse the arguments against this account, which were discussed in the first section of this chapter. Such instrumental arguments ultimately fail to limit universal duties to feasible proportions, especially in cases like that of refugee influx.

The special weighting of agent-centred claims, then, cannot be coherently defended on egoistic or ethical grounds. If self-interest trumps universal ethics, then it becomes difficult to sustain any commitment to ethics at all. Alternatively, if one accepts a combination of particularist and universalist values, then basic rights or their equivalent must have priority over particularist claims. Finally, instrumental justifications for special duties fail to provide sufficient grounds for restricting the requirements of universal morality. In short, there seem to be no clear criteria for balancing the claims of universal ethics against non-universalist considerations, without conceding priority to the former. Fishkin's account seems to be based on his own intuitive feelings about the appropriate level of ethical duty, without any convincing justification to back up the account.

What these arguments suggest is that the demands of universalist ethics cannot be curtailed without changing the substance and/or justification of universalist theories. Universalist theories are grounded in a conception of individuals as meriting equal consideration. And this commitment to moral equality cannot simply be watered down by introducing egoistic or particularist claims. Such attempts to combine universalism with special duties create muddled amalgams of theories with very different premises. Universal duties cannot be limited by invoking agent-centred claims, for this subverts the core commitment of universalism to the impartial consideration of the rights and interests of all individuals. And it contradicts the universalist commitment to a conception of human beings as morally equal. A theory of ethics that privileges the claims of some over others – that abandons the requirements of impartiality – cannot be coherently combined with a universalist theory. The only means of limiting the requirements of universal ethics is to argue from the other direction: to change the substance and justification of universalist theories, rather than to take universalist ethics as a given and impose limitations on grounds of self-interest or particularism. Hence the possible routes to constraining the requirements of ethics are either to change one's definition of ethical duty, for example by limiting universalism to a list of basic rights (see previous section); or to change the way in which universalist theories are grounded – a possibility that will be developed in Chapter Six.

The Dichotomy between Impartial and Personal Perspectives

These observations lead us to a more general problem with the attempt to limit the requirements of universal ethics. This second point concerns not so much the criteria for balancing universalist and particularist or self-interested claims, but rather the relationship between the two. One problem with Fishkin's argument for limiting universal duties was that he implied that these requirements, and the particularist considerations which limit them, are determined independently of one another. In other words, the balance between universalist and particularist concerns is characterised as a trade-off between two conflicting sets of interests. This account precludes from the outset the possibility of universalist duties influencing particularist considerations. If one defines the limits to morality exclusively on the basis of the agent's self-interest, there is no scope for such agent-centred concerns being influenced by the demands of impartial morality. Fishkin's concepts of zones and thresholds fail to recognise the dynamic relationship between self-interest and impartial ethics. They do not allow for any interaction or mutual influence between the partial and impartial spheres.

The problem of a supposed split between impartial and personal perspectives is clearest in the case of Fishkin's theory, but it equally applies to the theories of basic rights and Miller's particularist/universalist theory discussed earlier in the chapter. In the case of basic rights theories, the impartial perspective was captured by the commitment to a core list of universal rights, which served to constrain pursuit of personal or particular interests. And in Miller's theory, the attempt to incorporate a commitment to universal rights within a particularist ethical theory led to incoherence precisely because he retained this assumed dichotomy between two different perspectives. His acceptance of a notion of universally valid, impartial norms could not be consistently combined with a commitment to a particularist perspective that could trump these universalist considerations.

This notion of a dichotomy between two independently defined sets of considerations is of course parallel to the characterisation of the refugee policy debate outlined in the Introduction. In that case, I argued, the discussion on responses to refugee influx is constrained by the assumed conflict between refugee rights and national interest. The parallel between the dichotomy conception of national interest/refugee rights and self-interest/universal ethics is no coincidence. The assumed separation of a universal, impartial perspective and a self-interested, particularist sphere is widespread in liberal thought, and has undoubtedly shaped our wider assumptions about the relationship between ethics and self-interest. Whether at the level of individual or national interests, this characterisation encourages us to see the personal perspective as exclusively agent-centric, the national perspective as solely domestic oriented. And this assumed dichotomy can be seen as at least partially responsible for many of the problems with universalism discussed in this and the previous chapter. I shall illustrate this claim by briefly recapitulating the problems of motivation and thin universalism raised so far, from the point of view of this dichotomy between self-interest and ethics.

First, on the question of motivation, the assumed dichotomy makes it difficult to encourage an extension of universal duty where it is seen as conflicting with self-interest. As I argued in Chapter Two, this has the effect of rendering universal rights theories hopelessly unfeasible: not only do they impose a set of stringent duties, but they hold out little prospect of motivating people to comply with these. The separation of self-interest and the requirements of ethics creates serious practical problems of motivating compliance with duties to non-nationals.

Second, the various attempts by thin universalist theories to address the problem of motivation are again hampered by the dichotomy characterisation. Where universalism is combined with particularist or egoistic considerations, what is being attempted is the simultaneous defence of two independent and separately justified perspectives. And a balance between the two is bound to lead to incoherence and practical confusion where the demands of the two conflict. In such cases, the theory must claim either that universal ethics trumps egoism, or vice versa. In the former case, the outcome may be theoretically coherent, but it does not address the problem of motivation. In the latter case, where egoism trumps universal ethics, this must imply the abandonment of a coherent commitment to universalism. Theories of particularism or egoism as trumping universal ethics contradict the basic premises of universalism.

These two main implications of the assumed dichotomy between universalism and particularism – the problem of motivation, and the inability to combine the two considerations in any acceptable fashion – strongly suggest that we should search for an alternative account. An adequate account of duties to refugees needs to avoid the problems of incoherence and unfeasibility raised in the discussion of right-based universalism and thin universalism. I hinted above that universalist theories could in principle avoid these problems in two possible ways: by changing their content, or by grounding their claims in a different way.

The first route would require a revision of first order conceptions of the nature and scope of duties to non-nationals. This chapter considered several such attempts to alter the content of universalist theories, but none was successful. Liberal universalism simply does impose stringent demands, and it seems impossible to alter this without rendering the theory incoherent. The shortcomings of liberal universalism cannot be overcome by introducing particularist values. Retaining this form of universalism requires a consistent application, or else we might as well abandon this conception of morality altogether.

The second response of providing a better account of motivation could in principle address the problem of feasibility without abandoning the assumed split between personal and impartial perspectives, or the universalist grounding of such theories. I shall consider the first, less drastic revision of liberal universalism in the next chapter on social contract theory. These theories define and justify duty on the basis of a notion of consent. People are obliged to conform to a set of rules to which they have given their (hypothetical) consent. As I shall explain in the next chapter, social contract theories attempt to solve the problem of motivation by tying duty to agreement. The content of duty varies depending on what people agree to (or would agree to under specified conditions). However, the basic moral justification for most social contract theories remains a liberal universalist commitment to a conception of individual as free and equal. Consent is valued (in most cases) because it enables individuals to realise their capacity for reason or autonomy. So social contract theories retain two of the central premises of liberal universalism: a universalist grounding, and an assumed dichotomy between impartial and personal perspectives.

It is important to consider whether social contract theories are able to define an adequate conception of duties to refugees while retaining these two premises. For if they can provide an account of duties to refugees that is conceptually coherent, empirically plausible, and normatively desirable, then there will be no need to further challenge universalist assumptions about the foundations of liberal theory. If social contract theories are successful in this task, then the critique of liberal universalism will be limited to the forms of right-based universalism discussed in this and the previous chapters. In this case, there would be no need to probe second order liberal universalist assumptions. The discussion of social contract theory will demonstrate why a more radical, second order critique is necessary. And it will elucidate the more profound flaws common to all liberal universalist theories of duties to non-nationals.

Notes

[1] Jack Donnelly, *Universal Human Rights in Theory and Practice* (Ithaca, 1989), p. 42.
[2] Alan Gewirth, *Human Rights: Essays on Justification and Applications* (Chicago, 1982); Henry Shue, *Basic Rights* (New Jersey, 1980).
[3] Gewirth, *Human Rights*, p. 12.
[4] Ibid.
[5] Shue, *Basic Rights*, p. 19.
[6] Ibid., p. 20.
[7] Ibid, p. 114.
[8] Henry Shue, 'Mediating Duties', *Ethics*, 98 (1988): 687–704, p. 689.
[9] Ibid., pp. 690–1.
[10] Ibid., p. 696.
[11] Ibid., p. 26 and p. 67.
[12] Ibid., p. 20.
[13] Ibid., p. 115.
[14] Ibid., p. 114.
[15] Donnelly, p. 41.
[16] Ibid.
[17] Bernard Williams, *Moral Luck* (Cambridge, 1981), p. 14.
[18] Ibid. Williams' point is not simply that the demands of impartial ethics are unreasonable in the sense of demanding inordinate or overly stringent sacrifice or heroism. It is the more radical claim that failure to respect the strictures of impartial ethics may not be unethical at all. Indeed, ground projects 'may be altruistic, and in a very evident sense moral.' (p. 13) This second claim is based on Williams' argument that the impartial perspective is a misrepresentation of moral agency, which leads to an artificial dichotomy between self-interest and impartial ethics.
[19] David Miller, *On Nationality* (Oxford, 1995), p. 51.
[20] David Miller, 'The Ethical Significance of Nationality', *Ethics*, 98:4 (1988), p. 647.
[21] Miller, *On Nationality*, p. 74.
[22] Ibid.
[23] Miller, *On Nationality*, p. 49.

24 Ibid., p. 75.
25 Ibid.
26 Miller, *On Nationality*, p. 79.
27 Ibid., p. 79.
28 Ibid., p. 78.
29 Ibid., p. 77.
30 Shelly Kagan, *The Limits of Morality* (Oxford, 1989), p. 262.
31 James S. Fishkin, *The Limits of Obligation* (New Haven, 1982); and 'Theories of Justice and International Relations: The Limits of Liberal Theory', in Anthony Ellis (ed.), *Ethics and International Relations* (Manchester, 1996), pp. 1–12. A similar line of argument is pursued by Brian Baxter, 'The Self, Morality and the Nation-State', also in Ellis, *Ethics and International Relations*.
32 Fishkin, *Limits of Obligation*, p. 72.
33 Fishkin, 'Theories of Justice and International Relations', p. 4.
34 Ibid., p. 7.
35 Kagan, p. 6.

Chapter Four

Social Contract Theory and Moral Motivation

Social contract theory can be classified as a variant of liberal universalism, but one that is more explicitly concerned with the question of motivation. Social contract theories claim to ensure that people will be motivated to comply with rules of justice. The way in which theorists justify this claim varies, but all contractarians share a commitment to the notion of consent. By securing the consent of participants, contract theories claim to ensure cooperation with rules of justice. For most social contract theorists, consent has a dual role: it both generates morally desirable norms; and it ensures that people have good reason to obey these norms. In other words, achieving agreement on rules of justice produces a coincidence between what people should do and what they will be motivated to do. As such, social contract theory would appear to be a good candidate for defining duties to refugees. It is liberal universalist in substance;[1] but also claims to address the problem of feasibility, through ensuring consent to its terms of justice.

This chapter will consider whether social contract theories can provide a good framework for characterising duties to non-nationals. Of primary interest for us at this stage of the argument is the question of motivation and the role of consent in social contract theory. We need to examine whether or not social contract theories can address the problem of motivation whilst retaining a liberal universalist conception of duties to refugees.

The Goals of Social Contract Theory

Before examining specific theories, it is worth making a few general comments about the structure and aims of social contract theory. Social contract theory, or contractarianism, has a long tradition in liberal political thought dating back to the seventeenth century,[2] and has recently been revived in the works of Rawls, Scanlon and Barry.[3] Contract theory originally revolved around the question of political obligation and aimed to ensure the negative freedom of citizens from encroachment by the sovereign.[4] Yet there was also an important related question of how to ensure cooperation between individuals who were – according to most theorists – naturally self-interested, and who were competing for scarce resources. Under these conditions, or what Hume termed the 'circumstances of justice', cooperation could only be ensured by means of a set of rules for regulating conflict between competing interests or conceptions of the good. In other words, the natural self-interest of individuals and the scarcity of resources necessitated rules of justice.[5] It is this concern with principles for regulating social interaction that has been the central preoccupation of recent social contract theory. Contractarianism in political theory has come to be used as a hypothetical device for justifying one particular set of rules or principles for regulating social interaction over others. The basic rules for regulating social interaction are derived from a hypothetical agreement of parties to a contract.

Understood in its broadest sense, then, the social contract is a hypothetical agreement between individuals about the rules that should govern their social cooperation. But beyond this general function of ensuring agreement, social contract has more specific uses in different theories. Contractarians tend to argue for the significance of the contract for two different types of reason. First, they may see the contract as a device for ensuring compliance with a set of rules in order to avoid conflict. The contract guarantees the cooperation of all participants, and therefore ensures stability and may also maximise the individual benefits of cooperation. A second reason for valuing the contract is because of the moral significance of autonomy. On this account, what is important about the contract is not so much that it ensures a stable outcome, but that it defines terms of justice that rational agents would (at least hypothetically) agree to under conditions of equal autonomy. On this account, the significance of the contract is that it guarantees morally just terms, i.e. terms that contractors would consent to *qua* rational and autonomous actors.

While most social contract theories draw on some combination of these two notions of consent, the distinction between the two is nonetheless important. Placing relative emphasis on either the problem of conflict, or the moral value of autonomy, will have a bearing on the practical norms that one derives from the contract, and on the question of motivation. Regarding the content of the norms chosen, to put it simply, if conflict is defined as the basic problem for political theory, then the motivation to comply with rules of justice will usually be derived from the self-interested desire to avoid conflict or to maximise individual gains. This is the approach adopted by Hobbes, and more recently Gauthier. In their theories, the content of justice will be defined according to the self-interest of the parties, and the scope of justice will be contingent on the existence of conflict between individuals. Non-nationals will only be included in the contract if they threaten the stability of the society in question, or if their cooperation in some way brings additional benefits to current members. On the other hand, if consent is motivated by ethical considerations – as in the case of Barry's theory, and on some interpretations of Rawls – then terms of justice are likely to be defined on the basis of a commitment to fairness or impartiality. In this case, the scope of the contract may also incorporate a wider sphere of individuals, and the terms of justice are more likely to include a commitment to the rights of non-nationals.

These two ways of deriving a theory of justice from consent also reflect different conceptions of the relationship between justice and motivation. The first takes existing motivation as a starting point, thence deriving terms of justice. On this account, terms of justice are an extension of the desire to avoid conflict or to preserve one's life or liberty. The second approach defines a moral conception of justice, and then tries to show how and why people will be motivated to respect its strictures. As one commentator has more cynically put it, in social contract theory 'two winning moves are possible: either interest must be reduced to duty, or duty must be derived from interest'.[6]

The paramount concern of this book is to find a theory that allows for a conception of duties to non-nationals, and the conflict-based model seems unlikely to be able to provide this. Indeed, as I shall argue in the discussion of Hobbes, a morally adequate theory of international justice must be (at least partly) morally driven, rather than based on egoism. So Rawls' and Barry's morally driven theories seem to provide the best hope for deriving a global conception. Nonetheless, it is useful to start by examining Hobbes' theory, in order both to grasp the structure of contract theory, and also to understand the deficiencies of the conflict-based account. The theories of Rawls and Barry can be best understood through contrasting them with the purely egoistic account of Hobbes.

Deriving Duty from Interest: Hobbesian Theories

The best known example of deriving duty from self-interest is that of Hobbes' social contract theory, which produces a theory of justice which has been characterised as 'justice as mutual advantage' or justice as a *modus vivendi*.[7] Hobbes starts from the assumption that people's motives for entering into a social contract are purely self-interested. In Hobbes' *Leviathan*, people sacrifice a portion of individual freedom and enter a social contract in order to ensure their own preservation.

> The finall Cause, End, or Designe of men (who naturally love Liberty, and Dominion over others,) in the introduction of that restraint upon themselves, (in which wee see them live in Commonwealths,) is the foresight of their own preservation, and of a more contented live thereby.[8]

Compliance with a set of rules for regulating social interaction is preferable to risking death in a violent and anarchical state of nature. Indeed, the object of *Leviathan* is 'without other design, than to set before mens eyes the mutuall Relation between Protection and Obedience'.[9] Hobbes' political theory is constructed on the basis of what he understands to be human motivation, and moral duty is simply an extension of self-interest. As such, self-interest necessarily coincides with duty, and the rules of justice generate motivation on purely egoistic grounds.

Hobbes does not offer his contractors a choice between different sets of rules: those entering society face a more stark choice between almost unconditional obedience to the existing Sovereign, or a return to the dreadful state of nature. Nonetheless, his theory of human motivation and reason yields a particular theory of justice. Given that the only reasons for accepting rules constraining individual freedom is that they promote the individual's self-interest, then by definition it must be advantageous to the individual to comply with just rules. The existence of mutual advantage is a necessary condition for ensuring obedience. Significantly, it is also a sufficient condition for those rules to be just: justice is no more than a set of mutually advantageous rules for regulating social intercourse. As the contemporary Hobbesian David Gauthier writes, 'not only do we undertake obligations only for prudential reasons, but the undertaking extends only to what we have prudential reasons for carrying out'.[10]

The Moral Critique

We should consider implications of such a theory for the nature and scope of duties to refugees. Can the Hobbesian theory of justice account for duties to non-nationals, and adequately characterise their relationship with duties to compatriots? Barry's critique highlights two main problems with the theory which are relevant here. Firstly, justice as mutual advantage does not establish criteria for rules that correspond to what we would normally consider to be just or fair. In the words of Barry, it fails 'to correspond in crucial respects to what is normally considered to be just'.[11] Justice as mutual advantage implies that complying with rules of justice will only be *relatively* advantageous to each individual, compared with their situation in the absence of these rules. If those choosing principles of justice start from unequal positions in terms of wealth or power, then a mutually advantageous contract may produce fundamentally inegalitarian rules. Justice as mutual advantage has nothing to say about what sorts of distributions are fair, or how the benefits and burdens of social cooperation should be shared. It provides no moral basis for claims to equal or fair treatment, except insofar as such principles may be necessary to ensure that the rules of justice are mutually advantageous to all parties to the contract. Yet in the absence of equal starting points, weaker individuals may agree to principles that produce a relative improvement in their situation, but which do not correspond to what we would consider to be just principles. As Barry writes, 'so long as even very rough equality of strength obtains among the parties to rules of justice, the rules recommended by justice as mutual advantage will tend to correspond to those that we would ordinarily think just ... Where this rough equality fails to obtain, the correspondence will break down'.[12]

In this scenario, the terms of justice would be worked out on the basis of characteristics that most liberals would consider to be morally arbitrary, such as political power, wealth, intelligence or physical strength. The agreement reached may well incorporate favourable treatment for the more powerful. The possibility of such a scenario makes the extension of justice as mutual advantage to refugees highly problematic. Assuming that they are in fact admitted to a state, individual or small groups of refugees will tend to be in a weaker bargaining position, and therefore unable to secure fair terms. The receiving state will be able to decide how many refugees to admit, and under what conditions. If justice is an extension of self-interest, is not at all clear that those granted asylum will get fair or even tolerable treatment. If one were to follow the logic of a theory of justice based on self-interest, the standard of treatment of refugees would be significantly lower than is currently the case.

More seriously, it is probable that refugees would not be included in the contract at all. If the scope of justice is determined merely by considerations of mutual advantage, then the inclusion of refugees will depend on the extent to which those in the receiving country are dependent on the cooperation of refugees. In the case of a *national* social contract, it has traditionally been argued that compatriots are more dependent on one another's cooperation to avoid conflict, and that it is therefore in their interest to establish and maintain mutually acceptable rules. But there will be little or no motive to establish fair terms of justice with those on whom one is not dependent in this sense, for example refugees. Individual or small groups of refugees do not generally pose a threat to stability, and thus their cooperation is not required in order to prevent conflict; and they are often perceived as lacking the resources to make a positive contribution to society, unable to provide goods which would benefit the members of the society in question. Refugees are therefore seen as lacking the skills or resources to render their inclusion mutually advantageous to the receiving society. The country of refuge is not dependent on their consent to ensure peace or to generate additional resources. This question of dependence has raised problems for Hobbesian social contract theories at the domestic level. Gauthier, for example, writes of his own theory that 'animals, the unborn, the congenitally handicapped and defective, fall beyond the pail of a morality tied to mutuality. The disposition to comply with moral constraints ... may be rationally defended only within the scope of expected benefit'.[13] Following this logic, it would also be rational to exclude refugees from a system of reciprocal benefit. Those currently outside the sphere of interdependence are unlikely to be included in a social contract motivated by self-interest, let alone one whose terms are fair.

The only way theories of justice as mutual advantage can establish their applicability to the international sphere seems to be by showing that receiving states are in fact dependent on the cooperation of refugees. The refugee policy debate would then revolve around an empirical question of the actual reliance of nationals on non-nationals. It would be extremely difficult to establish a case for admitting refugees on these grounds. Perhaps one could imagine an extreme case where the presence of refugees outside of the relevant state would pose a threat to national security. In this case, establishing mutually advantageous rules for regulating cooperation between refugees and nationals may be in the interest of the receiving country. But this is a rather far-fetched scenario. Moreover, the extension of justice to these refugees would be entirely contingent on the coincidence of self-interest and the terms of the contract. It would not establish principles of justice for regulating interaction with refugees in general, but merely with regard to particular caseloads. Refugees who did not pose a similar threat to security would not be included in such an agreement.

A second possible route for establishing dependence would be to argue that refugees had resources or skills which were useful or necessary for the receiving state. In this case, entering into a contract with refugees would be advantageous to nationals because of refugees' positive contribution to society. This type of consideration clearly influenced a number of western European states in the 1950s and 1960s, when they absorbed large numbers of immigrants to provide labour in a period of economic growth. Yet as with the previous example, admittance of refugees would be a function of the extent to which the admittance of refugees would be advantageous from a purely self-interested perspective. In many cases the self-interest of nationals would not coincide with the interests of refugees. This motive for admitting refugees does not provide a consistent and reliable basis for grounding duties to refugees, and represents an extremely impoverished account of the nature of our duties to refugees.

An alternative to arguing for dependence on refugees would be to concede that refugees fall outside the sphere of justice, and define duties to refugees as a question of humanity, rather than one of justice. Again, this is a profoundly unsatisfactory option. It would imply that all those who are too weak or unimportant to be included in the contract would not be the subject of justice but rather of charity or supererogatory duties. This category would presumably include the congenitally handicapped as well as refugees. Given that these categories would normally be considered to be the subjects of some form of justice or fair treatment, their exclusion from the scope of justice demonstrates the inadequacy of theories of justice as mutual advantage. This inadequacy is a clear consequence of attempting to derive duty from self-interest.

The Problem of Compliance

Before abandoning justice as mutual advantage, it is useful to consider a second problem which further casts doubt on the theory's account of individual motivation. Quite apart from the scope of the contract or the fairness of its terms, it is difficult to see how the rules established by justice as mutual advantage would generate motivation to comply with all of the rules all of the time. Several commentators have argued that this creates a 'free rider' problem: assuming that everyone else (or most people) cooperate, it may be in my self-interest not to cooperate, at least in certain instances.[14] Justice as mutual advantage has the structure of a prisoner's dilemma, in which the social contract is agreed to because cooperation is preferable to conflict. But if everyone else cooperates, then it may be rational for me not to cooperate, provided that my non-cooperation does not jeopardise the stability of the whole agreement. As Barry writes:

> Settlements underwritten by justice as mutual advantage are no more than truces. As soon as one side or the other feels it can improve its position, there is nothing to restrain

it so long as (measured within its own conception of the good) the prospective gains outweigh the anticipated costs.[15]

He concludes that the 'pursuit of advantage does not provide an adequate motive for compliance with rules that would be mutually advantageous if generally observed'.[16] In other words, the exclusive dependence on self-interest to motivate compliance creates a very fragile system of social cooperation. The system is fragile in the sense that just rules does not seem capable of generating motivation compliance on every occasion. Thus not only do the rules derived from self-interest fail to correspond in important respects to what we would normally consider to be just. Even if we accept the adequacy of justice as mutual advantage as a system for regulating social interaction, it is not at all clear that the system would be stable.

Many commentators have attributed both of these weaknesses – the moral inadequacy of the theory of justice, and the failure of just rules to generate motivation – to the simplistic nature of Hobbes' theory of motivation.[17] As we shall see, this has led several political philosophers to supplement the theory with a more complex account of human motivation. In doing so, they have avoided the problem of making compliance contingent on the individual's egoistic interest in obeying every rule on every occasion. Richer theories of motivation can also provide non-egoistic reasons for agreeing to a particular set of rules, thereby allowing for a fairer conception of justice, and for the inclusion in the contract of those with whom it is not in one's self-interest to cooperate. This would open up a possibility for including refugees in a social contract. The next section will consider Rawls' attempt to base his theory of justice on a more complex account of motivation.

Rawls and Justice as Fairness

Rawls' theory of 'justice as fairness' has a rather different conception of the conditions under which people should select principles of justice. His contract is designed to yield fairer terms of justice, which do not discriminate between individuals on what liberal universalists would consider to be morally arbitrary grounds. Unlike Hobbes, the terms of justice do not establish a mere *modus vivendi* between individuals with conflicting ends. Instead, he introduces certain hypothetical conditions to ensure that his contractors will choose terms of justice that do not discriminate on grounds of wealth, talent, social status, gender or race. Rawls' theory is Kantian in inspiration, basing its theory of justice on a conception of individuals as autonomous choosers of their own ends. It therefore avoids the moral deficiencies of the Hobbesian account, and would appear to offer a better basis for deriving a contract that recognises duties to refugees.

Motivation and the Veil of Ignorance

Rawls' theory of justice can be understood as an attempt to combine two theories of the role of consent: a Humean account of the circumstances of justice; and a Kantian commitment to a conception of individuals as free and equal. The Humean premise implies that justice is required to solve a problem of conflict, thus making the application of rules of justice contingent on the 'circumstances of justice'. In contrast, the Kantian element suggests a moral commitment to a universalist conception of individuals as worthy of equal consideration, and hence a global contract. It is worth considering how Rawls incorporates each of the two strands, and examining their implications for international justice and duties to refugees.

First, as observed above, Rawls explicitly embraces a Humean interpretation of the 'circumstances of justice'.[18] He argues that there are certain 'background conditions' which give rise to the need for principles for choosing arrangements to regulate social interaction. These circumstances obtain 'whenever mutually disinterested persons put forward conflicting claims to the division of social advantages under conditions of moderate scarcity'.[19] This would imply that justice is required to solve a cooperation problem: it is required to avoid conflict between persons of roughly equal strength competing for scarce resources. On this account, society is no more than what Rawls sometimes refers to as a 'cooperative venture for mutual gain',[20] with justice simply a set of rules for avoiding conflict and ensuring social stability. It should be noted that a consistent application of the circumstances of justice account would yield no more than a *modus vivendi*. If the need for stability were the sole reason for advocating justice, then one could solve the problem with recourse to a Hobbesian theory of justice. And if one assumes that parties to the contract are mutually disinterested people competing for scarce goods, then one would expect them to agree to some form of justice as mutual advantage.

Yet Rawls' theory of justice aims to do more than provide rules for ensuring stability and cooperation. If justice were required solely to avoid conflict caused by scarcity and natural selfishness, then Rawls would not require his parties to choose principles from behind a veil of ignorance. The veil of ignorance requires the parties to adopt what amounts to an impartial ethical perspective. The parties have no knowledge of their social and economic status, natural assets, psychological disposition or conception of the good. The veil of ignorance is designed to avoid an 'outcome biased by arbitrary contingencies', in other words to preclude principles that are chosen on the basis of partial considerations.[21]

But although Rawls introduces a moral component, it is kept separate from the motivation of the parties to the contract. While the parties are obliged to adopt the impartial perspective represented by the veil of ignorance, this ethical perspective is independent of their self-interested rationality. Contractors in the Original Position are thus motivated by prudence or self-interest. The moral component of the choice of principles is guaranteed by the imposition of an external mechanism which ostensibly has no basis in the psychological make-up of the parties. Thus

Rawls introduces a sharp division between impartial and self-interested perspectives. The impartial perspective is captured by the fact that people voluntarily take on the veil of ignorance, which avoids an outcome influenced by morally irrelevant factors. While the self-interested perspective is captured by the rationality of the parties.

The Circumstances of Justice

One way of applying Rawls' theory of justice to the international sphere is to emphasise the significance of the circumstances of justice in deriving terms of justice. On this account, the scope and content of justice would be determined on the basis of empirical criteria. Namely, it would depend on the existence of a situation in which individuals with roughly equal power were competing for scarce resources. While establishing the existence or not of these empirical conditions would appear to be a relatively straightforward matter, there has been some controversy over whether or not the relevant conditions hold in the international sphere; and, if they do, whether they are characteristic of relations between individuals, or between states.[22] I shall consider in turn the possibility of deriving a global or an inter-state contract from an argument about empirical conditions.

The first possibility is that the argument for a global contract theory be based on a claim about the existence of circumstances of justice between all individuals. This interpretation of the global implications of the theory of justice has been most famously pursued by Charles Beitz.[23] Beitz challenges Rawls' assumption that justice should be limited to relations between individuals at the domestic level. He argues that Rawls derives this conclusion about the limited scope of justice from an incorrect empirical claim about the self-sufficiency of states. Beitz argues that there is a substantial degree of economic interdependence between states, which creates a 'non-voluntary society-wide system of economic institutions which defines starting positions and assigns economic rights and duties'.[24] Beitz argues that these institutions constitute a basic structure which should be regulated by Rawls' principles of justice because 'by defining the terms of cooperation, they have such deep and pervasive effects on the welfare of people to whom they apply regardless of consent'.[25] Given the extensive and nonvoluntary nature of interdependence, then, the principles of distributive justice must apply 'in the first instance to the world as a whole, then derivatively to nation-states'.[26]

However, we should be careful about following Beitz down this path. Beitz appears to misunderstand the significance of interdependence in the work of Rawls. On Rawls' account, empirical assumptions about the level of interdependence between individuals do play an important role in determining the scope of justice. But the relevance of economic and social interdependence stems not so much from the ethical significance of human interaction, but rather from the need to ensure cooperation between people with different interests or conceptions of the good. Interdependence creates a need for agreement on principles for regulating social interaction because without such principles there would be conflict for scarce resources. It is not significant for ethical reasons, as Beitz seems to suggest. Beitz is conflating an argument about the *ethical* significance of interdependence with an argument about the circumstances of justice.

This confusion leads Beitz to misapply Rawls' theory in his prescriptions about the scope and content of justice. His misunderstanding of the notion of interdependence as employed by Rawls leads him to characterise all individuals as interdependent at a global level. Now such a form of global interdependence may be relevant in an ethical sense. For example, one could argue that the actions of each individual could potentially affect the well-being of any other person, and that this (potential) interdependence of all human beings provided ethical grounds for regulating the interaction of all individuals in a global theory of justice.[27] But this does not follow from Rawls' conception of interdependence, which describes a state of actual dependence on others, requiring cooperation to ensure stability. On this conception, it is certainly not the case that all individuals are dependent on one another. In fact, as Rawls himself argues, this situation of mutual dependence is more characteristic of relations between states.

Rawls himself has derived rather different international practical implications from his theory of justice. In his 'Law of Peoples', Rawls argues that principles of justice should be worked out in the first instance for the 'basic structure of a closed and self-contained democratic society'.[28] Only once this is done will the parties consider principles of international justice, extending outwards to construct principles for the 'law of peoples'. In this second stage, the parties to the contract represent the societies of peoples who have already worked out their domestic principles of justice. They do not deliberate behind a veil of ignorance, but select inter-national principles in full knowledge of their nationality and the terms they have agreed to at the domestic level. The principles agreed to are far looser than the conception of justice as fairness. Notably, they omit the egalitarian and redistributive features of the domestic conception. The resulting conception of the law of peoples is based on 'familiar principles' of international law, including the right of states to self-defence; duties of non-intervention, observance of treaties and certain restrictions on the conduct of war.[29] Rawls does also includes a general commitment 'to honor human rights', which are later listed as 'such basic rights as the right to life and security, to personal property, and the elements of the rules of law, as well as the right to a certain liberty of conscience and freedom of association, and the right to emigration'.[30] But these rights are not nearly as comprehensive as those enjoyed by participants in the domestic contract – indeed, Rawls stresses that they must not be 'peculiar to our Western culture', but acceptable to those from what he terms 'well-ordered' non-liberal societies.[31] In essence, this amounts to limiting the conception of justice at the international level to a *modus vivendi*. Terms of justice are designed to ensure a stable international environment, in which states can get on with the more important business of ensuring domestic justice and stability.

A frequent criticism levelled at Rawls' international theory is that his focus on the domestic basic structure leads him to treat groups of people rather than individuals as the relevant moral unit in the international sphere.[32] Rawls does not provide a conception of duties to those outside of the relevant sphere of social cooperation, thus wholly overlooking the question of duties to non-nationals and to refugees. This omission of duties to individual non-nationals is largely explained by the narrowly defined purpose of Rawls' principles for international cooperation. The law of peoples is not designed to achieve global fairness or rectify violations of human rights, but rather, as a means of establishing rules between societies that *already* meet basic human rights standards. '[D]efense of well-ordered peoples is the first and most urgent task'.[33] Well-ordered states can find sufficient common consensus to agree to principles which will provide the best international context for realising domestic justice. The principles adopted for the international sphere are thus seen as secondary to the central question of achieving stability and consensus on principles of justice for the basic structure. The main impetus for considering questions of international justice seems to stem from its potential threat to these domestic arrangements. The neglect of individual justice is therefore not an aberrance. Rather, it can be understood as the logical outcome of a conception of justice as triggered by the circumstances of justice that hold between states.

Morally Driven Agreement and the 'Strains of Commitment'

However, we have seen that there is another interpretation of Rawls, which emphasises the Kantian rather than the Humean strand of his theory. On this account, Rawls is committed to a conception of individuals as free and equal, and it is this *moral* premise that should determine the nature and scope of justice. As Pogge argues, for example, Rawls' neglect of individual justice beyond borders is inconsistent with his 'conception of all human beings as free and equal morel persons'.[34]

This emphasis on the moral element in Rawls' theory raises an important question about the foundations of his commitment to Kantian ethics. In his recent work, Rawls has argued that his conception of justice should not be understood as grounded in a metaphysical account of the essential and universal characterstics of human beings. Rather, this conception is derived from the shared values of individuals of a certain cultural context. Thus the moral values embodied in the veil of ignorance are not universally valid, but describe the moral beliefs of inheritors of liberal democratic institutions and a liberal tradition of political thought.

Now on this non-metaphysical reading, justice as fairness must be understood as deriving its ethical content from the intersubejctive values of contractors. As such, justice as fairness will only be chosen by those committed to the liberal conception. And commitment to this conception is clearly contingent on the historical and cultural context of the contractors. It is most likely to be agreed by citizens of liberal democracies, and not members of non-liberal non-democratic states. Once again, this seems to pull us back from a global contract to one agreed between members of liberal democratic societies. The applicability of the veil of ignorance is thus limited to particular societies, and – short of a major shift in the values of all non-liberal societies – will not be applicable to the global sphere. And without the application of a veil of ignorance, justice will be determined on the basis of the need to avoid conflict. Hence it will be a contract between states, and one that establishes no more than a *modus vivendi*. We seem to be left again with a morally inadequate conception of duties to non-nationals. The moral component of Rawls' theory, then, does not seem to yield a global contract, at least not in his later work. Having rejected a metaphysical conception, the scope and content of his theory of justice as fairness is contingent on the existence of shared values.

But could one derive a global conception of justice from Rawls' earlier work, prior to his explicit abandonment of a metaphysical conception? In other words, if the commitment to Kantian ethics is understood as universally valid rather than derived from shared values, could this yield an adequate conception of duties to refugees? A global application of Rawls' theory of justice as fairness would require imposing a veil of ignorance on all individuals, or on the representatives of each state. Contractors would be denied knowledge of their nation's gross domestic product, natural resources, geopolitical situation, and so on. They would presumably agree to radical redistribution of wealth between states, and international institutions would distribute goods on the basis of the two principles of justice. Contractors would also be deprived knowledge of whether or not they were actual or potential refugees. Presumably this would encourage them to introduce an extensive set of refugee rights, with provisions far more generous than those currently in place.

Now the problem with such an agreement would be that it would be unlikely to secure continued compliance one the veil of ignorance was lifted. It should be recalled that Rawls' procedure assumes that parties are motivated by rational self-interest. The moral component of their agreement, which ensures that *fair* terms are accepted, is only guaranteed by the imposition of a veil of ignorance. But once the terms of justice have been agreed upon, the veil is lifted and people are once again aware of their socio-economic situation and personal characteristics. And given their self-interested motivation, those who are privileged in terms of natural assets, wealth or social status will be unlikely to be motivated to continue to comply with the chosen terms.

The problem of continued compliance outside of the Original Position gives rise to what Rawls has termed the 'strains of commitment'.[35] The principles of justice chosen in the Original Position must be acceptable once the veil of ignorance has been lifted. This means that those who are worst off under the terms should nonetheless still consider that the chosen principles of justice are better than other principles that could have been selected in the Original Position. Hence those who lose substantial privileges as a result of the redistributive implications of the principles should nonetheless continue to comply with them. This implies a requirement of unanimous agreement for the principles not only in the original position, but also once people are aware of their actual position and natural assets, social and economic status, and so on. In fact, the test of the strains of commitment is far more challenging for Rawls' theory of justice than ensuring the relevant terms are chosen in the Original Position. As Barry argues, the test has a crucial role in ensuring consent for principles. As he writes, 'the implicit criteria determining what principles are consistent with the "strains of commitment" test are actually the criteria for principles of justice'.[36] Only the strains of commitment test will ensure cooperation once people know about their characteristics and socio-economic status.

Barry argues that this problem arises because of Rawls' assumption of self-interested motivation. It is his characterisation of the parties to the contract as unmotivated by moral considerations that obliges Rawls to impose a veil of ignorance. Barry argues instead for a conception of motivation that includes a moral component. This would render the veil superfluous.

> Where the parties are assumed to be pursuing their own interests, a veil of ignorance is essential. But where they are assumed to be motivated by the desire to reach an agreement on reasonable terms, a veil of ignorance is an optional feature – a heuristic device which can be resorted to on occasion but does not have to be relied on to create solutions.[37]

Barry favours a procedure for agreeing terms of justice that resembles Rawls' strains of commitment test, rather than his Original Position.[38] The next section will consider whether the theory he produces – justice as impartiality – can produce a better conception of duties to refugees.

Justice as Impartiality

Barry's theory of justice as impartiality in many ways resembles Rawls' theory of justice. Indeed, Barry characterises Rawls' theory as a variant of justice as impartiality: it is 'the best-known, most influential, and the most fully developed variant of justice as impartiality'.[39] The main difference between Barry's theory and the early work of Rawls lies in the procedure for agreement to terms of justice. Rather than representing the impartial or moral perspective through the imposition of a veil of ignorance, Barry assumes that the parties to the contract are aware of their social and economic status and natural assets. Nonetheless, they are able and willing to abstract from these morally arbitrary characteristics and choose fair principles. There is no device for making a sharp distinction between moral motivation and self-interested rationality: impartial and personal perspectives are assumed to coincide in Barry's conception of reason. Barry prefers to conceive of contractors as motivated by the desire for fairness. On this account, the impartial perspective is not conceptually or psychologically distinct from the interests of contractors. Rather, it is assumed that the contractors have an interest in or desire to accept impartial terms.

In terms of its characterisation of individual psychology, Barry's failure to make a clear distinction between egoism and altruism seems at least *prima facie* to be a more accurate portrayal of people's motivation: reasons for action invariably involve a complicated mixture of egoism and altruism, and it is difficult in practice to disentangle one from the other. However, at the conceptual level it creates a new set of problems for Barry's account. Not only does his theory still rest on an assumed dichotomy between self-interest and impartial ethics. Paradoxically, his attempt to deny the dichotomy through the notion of a desire for fairness leads to a number of serious practical problems with his account. By blurring the conceptual distinction between self-interested and ethical motivation in his procedure for selecting principles, he is unable to explain impediments to motivating the global application of justice. Moreover by linking motivation so tightly to terms of justice, his theory risks being counter-productive. Where the relevant motivation is not triggered, there will be no terms of justice at all.

The Desire for Reasonable Agreement

Barry argues that people are motivated to agree to his criteria for just rules precisely because of their desire for reasonable agreement. The concept of 'reasonable agreement' is the key phrase in this formulation, and needs some unpacking. Barry takes this construction from Scanlon's 'contractualist' account of morality, according to which the nature of moral wrongness can be stated as follows:

> An act is wrong if its performance under the circumstances would be disallowed by any system of rules for the general regulation of behaviour which no one could reasonably reject as a basis for informed, unforced general agreement.[40]

This rather skeletal statement calls for several explanatory remarks. First, the agreement must be one that is informed in the sense of not being 'based on superstition or false belief about the consequences of actions'. Second, it should be unforced in order to rule out coercion to agree to terms from a weaker bargaining position. And thirdly, the notion of that which can be 'reasonably rejected' is designed to 'exclude rejections that would be unreasonable *given* the aim of finding principles which could be the basis of informed, unforced general agreement'.[41] A rejection will be reasonable only if it is based on the desire to find principles which others similarly motivated could not reasonably reject. It is therefore assumed that all parties to the contract are similarly motivated. Scanlon prefers the stronger condition 'no-one could reject' to 'every-one could accept' in order to rule out agreements involving substantial levels of self-sacrifice for some people. It is possible that some would voluntarily sacrifice their own interests in accepting an agreement, on terms that it would be perfectly reasonable for them to reject. This is a possibility that Scanlon wants to avoid.

While acknowledging that Scanlon intends his contractualist construction as a conception of the nature of morality, Barry employs it for a narrower purpose. He sees the construction as a 'device for talking about what is fair, on a certain fundamentally egalitarian conception of fairness'.[42] Barry does not consider the notion of contractualism to be a complete theory of the nature of morality, but it is one that captures the notion of fairness which is at the heart of his theory of justice. Scanlon's construction can be seen as a device for agreeing to a conception of justice, and Barry argues that the theory chosen will be justice as impartiality.

Justice as impartiality certainly appears to be a more plausible candidate for grounding duties to refugees than justice as mutual advantage. The notion of *reasonable* agreement ensures that the terms established under the contract are not contingent on power or other morally arbitrary characteristics. And since self-interest is no longer the sole motivation for compliance, one would expect parties to the contract to agree to fair terms for vulnerable groups such as refugees. Justice as impartiality does in this sense correspond more closely to what liberals would normally consider to be just. But are the assumptions it makes about motivation plausible, and will this conception of motivation be generated by the criteria for just rules?

The plausibility of Barry's theory of motivation will hinge on whether a desire for reasonable agreement really does motivate people in the requisite sense, or at the very least whether people can be encouraged to develop such a motivating desire. Barry holds that the desire for reasonable agreement presupposes the existence of 'the desire to live in a society whose members all freely accept its rules of justice and its major institutions'.[43] Barry does not provide an account of the source of this desire in *Justice as Impartiality*, or its relationship to more narrowly defined self-interest. He apparently takes the existence of this type of motivation as an uncontroversial fact of human psychology. 'I do not think the agreement motive presents a serious problem. The desire to be able to justify actions and institutions in terms that are in principle acceptable to others is, fortunately, widespread'.[44]

But as with other liberal universalist theories, as soon as one attempts to apply his conception to the international sphere, it appears to be completely unfeasible. Even assuming that justice as impartiality would be selected as a principle for regulating interaction at the domestic level, it seems far-fetched to assume that people would be motivated to extend the scope of this agreement to govern interaction with non-nationals. Such extension would mean that refugees would have an effective veto on unfair or partial terms governing their rights. Refugees would be justified in 'reasonably rejecting' terms that did not treat them with impartiality, thus implying the duty to extend the same treatment to all actual and would-be refugees as that already afforded to current nationals. As I have already argued in other cases, such an arrangement would not motivate the compliance of the citizens of receiving states. They would be extremely reluctant to extend their domestic terms of justice to govern the treatment of non-nationals.

The recurrence of this problem of motivation is in one sense not surprising: we have encountered similar problems of feasibility in Chapters Two and Three. Yet Barry's theory did initially seem to hold out the prospect of addressing the problem of motivation. He claimed that his account – unlike that of Rawls – would show why people would be motivated to comply with impartial justice. Barry argued that the desire for fairness would guarantee a practical commitment to engage in his procedure for selecting rules of justice, and to continue to comply with these rules. But his empirical claim that people are motivated by the desire for fairness is not justified, at least not as regards the extension of justice to non-nationals.

This is a rather worrying problem for Barry's theory. For the effective functioning of his contract presupposes that the parties will be motivated in the relevant sense. The existence of the desire for reasonable agreement is preconditional for securing agreement to justice as impartiality. So if this empirical precondition is not met, his terms of justice will not gain the consent of the parties, and justice as impartiality will not apply. The application of the terms of justice is contingent on the existence of the correct type of motivation. Perhaps Barry is right to assume that the desire for fairness motivates parties at the domestic level. But this desire certainly does not extend to agreement at the international level. And given this, there is a risk that he will be unable to derive any terms of justice whatsoever for the global sphere. If agreement on terms is conditional on the existence of a desire for fairness, then parties are unlikely to agree to any rules of justice for regulating interaction with non-nationals.

Moreover, there is a second problem with extending motivation to the international sphere. The problem of motivation is of course common to all the theories of liberal universalism we have discussed so far. But in Barry's case, the difficulty is exacerbated by his failure to distinguish conceptually between moral and self-interested motivation. By combining the two elements in the notion of the desire for fairness, Barry makes it difficult to locate the impediments to motivation at the international level. In other words, there is no way of explaining why the desire for fairness is more reliably triggered at the national than at the international level. With Rawls' theory, it was at least possible to separate out the self-interested from the ethical component, and attempt to explain why self-interest might impede motivation to apply principles internationally. But for Barry, the coincidence of self-interest and moral motivation in the desire for fairness makes it difficult to explain the limits of moral motivation to extend terms of justice to refugees. The desire for fairness does not differentiate between the significance of agreement on terms of justice at the domestic and the international sphere. It simply assumes that parties to the contract will be impartial between the two, an assumption that is clearly empirically incorrect.

Having discussed some of the practical and heuristic problems created by Barry's conception of motivation, I would like now to probe what I consider to be the source of these problems in his theory: namely, Barry's underlying assumptions about reason and desire. For the practical problem of feasibility generated at the international level stems from a fundamental deficiency of his theory that is also common to Rawls' theory of justice. Both are committed to what I shall term a 'rationalist' theory of motivation. *Prima facie*, this may appear to be a strange claim: after all, Barry talks about a 'desire' for fairness, implying that moral motivation is based on sentiment rather than reason. But I shall argue in the next section that, like Rawls, Barry's theory of motivation can only be coherent if it assumes that agents are motivated by reason. Barry and Rawls' theory are both implicitly committed to an assumed split between an impartial perspective and a personal viewpoint. This split creates problems for explaining motivation to comply with terms of international justice. While the two theorists attempt to patch up the problems created by this assumed split in different ways (Rawls through the veil of ignorance and Barry through blurring moral and self-interested motivation), both are fundamentally flawed by their implicit attachment to this simplistic conception of moral agency.

The Source of the Desire for Fairness: Egoism, Sentiment or Reason?

What, then, is this underlying theory of motivation that causes problems for both Rawls' and Barry's accounts? There are three traditional accounts of the sources of moral motivation: it could be held to be located in self-interest, sentiment, or a more moral conception of rationality.

The first option for Barry, then, would be to derive the desire for fairness from self-interest. This possibility is clearly ruled out by Barry in his rejection of egoistic social contract theories. More specifically, in a discussion of Rawls' work, Barry agrees with what he understands to be the latter's assumption that there 'is an independent motive for behaving justly stemming from the recognition of others as having legitimate claims to have their interests taken into account'.[45] This independent motive is not based on considerations of mutual advantage or reciprocity, but would seem to be an altruistic concern, that is to say, a concern for the well-being of others which is not reducible to self-interest or prudence. It should be noted that Barry's rejection of a purely self-interested account of motivation is somewhat qualified by an acknowledgement that 'the experience of dependence on others is an important predisposing factor' in creating the desire for fairness,[46] and hence that it is 'more likely to come to the fore in conditions of approximately equal power than in conditions of radical inequality'.[47] While this notion of predisposing conditions is evocative of Hume's account of the 'circumstances of justice', Barry seems to attribute less weight than does Hume to the significance of conditions of dependence or equality in motivating justice. His argument seems to be that the desire for fairness exists regardless of these empirical conditions, although it is likely to be stronger where rough equality of strength between the parties obtains.

Yet Barry must also forego a sentiment-based account of motivation. As Scanlon argues, the type of motivation required for a contract based on reasonable agreement cannot be based on sympathy. The utilitarian notion of sympathy is unlikely to yield consistent and even-handed treatment of all individuals.[48] It can motivate us 'because of our sympathetic identification with the good of others. But as we move from philosophical utilitarianism to a specific utilitarian formula as the standard of right action, the form of motivation that utilitarianism appeals to becomes more abstract'.[49] In other words, motivation generated by sympathetic identification does not seem to be triggered by the more abstract notion of aggregate well-being. By contrast, the desire for fairness is impartial in its choice of objects, and is concerned with justifying action on the basis of what would normally be considered as just. Presumably this makes it a better candidate for accounting for people's desire to perform duties to a more abstract set of objects, with whom they have no particular identification. It would certainly be more effective at motivating people to accept refugees with whom they have no particular sympathy or affinity. Assuming that the desire for fairness does have motivational force, it would seem to trigger moral motivation more *systematically* than sympathetic identification.

Both the sentiment and the self-interest based theories of motivation would seem to yield an overly partial or particularist conception, which would not be appropriate for generating compliance with impartial justice. So if the desire for fairness is not based on either sympathy or egoism, it must have at its source some concept of reason. On this account, Barry's theory of motivation would be more akin to the Kantian variant: reason, rather than sentiment or self-interest, motivates us to comply with the requirements of morality. Our commitment to impartial justice is generated by rational deliberation on the requirements of universal morality. I shall discuss the more general problems with the Kantian account in Chapter Five. The point I want to make here is that Barry's theory of motivation must embrace some such conception of reason. If morality is defined as adopting an impartial perspective, then only a reason-based account of motivation will supply the appropriate motivation.

Now a Kantian conception of reason, as we have seen, would produce a commitment to the impartial application of terms of justice. This would mean that those engaging in practical deliberation on the requirements of justice would be motivated by a conception of justice that did not differentiate on the grounds of nationality, race, wealth, and so on. And refugees would thus be included in the scope of the agreement on terms of justice. If the moral component of motivation is guaranteed by impartial reason, then the empirical limitations of moral motivation must be explained by self-interest or sentiment. It is these partial or particularist considerations that constrain motivation to extend justice to non-nationals. This would seem to tally with Barry's account – indeed this characterisation of a conflict between particularist considerations and impartial justice seems to explain why the desire for fairness is not so reliably triggered at the international level.

But this unfortunately takes us back to the problem with the Rawlsian account. In the discussion of Rawls, we saw that the application of justice as fairness was contingent on continued commitment to terms agreed behind a veil of ignorance. Rawls' separation of self-interested rationality on the one hand, and an externally imposed veil of ignorance on the other, made it difficult to understand why people would comply with terms once the veil of ignorance was lifted. Barry's theory aimed to overcome the problems caused by this division of self-interest and impartiality, combining the two in a description of the desire for fairness. Yet once we unpack Barry's notion of the desire for fairness, we encounter exactly the same problem. Justice is motivated by impartial reason, and as such should not differentiate between national and non-national subjects of justice. But this form of moral motivation is constrained by particularist considerations – be they egoistic, or related to sympathetic identification with a particular group of people. And this produces a division between the personal perspective and the requirements of impartial justice. This split is along precisely the same lines as the division between the veil of ignorance conception of impartiality and the self-interested rationality of the parties that we found in Rawls.

To make matters worse for Barry, his attempt to plaster over this split gets him into a fresh set of difficulties. As I suggested earlier, his notion of the desire for fairness simply obscures the division, exacerbating the problem of explaining limited motivation. By presenting a conception of motivation that merges egoistic and moral reasons for action, it is difficult to pinpoint the impediments to extending motivation to non-nationals. And this explanatory weakness in turn makes it more difficult to find ways of encouraging motivation to expand the scope of justice.

In addition this practical problem of pin-pointing impediments to encouraging motivation, as we have seen, there is a structural problem with Barry's theory of motivation. By combining self-interest and altruism in the single concept of the desire for fairness, he creates a rather brittle theory of motivation, which cannot allow for the legitimacy of or even evaluation of compromise or 'second best' options. It has been argued that once the desire for fairness is triggered, it is more systematic than more emotional sources of motivation, notably feelings of sympathy. This was described by Scanlon as a virtue, as motivation is thus not dependent on unreliable and morally arbitrary identification with particular people or situations. Yet the quality of being systematic works the other way: if the desire for fairness is not triggered in its pure form, there is no nuanced or weaker version of the desire which will motivate people to accept second best terms. While terms of justice may be more or less fair, and their scope may cover a smaller or greater range of people, the desire for fairness does not recognise the significance of these differences. Where the desire for fairness is triggered, rules of justice will apply impartially to all people, regardless of nationality. Where it is not, justice will not apply at all. Barry's framework seems to rule out non-systematic or less than full-scale principles of justice. Justice must be full-fledged impartiality, embodied in the condition of reasonable rejectibility, or it is not justice.

Both Barry and Rawls face problems generated by the assumed split between personal and impartial perspectives. This makes it difficult to explain motivation to extend justice to non-nationals. Hence these morally driven social contract theories fail to address the problem of motivation. Indeed, in tying agreement so closely to justice, through the notion of consent, they are left with a rather stark choice as exemplified in the different interpretations of Rawls: either a Hobbesian account in which justice is based on egoistic motivation and is limited to the domestic level; or a Kantian account in which justice is global in scope, but does not generate motivation. In the latter case, we are back to the problem of the feasibility of liberal universalist theories. But we also have an additional problem, generated by the close link between justice and consent. If the relevant motivation is not forthcoming, then the contract cannot function. This problem, as we saw, was especially acute in the case of Barry's theory. Since on his account justice is so closely tied to a certain kind of motivation, once this motivation fails to be triggered, justice as impartiality simply will not apply.

One way of understanding this problem of motivation is by considering the role of the procedure in social contract theory. Contractarianism derives a procedure for selecting terms of justice from some background conception of fairness or impartiality. It then puts forward this procedure as a stand-alone, self-justifying device for testing the fairness of rules of justice. Thus Rawls justifies his terms of justice by the fact that they would be agreed from the Original Position, and Barry justifies his norms by virtue of the fact that they are not reasonably rejectable. But these procedures are detached from any richer ethical justification, for example an account of why contractors would value justice or fairness. And this detachment of the procedure from a background justification places an excessive emphasis on procedure, creating problems when the procedure fails to function. If people are not motivated to adopt an impartial perspective, then the ideal rules of impartial global justice will fail to be generated. And the stand-alone contract has no mechanism for defining alternative terms of justice that achieve partial or second best distributions. The impartial perspective is an ideal conception of moral agency abstracted from the very values and goods from which it was derived.

As a concluding thought, we should consider why social contract theories seemed to offer such good prospects for addressing the problem of motivation in the first place. Their reputation for generating compliance with terms of justice was earned through their apparent success in the domestic sphere. For at this level, there is likely to be a far greater coincidence between the need for stability, and the moral goal of ensuring impartial justice. Social contract theory for the domestic sphere seems to solve both the problem of conflict, and to ensure fair principles. However, the apparent facility for addressing both of these problems did not extend beyond the national level. The overlap between the need for stability and the goal of securing individual justice seemed to break down when it came to questions of global justice. The confidence of social contract theorists that there is a coincidence between these two functions leads many to tie motivation to justice in a rigid way. The epitome of this tendency can be found in the work of Barry, and his notion of the desire for fairness. These high expectations are not fulfilled at the global sphere, and the rigidity of the link between the two makes it impossible to effect a partial retreat from the relevant terms of justice. There is no scope for ratcheting down the requirements of impartial justice, short of rejecting them wholescale.

The Limits of Liberal Universalism

The critique of social contract theories presented in this chapter should now be considered in conjunction with the discussion of right-based theories in Chapters Two and Three. For by now our broader critique of liberal universalist theories should be taking a more coherent form, and we need to start extracting the common elements.

The main weakness of liberal universalism examined in Chapter Three, it should be recalled, related to its inability to incorporate a commitment to the significance of particularist ties and values. The concern to include such values was triggered by the practical problem of motivation as defined in Chapter Two. But this concern could not be addressed by theories of thin universalism: these theories either encountered the same problem of motivation (in the case of basic rights theories), or were based on untenable mixtures of universalist and particularist grounds. Such mixed premises produced both theoretical incoherence and practical confusion. The failure of thin universalism to produce a conception of duties to refugees that was both internally coherent and practically feasible left us with three options. We could consider changing either the content of the ethical theory; or our account of motivation; or the foundations of the theory.

On the first possibility, Chapter Three already represented an attempt to change the content of the theory, examining theories that tried to ratchet down the demands of liberal universalism. None of these theories succeeded in redefining the demands of morality in a way that was practically feasible and internally coherent. Yet any further modification of the content of liberal universalist theory would be highly problematic. Given the book's goal of finding a normatively adequate conception of duties to refugees, we need to retain a substantive commitment to universal rights. We saw in Chapter Two that a conception of individuals as free and equal was the best way of grounding that commitment. So while it is recognised that this commitment to a liberal universalist conception generates unfeasible requirements, a rejection of this substantive conception would imply abandoning the normative criterion, as set out in the Introduction.

The second option was to search for an alternative account of motivation, which would generate compliance with these substantive liberal universalist duties. If the problem of motivation were solved in this way, then there would be no need to modify the substantive content of universalist ethics. The possibility of revising the account of motivation whilst retaining a commitment to liberal universalism was considered in this chapter. Social contract theories were an attempt to show how people would be motivated to comply with terms of justice. But linking motivation to justice in this way led to two possible outcomes, both of which were problematic: either people were motivated to comply with morally deficient terms of justice; or the terms were more palatable but failed to motivate compliance for the international sphere. Social contract theories held out the promise of ensuring motivation to respect the demands of liberal universalism. In order to achieve this coincidence of ethics and motivation, they structured their theories so that the procedure for deriving terms of justice presupposed willingness to comply. Paradoxically, this tight relationship between justice and motivation meant that once the relevant motivation was not forthcoming, the procedure would break down and it would be impossible to derive any terms of justice at all.

Before going on to consider the third possible route for finding an adequate conception of duties to refugees, it is worth drawing out the common theme that unites the criticisms of liberal universalism advanced so far. In Chapter Three, I reached the conclusion that liberal universalism could not incorporate a commitment to particularism; in this chapter is was argued that it could not provide an adequate account of why people should be motivated to respect the terms of impartial justice. But the discussion has done more than simply produce a list of separate flaws in these accounts. The strand running through the critique is the set of problems flowing from the assumed dichotomy between personal and impartial perspectives. I suggested in Three that the reason why particularist and universalist values could not be coherently combined related to their very different assumptions about moral agency and the source of moral beliefs. Liberal universalism assumes that the moral agent must adopt an impartial perspective, abstracting from her particular values and interests. If one is committed to this conception of two separate perspectives, it will not be possible for particularist considerations to legitimately over-ride impartial ones – at least not for questions of basic or core rights. The two must be characterised as in conflict with one another.

The accounts of motivation discussed in this chapter likewise seem to suffer from their commitment to the personal–impartial divide. The morally driven social contract theories simply fail to explain why the individual would be motivated to comply with the global application of rules of justice as impartiality or fairness. And this is linked again to a separation of the requirements of an impartial perspective and the personal sphere. In Rawls' theory, the gap between the two was clearly evident: motivation was kept separate from moral duty through the procedural division between the rationality of the parties and the veil of ignorance. Barry merged the two in his procedure, but retained a conception of impartial moral agency. The difference was that he assumed that people simply would be motivated to respect the requirements of impartial morality. But this empirical claim was unfounded, and merely served to beg the question of how to explain why people were less motivated to extend duties to non-nationals.

So the common strand in the critique seems to revolve around a faulty conception of moral agency. And this brings us to the third possible option for providing an adequate conception of duties to refugees: challenging the foundations of liberal universalism. The discussion thus far seems to suggest that the best way of overcoming the problems of liberal universalist accounts would be to challenge the assumed dichotomy between the personal and impartial perspectives. This will require unpacking in more detail the assumptions about moral agency and motivation that underlie these theories. More specifically, we must examine assumptions about the role of impartial reason in defining and motivating morality, and how this conception of reason is related to the personal or particular perspective. These issues are dealt with in the next chapter.

Notes

1   This is true of most social contract theories, Hobbes being a notably exception – his theory certainly does not produce liberal prescriptions, although the structure of his contract was replicated by other contract theorists to produce more a liberal conception of justice.

2   For a history of contract theory, see J.W. Gough, *The Social Contract: A Critical Study of its Development* (Oxford, 1936).

3   John Rawls, *A Theory of Justice* (Oxford, 1971); Thomas M. Scanlon, 'Contractualism and Utilitarianism', in Amartya Sen and Bernard Willliams (eds),*Utilitarianism and Beyond* (Cambridge, 1981), pp. 103–28; Brian Barry, *Justice as Impartiality* (Oxford, 1995); Robert Nozick, *Anarchy, State and Utopia* (Oxford, 1974) – although this latter can be categorised as libertarian rather than liberal. The contractarian approach is also, arguably, employed in the theory of Habermas. See Chapter Five for a fuller discussion of this.

4   Gough, p. 148.

5   For Hume's development of the notion of the 'circumstances of justice', see his *A Treatise of Human Nature* (London, 1969), pp. 535–49.

6   Gordon J. Schochet, 'Intending (Political) Obligation: Hobbes and the Voluntary Basis of Society', in Mary Dietz (ed.), *Thomas Hobbes and Political Theory* (Kansas, 1990), pp. 55–73.

7   See, respectively, Brian Barry, *Justice as Impartiality*; and Thomas Pogge, *Realizing Rawls* (Ithaca, 1989), p. 101.

8   Thomas Hobbes, *Leviathan* (London, 1957), p. 87.

9   Ibid., p. 391.

10   David P. Gauthier, *The Logic of Leviathan: The Moral and Political Theory of Thomas Hobbes* (Oxford, 1969).

11   Barry, *Justice as Impartiality*, p. 48.

12   Ibid., p. 45.

13   David P. Gauthier, *Morals By Agreement* (Oxford, 1986), p. 268.

14   See Rawls, *Theory of Justice*, pp. 267–70.

15   Barry, *Justice as Impartiality*, p. 39.

16   Ibid., p. 48.

17   S.M. Brown, for example, describes it as 'incredibly crude and plainly false'. See 'Hobbes: The Taylor Thesis' in Preston King (ed.), *Thomas Hobbes: Critical Assessments* (London, 1993), p. 101. Rawls takes a more lenient view, viewing Hobbes' account of motivation as no more than a 'common foothold for political argument'. See John Rawls, 'The Idea of an Overlapping Consensus', *Oxford Journal of Legal Studies*, 7:1 (1987), p. 2.

18   Indeed, he writes that his conception of the circumstances of justice 'adds nothing essential' to Hume's account. See Rawls, *A Theory of Justice*, p. 127.

19   Ibid., p. 128.

20   Ibid., p. 126.

21   Ibid., p. 141.
22   David R. Mapel, 'The Contractarian Tradition and International Ethics', in Terry Nardin and David R. Mapel (eds), *Traditions of International Ethics* (Cambridge, 1992), pp. 180–200.
23   Charles R. Beitz, *Political Theory and International Relations* (Princeton, NJ, 1979); Charles R. Beitz, 'Justice and International Relations', in Charles R. Beitz, Marhsall Cohen, Thomas Scanlon and A. John Simmons (eds), *International Ethics* (Princeton, NJ, 1985), pp. 282–311; and Beitz, 'Sovereignty and Morality in International Affairs', in David Held (ed.), *Political Theory Today* (Oxford, 1991), pp. 236–54.
24   Beitz, 'Justice and International Relations', p. 303.
25   Ibid.
26   Ibid., p. 305.
27   See, for example, Onora O'Neill, *Towards Justice and Virtue* (Cambridge, 1996), pp. 105 and 113–21.
28   John Rawls, 'The Law of Peoples', in Stephen Shute and Susan Hurley (eds), *On Human Rights* (New York, 1993), p. 46.
29   Ibid., p. 55.
30   Ibid., p. 68.
31   Ibid., p. 70. Indeed, it is difficult to see how Rawls can derive even this limited conception of human rights as part of his 'law of peoples', given that contractors are strictly only interested in ensuring international stability. Perhaps he considers that international respect for human rights is a means of preventing conflict, but he does not advance this as a justification. The only comment he makes on possible motivation to agree to the international respect of human rights is that 'systematic violation of these rights is a serious matter and troubling to the society of peoples as a whole'. (p. 68) But he does not explain what he means by this in his 1993 essay.
32   Mark R. Wicclair, 'Rawls and the Principle of Nonintervention', in H. Gene Blocker and Elizabeth H. Smith (eds), *John Rawls's Theory of Social Justice: An Introduction* (Athens, Ohio, 1980), p. 297; Brian Barry, *The Liberal Theory of Justice* (Oxford, 1975), p. 133.
33   Rawls, 'Law of Peoples', p. 73.
34   See Pogge, *Realizing Rawls,* p. 240. In fact, Pogge's grounds for 'globalising' Rawls' theory are extremely ambiguous – they seem to comprise a mixture of a Kantian metaphysical conception of persona, and an empirical claim about shared values.
35   Barry, *Justice as Impartiality*, p. 52.
36   Ibid., p. 67.
37   Barry, *Theories of Justice*, p. 331.
38   As Barry writes, it 'constitutes an independent version of justice as impartiality, and one that would if systematized lead us to the theory proposed by T. M. Scanlon'. See *Justice as Impartiality*, pp. 112–3.
39   Barry, *Justice as Impartiality*, p. 8.
40   T. M. Scanlon, 'Contractualism and Utilitarianism', in Amartya Sen and Bernard Williams, eds., *Utilitarianism and Beyond* (Cambridge, 1982), p. 110.
41   Ibid., p. 111.
42   Ibid., p. 113.
43   Barry, *Justice as Impartiality*, p. 164.
44   Ibid., p. 168.
45   Barry, *Theories of Justice*, p. 324.

46 Ibid., p. 289.
47 Ibid., p. 290.
48 Scanlon, 'Contractualism and Utilitarianism', pp. 115–6.
49 Ibid., p. 115.

Chapter Five

The Role of Reason in Moral Motivation

The critique of liberal universalist theories developed in the last three chapters has focused on the failure of these theories to meet the three criteria for an adequate account of duties to non-nationals. None of the theories discussed can offer a normatively desirable first order account, which is both practically feasible and internally coherent. After outlining the problem of practical feasibility encountered by pure liberal universalism, the discussion examined whether this problem could be addressed by altering the content of liberal theory, or changing its account of motivation. As I argued at the end of the last chapter, neither of these tactics worked, and it is necessary to turn to the third, more radical route. This will involve challenging the liberal universalist account of the sources of moral norms and moral motivation. In particular, I will challenge the notion of a dichotomy between an impartial perspective, in which the moral agent is motivated by reason; and a personal perspective, which comprises the person's partial interests, ties and particular characteristics.

This chapter pursues such a critique of the dichotomy model by challenging liberal universalist assumptions about the role of reason in defining and motivating moral action. The chapter will argue that the failure of these theories to provide an adequate theory of motivation can be traced to the importance they attach to reason in both motivation and in defining morality. By exaggerating the role of reason in motivation, they fail to provide a plausible account of moral agency, and to account for the significance of particular ties. And by inflating the role of reason in defining morality, they fail to account for the diversity of moral norms in different cultures, and the influence of intersubjective values and beliefs on conceptions of justice. The non-rationalist account outlined in this chapter will be far better placed to explain the significance of personal characteristics and ties in motivating moral action, and the role of intersubjective values in defining the moral perspective.

Reason and Moral Motivation

Rationalism: Some Initial Doubts

The main target of criticism in this chapter is a group of theories that will be labelled 'rationalist'. On the definition used in this thesis, a rationalist theory is one that accords a central role to reason in motivating moral action.[1] Such theories are usually contrasted with theories of motivation that accord a central role to feeling or sentiment. In this context, 'reason' will denote the activity of reasoning, specifically the exercise of logical or cognitive categories and rules to deliberate from premises to conclusions. And practical reason will refer to rational deliberation from premises to conclusions about what one should do.

According to the rationalist view, it is reason (rather than desire) that moves us to act in accordance with the requirements of morality. Moral motivation is not dependent on the presence of interest or desire, but is guaranteed by the agent's rationality and her beliefs about the requirements of morality. The motivation to act in accordance with the requirements of morality 'comes from the requirements themselves'.[2] According to Nagel, the agent is motivated precisely because she recognises that this is the morally correct action. Motivation is not contingent on any independent component of human nature, such as a Hobbesian fear of death, or sympathy, as in the case of Hume. It is the moral nature of the requirements that motivates, rather than the existence of other conditions or dispositions.[3]

We have already seen how this emphasis on reason is a central feature of theories of impartial justice. According to these accounts, the moral agent is abstracted from her particular situation and characteristics and is moved by reason, rather than personal desires or attachments. Whether this form of abstraction involves subjecting one's maxims to the test of universalisability, deliberating behind a veil of ignorance, or considering which norms would be the object of reasonable agreement, the rationalist account claims that the agent is moved to respect the requirements of morality through reason. Rational deliberation on the requirements of morality is sufficient to motivate the agent, so motivation is possible without any additional sentiment or self-interest. What is being claimed by the rationalist, then, is that reason alone can provide the agent with reasons for respecting the requirements of morality. The agent is motivated to act morally simply by exercising certain cognitive capacities, specifically by engaging in practical reasoning about what action she ought to take.

It should be emphasised that on this account, the role of reason is not simply instrumental to realising pre-given desires (for example, personal interests or goals). For if reason were simply a device for working out how to achieve certain given ends, then it could not claim motivating force. In this case, it would be the original desires, rather than reason, that motivated action. And it is precisely this point that critics of rationalism find implausible. Anscombe, for example, argues that practical reasoning simply involves reasoning from a given premise or set of premises to conclusions about what one should do. It is the general moral premises from which one reasons that contain the conception of moral duty. While it is possible that an agent could employ reason to deliberate from general moral premises to a conclusion about what moral action to take, she will only be motivated to engage in this type of reasoning if she has already accepted the moral premise in question. And as Anscombe writes, 'it is clear that such general premises will only occur as premises of practical reasoning in people who want to do their duty'.[4] A similar point is made by Williams when he argues that rational deliberation cannot motivate us to perform a moral duty, unless we are already motivated to engage in this form of deliberation and to accept the conclusions it may yield. In other words, we must be committed to the value of this type of deliberation in order to be motivated by its conclusions. A reliance on practical reason as a source of motivation merely begs the question of what motivates us to engage in practical reasoning in the first place.

This point can be elaborated through considering Nagel's account of moral agency. He argues that adopting a moral perspective involves abstracting from and thus (temporarily) abandoning the personal point of view.[5] While Nagel holds that the agent does this out of respect for reason alone, the agent can surely only be motivated to abandon her personal perspective for reasons present to her in the personal perspective. But if this is the case, then it is not abstract reason alone that motivates action in accordance with the requirements of impartial ethics. Rather, we are motivated to adopt an impartial perspective by a reason or set of reasons already present in our personal perspective. The problem arises because the exercise of reason requires abstracting from certain personal characteristics or ties. If reason alone can motivate the individual to engage in this form of abstraction, then it is difficult to see how the person will initially be motivated to obey the dictates of reason. The switch from personal to impartial perspective requires the exercise of reason, yet this exercise of reason is not possible unless one has already adopted this viewpoint. Adopting the impartial perspective would appear to be both the precondition and the outcome of the exercise of reason.

What this suggests is that the rationalist account of motivation cannot be established merely by pointing to the role of reason in practical deliberation. The rationalist will have to show how reason can actually motivate us to accept the relevant premises of moral argument. In other words, if practical reason is understood as the use of logical rules to deliberate from premises to conclusions about what one ought to do, then moral motivation depends on one or both of the following conditions. First, as Anscombe suggests, it depends on the agent being motivated to accept the general moral premises from which she then reasons to practical conclusions. And second, it depends on the agent being motivated to commit herself to accepting the practical conclusions of a process of deliberation from these premises. In short, the question is that of how such deliberation can provide us with reasons to respect the requirements of morality.

Kant and the Problem of Moral Motivation

Rationalist theories of motivation need to overcome this sort of criticism by showing how reason can influence the agent's will. There have been a number of attempts to provide some form of rational link between reason and moral agency, although none of them ultimately succeed. A good route for understanding these accounts is through considering the problems faced by Kant's theory of motivation, and subsequent attempts of neo-Kantians to overcome this problem.

Kant asserts that the will can become moral or a 'good will' through the exercise of reason. Pure reason can exert influence over the will through qualifying its subjective rules of action or maxims. It is through subjecting these maxims to the directives of reason that the agent's will becomes good. The device through which subjective maxims are qualified by reason is the Categorical Imperative, which sorts through existing maxims to select those which are universalisable.[6] The Categorical Imperative commands us to: 'Act only on that maxim through which you can at the same time will that it should become a universal law'.[7] Or in its negative formulation, the requirement is that 'I ought never to act except in such a way *that I can also will that my maxim should become a universal law*'.[8] This formula provides a process of selection or test to establish which subjective rules of action qualify as moral. The good will comprises that which is left over from the will once all non-universalisable maxims have been discarded as rules for action.

Leaving aside the difficulties raised by the Categorical Imperative as a device for testing maxims, Kant's account faces a serious problem explaining how reason can transfer its influence to the will. In Kant's system, the reason shaping the will must be pure, in the sense of being untainted by the contingent and particularist considerations of the empirical world.[9] Pure reason belongs to the intelligible or noumenal world, and must be unconstrained by the phenomenal world if it is to be immune from the influence of partial and changing interests. By contrast, the practical reason normally exercised by the agent in the empirical world is influenced by such particularist considerations. The challenge is to show how this practical reason can be influence by pure reason – to construct a bridge between the intelligible and phenomenal worlds, in order that practical reason may become moral.

The connection between pure and practical reason is established through Kant's notion of free action. Free action denotes a series of empirical events whose cause is not empirically conditioned, but free. It is through such free action that the purity of reason in the noumenal realm is supposedly transferred to the realm of practical action. So *pure* practical reason – practical reason unconstrained by partial and contingent factors – is only possible if we assume the possibility of unconditioned causality. In the absence of such a concept of freedom, the will could not be rendered good.

But this still begs the question of how the agent is motivated to apply pure reason to the practical sphere. Such motivation must be generated in the phenomenal world, if it is to influence the action of actual wills. Yet on Kant's account, the phenomenal self is subject to partial and changing interest, so the motive to subject one's maxims to the test of the Categorical Imperative would not be pure in the desired sense. It must be the empirical will that decides to undergo the influence of pure reason, for otherwise pure reason could have no influence on conduct. But this presupposes the existence of an empirical disposition to be motivated to respect the requirements of the Categorical Imperative, a disposition which is in some sense prior to the influence of pure reason. Kant would reject this, claiming that pure reason must be capable of motivating the agent, without any pre-existing desire of the will to be so motivated. He retains a separation between the motivational constitution of the empirical will, and the structure of morality, but claims that the latter may nonetheless shape the former. And in so doing, his account of pure practical reason remains somewhat obscure. Kant argues that we must simply presuppose the possibility of the freedom required to render practical reason pure. But he gives no cogent justification as to why we should presuppose any such thing.

The question of how practical reason becomes pure is in fact a version of the problem encountered in the critique of rationalism outlined above. If reason is to be attributed motivational force, then there must be some account of how reason can influence the will. Yet the will can only accept such influence if it is already motivated in the relevant sense. Kant's attempt to overcome this circularity through the notion of free action is obscure at best, and simply fails to provide a plausible account of motivation.

Neo-Kantian Accounts

Before turning to non-rationalist accounts, it is useful to consider how some contemporary neo-Kantians have attempted to address the problem. Have any theorists managed to bridge this gap between empirical will and moral obligation through the notion of motivating reason – in other words, provided a tenable rationalist account? The various responses offered to this problem can be categorised along the lines established in Chapter Four to distinguish between different theories of justice. The various accounts discussed in that chapter of the relationship between personal and impartial perspectives are parallel to the account of the relationship between moral obligation and the will.

We should start by recalling how Hobbes derived moral duty from an egoistic conception of the will. On this account, there is no gap between reason, the will, and the requirements of morality. Reason is understood as prudential rationalist, that is, as instrumental to maximising self-interest, and moral duty requires no more than the rational pursuit of these egoistic ends. The gap between will and morality is closed, but at the price of accepting a morally warped theory of justice as mutual advantage.

A similar conception of rationality is adopted by Rawls, who also equates prudential reason with the individual will. Yet Rawls is not content with a theory of justice as mutual advantage, preferring a more Kantian, impartial conception of justice as fairness. Since prudential reason alone will not yield the appropriate terms of justice, Rawls is obliged to introduce an external filter for sieving out morally unacceptable considerations from the choice of rules of justice. The veil of ignorance serves as replacement to the Categorical Imperative, ruling out considerations that are partial and particularist. The individual's will is therefore constrained by a test of impartiality in the Original Position. Yet as Barry points out, the Original Position is entirely divorced from the actual motivation of the parties, understood as prudential rationality. This is why the real test of Rawls' agreement seems to be whether the terms of justice can withstand the 'strains of commitment' – the motivation to cooperate with terms once the veil of ignorance is lifted. In essence, Rawls' account exacerbates the problem faced by Kant, through widening the gap between the will and the requirements of morality. His concept of reason fails to provide any sort of bridge between the egoistic will and the perspective from the veil of ignorance, since it is simply instrumental to realising self-interest.

Now as we saw in Chapter Four, the Rawlsian account is able to close the gap between the will and morality – at least in Rawls' later work – by abandoning its cognitivist claims. Since reason cannot lead the will to respect morality, then the individual's will must be conditioned to be moral through some other means. Rawls establishes an empirical link between the will and the requirements of morality, through showing how both will and morality are shaped by the same social matrix. Commitment to moral norms is acquired through a particular social context and this same environment also shapes the individual's will. The veil of ignorance therefore loses its status as the embodiment of universalist impartiality, and becomes a device for representing the values of particular cultures – liberal democratic societies. In the later Rawls, then, morality influences the will not through reason, but through a particular process of socialisation. Motivation to respect the requirements of morality is not generated solely by the exercise of reason, but through some non-rationalist account of a will shaped by shared values.

A rather different neo-Kantian account of the relationship between will and morality is offered by Barry. Barry appears to retain a more theoretical conception of reason i.e. one that denotes the employment of cognitive capacities to deliberate from premises to conclusions, rather than a prudential conception of reason as an instrument for maximising self-interest. Yet Barry, as we saw, fails to acknowledge any gap between the requirements of morality and actual will. Reason is employed by the agent to deliberate on terms of justice in order to find rules that could not be reasonably rejected by anyone. Both the agent reflecting on these terms, and those subjects who are being considered as potential rejecters of the terms, are assumed to be motivated by a desire for fairness. And this desire corresponds exactly to both existing will, and the requirements of morality. In other words, there is a perfect coincidence of will and morality, achieved through the exercise of reason. But this coincidence is not achieved through pure reason influencing the will, as in Kant's account. Rather, it seems to be the case that the existing will *as it stands* is motivated to accept the requirements of reason. There is no gap between morality and the will because people do actually want to be moral. This account, it was argued in Chapter Four, is open to the objection of empirical implausibility. It is simply not true that people are motivated in this way, at least not for questions of duties to non-nationals.

A third neo-Kantian solution is to abandon the requirements of a link between the will and some specified conception of moral duty, as in the case of discourse ethics. These theories do not specify the content of moral duty, but only the procedure for deriving norms. They also claim that this procedure is not based on particular conceptions of morality, but is built into the structure of language. Discourse ethics thus denies any commitment to first order moral values. On this account, moral rules are not philosophically grounded but are the outcome of agreement through rational dialogue aimed at achieving consensus. The terms of this dialogue replace Kant's Categorical Imperative, and supposedly also the commitment to a particular first order conception of justice as impartiality.

Now discourse ethics is of course only relevant to this discussion if it can be classified as a liberal universalist theory, and more specifically if it can guarantee a commitment to some conception of duties to refugees. The answer to this question is complex, and I can only touch on it here. Put in the briefest terms, if discourse ethics *is* liberal universalist in the relevant sense, then it will face the same Kantian problem of a gap between will and the requirements of universalist moral duty. For on this reading, the procedure will necessarily generate agreement on a universally valid conception of duties to refugees, and thus create a problem of motivation. On the other hand, if it is *not* a liberal universalist theory – and its procedure does not guarantee agreement on duties to refugees – then the problem of motivation and the relationship between morality and the will does not arise, since there is no prescribed conception of moral duties. But in this case, discourse ethics should be considered as irrelevant to the discussion. For it would not guarantee that the outcome of dialogue in a particular community will produce our desired first order conception of duties beyond borders. In short, either discourse ethics is a purely formal procedure, immune from substantive moral commitments, and therefore does not count as a cognitivist theory; or it is a moral theory facing the same set of problems encountered by Kantian accounts. This issue will be tackled later on in the chapter.

In summary, the rationalist accounts considered fail to bridge the gap between will and morality in a convincing way. Reason in both its prudential and its theoretical sense is ill-equipped to motivate the will to respect the requirements of morality. We shall now turn to Humean theories and the 'belief–desire' theory of motivation to see if it provides a more satisfactory account.

The Humean Alternative and the Interdependence Thesis

Hume and the Belief–Desire Theory

If the rationalist theory is flawed, the obvious next step is to consider the traditional Humean rival, the 'belief–desire' account. In contrast to the rationalist account, belief–desire theorists reject the role of reason in motivation, asserting that action can only be motivated through desire. On this account, beliefs are merely passive representations of the world: they may supply information relevant to action, but cannot in themselves motivate action. Desires, on the other hand, are active and seek to change the world to conform to their aspirations, thus motivating action to bring about such change. As Hume writes: 'Reason being cool and disengaged, is no motive to action, and directs only the impulse received from appetite or inclination, by showing us the means of attaining happiness or avoiding misery.'[10] In Hume's view, people are motivated to be moral out of a specific type of desire or sentiment, sympathy. Not only is the existence of sympathy a necessary condition for moral motivation, it defines what morality is. This sentiment is logically prior to ethics, in that the disposition to sympathy creates or defines moral duty. In other words, the desire is not simply a condition of motivating moral action, but it determines what is of value. On the basis of our desires, we project onto the world the property of value. Moral value is thus not independent of or prior to motivation, as on the rationalist view, but is simply a projection of desires.

One problem with this account is the role it ascribes to desire in determining what is of value. If desire creates value, then the property of being valuable is no more than an ascription by a particular subject. There is no independent quality of 'valuableness' or 'good' which can be said to be a property of the object, beyond the fact that an individual desires it. The property of value is simply a mental state of the subject, a projection of the individual's desire onto objects. If this is the case, then the Humean theory will have problems accounting for the possibility of being mistaken about what is valuable. G. E. M. Anscombe uses the example of a person who desires to collect bits of bone three inch long for no reason other than that he thinks this is a desirable thing to do.[11] The collection of bits of bone is not instrumental to any other ends, but is perceived to be of intrinsic value to the individual. If desire creates value, then we would be committed to the view that collecting pieces of bone is a valuable activity, at least for this individual. But we would clearly want to question the value of collecting three-inch pieces of bone, even if we acknowledge the person's desire to do so. In order to ascribe value, we would need to define some quality or objective of this activity independent of the individual's desire that would justify its value. For example, we might argue that the pieces of bone had aesthetic value, or the act of collecting them was therapeutic for the individual. In the absence of such an additional reason or belief, the ascription of value by desire, as Charvet observes, renders the foundations of the value quite arbitrary.[12] More specifically, we would need to link desire to an independent conception of what it is rational or worthwhile to desire. This may require a theory of needs or some teleological account of the conditions for well-being or human flourishing. This would provide a test of value independent of the individual's desire, thus avoiding the arbitrariness and subjectivism of the Humean account. But it would also mean rejecting the purely desire-based account: for if desires could be shown to be irrational (according to the relevant conception of rationality/ the good), then they would not be the sole determinants of value in the world.

The second glaring weakness of the Humean account is its inability to account for the role of reason and belief in modifying or eliminating desire. To return to the case of the bone collector, we might want to influence his desire by demonstrating that this activity would not further his interests or well-being. Having determined that his ascription of value to this activity was irrational, we might attempt to make him understand that he was mistaken about the value of collecting pieces of bone.

And it would not be unreasonable to expect our arguments to influence the person's desire to collect three-inch pieces of bone. By supplying reasoned argument or additional information, in this case about the contribution of this collection to the individual's well-being, we might expect to be able to eliminate or at least modify the person's desire to collect pieces of bone. If this is a possibility, then the role of belief would go beyond that of simply guiding pre-existing or intrinsic desires. Reason and belief about what is valuable would be capable of modifying desires. On this account, beliefs and reason would provide criteria independent of desires which would at least in part determine what is of value. These beliefs and reason would also have a role in influencing desires. For if our beliefs about what is valuable change, so too will our desires. It follows that if beliefs and reason have a role in ascribing value, they must also influence desires. This would depart from the Humean account, which limits the role of reason to that of affecting beliefs about how best to *realise* our desires. On this alternative conception, reason would be capable of affecting both instrumental *and* intrinsic desires.

These two problems with the Humean account – its reliance on subjective states and its full-scale denial of any role to reason – in part account for the persistence of rationalist accounts. The pure Humean account implies a retreat into a form of subjectivism or emotivism, according to which neither reason, nor intersubjective beliefs, play any role in modifying subjective desires.[13] Now while this form of subjectivism is plainly unacceptable, neither do we want to return to the rationalist theories criticised in section one. What is needed is a theory of motivation that conceives of desires and reason as interdependent, a conception that can be found in the work of John Charvet.

The Interdependence of Reason and Desire

Charvet builds on both of these criticisms of what he terms the 'desire-fulfilment' theory, developing a theory of motivation that characterises beliefs and desire as interdependent. He criticises both rationalism and desire-fulfilment theory for conceiving of desire and reason as independent of one other. Belief–desire theorists, as we have seen, deny the role of reason in shaping desires in any more than an instrumental sense. While rationalists deny the role of desire in motivating moral action. By insisting on this separation of belief and desire in moral action, both rationalists and Humeans render the interdependence of the two in rational action unintelligible.[14] Charvet concedes the Humean argument to a point, agreeing that motivation requires the existence of a desire, and that beliefs play a role in guiding desires. But he departs from the belief–desire theory in attributing a more fundamental influence to beliefs: the role of these beliefs is not limited to that of providing information to help satisfy pre-existing desires. Beliefs play a more formative role in the development and shaping of desires from their very inception. Indeed, desire *arises* in the individual 'as a specific desire directed onto some object'.[15] Desire can only operate under the influence of beliefs. In turn, the belief system does not operate in isolation from desires, but is concerned with 'the progress and satisfaction of its owner's desires'.[16] The two systems are therefore distinct but interdependent. As Charvet writes: 'The impulsive force must be given a specific and directed form by belief and the activity of the belief must be guided by desire'.[17]

The claim here is that while the presence of a desire is indeed necessary for motivation, such desires are not fixed, but may be modified by both beliefs and reason. Beliefs and reason are therefore not simply instrumental in satisfying desires, but themselves influence and shape desires. Desires are *mediated* by the individual's cognitive structure and beliefs about the world.

Now it might be objected that this account offers no basic improvement on the Humean account. If motivation requires the existence of desire, then as we saw above, it is also the case that the individual must have a desire to adopt certain beliefs and to exercise reason in the first place. If this is true, then the beliefs and reason that modify desires are themselves motivated by desire. And in this case, desire can only be modified if the agent has a pre-existing desire to do so, in which case reason and beliefs are merely instrumental to realising desires.

This is true in a superficial sense, but it is also misleading in that it overlooks the diversity and complexity of the types of desire in question. Desires are not necessarily egoistic, and insofar as they have as their end the welfare of others or of society at large, they may be subject to modification by changing beliefs or engaging in reasoning about what is best for others.[18] Even prudential self-interest, for example the desire to be rich all of one's life, may lead one to modify existing desires through reason and beliefs about what is acquired to realise this desire. Deliberation on the best course for ensuring one is rich in old age may lead one to modify a desire to spend this week's salary on a holiday. In cases such as this, the more fundamental interest in promoting the welfare of others or of oneself in the long term can generate motivation to subject at least some of one's desires to rational scrutiny. And the outcome of this deliberation may result in the modification of one's desires. Thus reason will have changed desires and thereby affected what one will be motivated to do. But it will still be true to say that it is the *desire* that motivated the individual to act.

What this implies is that we must distinguish between two main categories of desire. As we have seen, some desires are abstract and general, for example the desire to promote the welfare of one's society, or the desire to be respected by others. These desires may generate additional, more specific desires which are understood by the agent to be instrumental to realising general desires. For example, the desire for respect may generate a desire to have one's work praised, or to be viewed as a good father. While these derivative desires may be modified by beliefs about how to gain respect in different contexts, the general desire is likely to remain more or less fixed.

In the case of moral motivation, two basic desires seem to be especially significant. The first is what can be termed the 'empathic' disposition.[19] This is a capacity to feel concern at the suffering of others. It is a psychological disposition which is developed in most children, initially as anxiety about the idea of loss of primary carers.[20] The empathic disposition motivates people to extend concern to others, thus explaining the possibility of sympathy-based morality. As the child develops his cognitive capacities, this disposition will be mediated through reason, which can indicate how best to act on this general concern. It can also help the child to channel empathy into more sophisticated forms of sympathetic identification. This cognitive capacity will enable him to progress from a feeling of anxiety or frustration at the suffering of an other, through empathy at the other person's suffering, to some idea about how he might assist in alleviating this suffering. In addition, as the child becomes familiar with the shared norms and values of his environment, the disposition to empathy may also be mediated by intersubjective beliefs about how best to channel empathy. In other words, the disposition will be given direction and content by the more elaborate set of moral views embraced by his community, and into which he will be socialised. As the philosopher Richard Wollheim writes:

> For what the community does is to fix, or pin down, the otherwise unregulated discernment of match or correspondence ... Even if the agent remakes these correspondences, reinvents them, which is what he will want to do if he is any way a critic of his society and its ways, they provide him with the initial exemplars of match.[21]

The second relevant emotional disposition is a desire for recognition or affirmation. The desire for recognition stems from a fundamental psychological need for affirmation, which motivates the individual to gain approval and respect from those around him. The search for this form of reassurance influences the individual's relation to her environment. Again, one can understand this through considering the development of this disposition in children. The need for affirmation generates a certain pattern of interaction between the infant and her environment. It motivates the infant to internalise the standards and rules conveyed by her parents as the criteria for achieving affirmation. Conformity with these standards will tend to provoke an affirming response from parents, thus fulfilling the need for affirmation and approval from her loved objects. As Axel Honneth writes: 'By putting oneself in the normative point of view of its interaction partner, the other subject takes over the partner's moral values and applies them to its practical relation to itself'.[22]

The need for affirmation, like the empathic disposition, is not simply a temporal stage in the child's development. It is an ongoing emotional need that motivates the individual to gain approval and respect from friends, relatives, school teachers, and eventually a wider social and professional community. Reason helps the individual to establish a link between this desire for affirmation and the required moral action. An agent motivated by this desire will engage in rational deliberation, reasoning from premises about the moral values she has internalised, to conclusions about what she should do.

Both of these desires are therefore shaped by the individual's cognitive structure, as well as her society's shared beliefs and vales.

Implications of the Interdependence Thesis for the Foundations of Ethics

The account outlined above holds that both reason and beliefs may mediate desires and thus play a role in moral motivation. The source of moral motivation, it was argued, should be understood as a set of general and abstract basic desires, which are then given more precise direction and specification by beliefs and reason. Beliefs and reason show how these desires may be fulfilled, and in turn help create and modify derivative desires. Beliefs in this context could include beliefs about the natural and social world (facts), as well as *moral* beliefs (norms).

Now the first thing to note is that the question of the *source* of these moral beliefs was left open. In fact, they may be understood as deriving from two possible sources. Moral beliefs may either be held to be universally valid claims (what can be termed 'cognitivism'), or they may consist of values that are particular to a given group of people ('non-cognitivism'). Secondly, it was not clearly specified in the account above exactly how *reason* could influence these beliefs. Again, there are two main possibilities. If one accepts that moral beliefs are universally valid claims, then one is likely to be committed to the view that these moral beliefs are derived from reason. This cognitivist view would hold that reason defines some or all moral duties. Alternatively, if one holds that moral beliefs are derived from shared values, then reason is likely to have a less significant role in shaping moral beliefs, for example it may be simply useful for ironing out inconsistencies between different values, or demonstrating their practical unfeasibility. In short, the interdependence thesis seems to leave open the matter of whether moral beliefs are universally valid or derived from shared values.

The answer to this question is important: it will have a bearing on the foundational status of liberal universalism. If we reject cognitivism, this will imply that the claims of liberal universalism are not universally valid, but specific to particular historical-cultural contexts. This is of course a central issue for any moral theory. Thus while I have outlined a non-rationalist account of motivation based on the interdependence thesis, we still need to clarify the issue of the *sources* of moral norms. For the question of whether these norms are intersubjective (and derived from shared beliefs) or universally valid (and derived from reason) will have important implications for the relationship between moral norms and motivation.

The Role of Reason in Defining Morality

The cognitivist claims that it is through reason that the individual comes to recognise her moral duty. The human capacity for reason enables her to derive certain universally valid principles for guiding action. By contrast, the non-cognitivist holds that reason plays a less decisive role in defining morality. Reason merely modifies beliefs and desires through applying certain logical rules of coherence, consistency, and so on. Both these positions, it has been argued, are in principle compatible with the interdependence thesis, although combining the interdependence thesis with a cognitivist account would commit one to an externalist view of the relationship between morality and motivation.

Attempts to Define Morality through Reason: The Kantian Route

One way in which theorists have attempted to derive morality from reason is through reasoning from the presuppositions of rational action to a principle of the universal right to freedom. In order to derive moral norms in this way, the agent would have to draw a number of inferences about moral duty, based on a conception of herself as a rational agent. Williams suggests a version of this form of reasoning, involving three steps.[23] First, the rational agent recognises her interest in freedom, and thus her interest in the absence of constraints on this freedom. Second, she claims a right to the conditions necessary for exercising this freedom. And third, she accepts the same right of other individuals, grounded in their similar interest in freedom. If this account is correct, then all rational agents are committed to accepting the principle of an equal right of humans to freedom. And this principle is derived from a process of reasoning from subjective interest to the obligation to respect the right of all rational beings to freedom. In other words, the moral duty is derived simply from the agent's recognition of her interest in freedom, qua rational being. All that is required to get from this premise of oneself as interested in freedom to the conclusion that there is a universal right to freedom is the recognition of others as relevantly similar, and rational deliberation will generate this practical conclusion.

As Williams argues, however, the steps from premise to conclusion require more than rational deliberation. While the first and third steps seem to be sound, it is the second step that is more problematic. The first step, it should be recalled, involved the agent recognising her interest in freedom, and thus in being free from constraint. The existence of such an interest seems to be plausible as a premise. And the third step involved a universalisation of the right to freedom. If the interest in freedom qua rational being grounds a right to freedom, then it follows that all rational beings with a similar interest should have a similar right. What grounds a right for one person must ground a right for others. The problem arises with the second step: the inference from the fact of having an interest, to the claim that others should respect one's right to having this interest realised.

The difficulty here is not so much that considerations like these are not used to ground rights in liberal theory. The point is that the inference from interest to right cannot be made simply through rational deliberation. Rather, it involves making a normative claim about the value of freedom. The simple fact of not wanting someone else to interfere with my freedom does not in itself generate any prescription about rights and duties – as Williams puts it, it is not 'enough to lead each agent into morality'.[24] There is no reason why others should recognise my freedom as a good, merely because I desire it. I can only conclude that they are morally bound to do so on the assumption that they should be committed to a conception of the self as worthy of freedom. In this case, I will indeed be committed to respecting similar characteristics in others, and thus recognising the rights of all rational beings. But again, this rests on a substantive moral belief about the value of freedom.

To illustrate this point, one could consider other sorts of characteristics apart from a capacity for autonomy that might also be deemed morally relevant, and thus ground alternative universal norms. For example, some cultures might value bravery or moral virtue, others humility before God, or deference to one's elders in all practical decisions. A more familiar example might be a society that values physical and economic security above freedom. Now in these cases, rational deliberation from subjective interests to universal norms would establish rather different moral obligations. For example, it might justify norms forbidding sexual freedom, or a hierarchical conception of rights based on age. Alternatively, in the case of the society that values security, members of this community might conclude through rational deliberation that there should be substantial constraints on freedom in order to promote the goal of national security or to increase national prosperity. It is quite plausible that the agent would consider capacities or interests such as these to be the morally relevant characteristic of human beings, and if so it would be rational to universalise these beliefs. The rationality that allows one to reason from premises to conclusions is no more than a set of formal rules, which only derive substantive content from moral premises. I am not denying that many, including myself, are committed to a conception of the individual as a free and rational agent. But the point is that this commitment is not derived from rational deliberation. It is premised on a substantive belief about the morally relevant features of human beings.

There is one alternative route for reasoning from subjective interest to rights without necessarily being committed to a view of persons as free. One could justify individual rights solely from considerations of mutual interest. In this case, the subject would not have to assume that her interest in freedom was morally worthy of respect by others, but simply posit that it would be in the mutual advantage of all to establish a system of reciprocal rights and duties to maximise the interests of all. This would of course require the empirical assumption that all participants in this contract did in fact have an interest in freedom, but it would not require a substantive normative commitment to the value of such freedom. Needless to say, this would lead us back to the Hobbesian conception of justice as mutual advantage, with its simplistic psychological assumptions and morally unacceptable terms of justice.

In summary, the attempt to derive moral norms through reasoning from subjective maxims to universal norms requires an additional commitment to certain morally relevant features of human beings. Since this substantive value could not be derived from reason itself, its source must lie in a commitment to a conception of the self as rational and free. And it is precisely this type of discussion over the morally relevant features of the self that is the object of first order debate between different moral systems. The alternative is to deny commitment to a particular conception of the self and return to the contingencies of a system of rules based on overlapping self-interest. Since neither account is satisfactory, we shall now turn to the second main variety of cognitivism.

Cognitivism and Discourse Ethics

Discourse ethics attempts to derive universally valid moral principles – or at least one such moral principle – from the structure of language. The universal validity of norms is established through a procedure that is presupposed in the rules of argumentation, rather than through a process of reasoning from subjective interests to universal maxims. The relationship between the validity of norms and discourse can be understood at two levels. First, participation in discourse presupposes that the agent accepts certain rules of argumentation, such as logical rules of consistency, the sincerity of speakers, equal rights of all to participate in discourse, question any assertion, and so on.[25] From these presuppositions, Habermas argues that one can derive a principle of universalisation (U), to which all participants of argumentation are implicitly committed. As he writes,

> Every person who accepts the universal and necessary communicative presuppositions of argumentative speech and who knows what it means to justify a norm of action implicitly presupposes as valid the principle of universalization.[26]

This principle (U) is a principle of argumentation, which grounds the universal validity of norms. For a norm to be universally valid, it must fulfil the condition established in (U), as follows:

> (U) *All* affected can accept the consequences and the side effects its *general* observance can be anticipated to have for the satisfaction of *everyone's* interests (and the consequences are preferred to those of known alternative possibilities for regulation).[27]

The principle (U) thus signifies a second level at which discourse is related to validity claims. Not only does discourse imply acceptance of (U), but norms that are agreed under the conditions stipulated in (U) are universally valid. The two levels of universal validity correspond to second order and first order moral principles. (U) is a second order principle which grounds the validity of moral norms. It establishes a universally valid *procedure* for agreeing substantive first order moral rules, a procedure which is supposedly free of substantive first order commitments. (U) is derived from the structure of language, and is thus neutral between different substantive norms. By contrast, the first order norms that are agreed through this procedure derive their validity from rational agreement between participants. The outcome of particular discourses is not determined in advance, but will vary depending on the particular social matrix of participants. Habermas does not see the task of the moral theorist as specifying substantive moral rules for societies, as, for example, Rawls does when he claims that his contractors will accept his two principles of justice. Habermas' principle (U) does not in itself generate any rights beyond the freedom to participate in discourse. Any additional rights must be justified through discourse.[28] Nonetheless, the outcome of such discourse is understood to have validity qua conforming with (U).

This of course means that discourse must meet a number of conditions, as set out in the hypothetical 'ideal speech situation' (ISS). The ISS is characterised by the even distribution of chances to perform various speech acts. This prevents any constraints on argumentative reasoning or participation. Moreover, the participants are motivated to arrive at consensus through the search for *valid* norms, and are thus open to be convinced by the force of the better argument. Consensus is rationally motivated only if it is achieved through the participants' free acceptance of arguments on the grounds of their rational cogency. Habermas does not claim that the ISS is often or perhaps even ever attained in practice. But these conditions are nonetheless presupposed when we engage in discourse, and it is precisely deviation from the ISS that gives rise to doubts about the validity of consensus.[29] Even in cultures where such principles of discourse do not seem to feature at all in the derivation of moral norms, Habermas claims that they are nonetheless still implicitly embedded in speech.[30]

Prima facie, Habermas' procedure appears to be fairly similar to the Scanlonian formulation of 'reasonable agreement' discussed in Chapter Four. Indeed, Habermas acknowledges that Scanlon's formulation is a step in the right direction, avoiding the Rawlsian split between rationality and moral motivation. Scanlon's contractors are motivated to reach rational agreement by the desire to justify their actions to others, or what Barry terms the desire for reasonable agreement. Nonetheless, Habermas argues that the Scanlonian approach is still committed to a contractarian assumption of individual participants engaging in monological deliberation. This implies a conception of the self as 'unencumbered' and reason as something exercised by isolated individuals, outside of social interaction. Habermas prefers a conception of the self as intersubjectively mediated, and rational deliberation as a dialogical exercise, through which participants revise or clarify perceptions of their interests by subjecting them to rational criticism from others.[31] Engaging in discourse also has an important practical function of avoiding the (possibly unintentional) distortion of others' interests. Discourse prevents participants from making inaccurate assessments of the interests or others, a problem that is encountered in monological interpretations of the Categorical Imperative.

In short, discourse ethics claims to address the weaknesses of the Kantian account, while retaining a cognitivist commitment to universally valid moral norms. It grounds its commitment to a principle of universalisation in the structure of language, rather than a transcendental account of the morally relevant capacities of all rational beings. And it justifies substantive moral norms through a dialogical process which rejects the individualist assumptions of most liberal accounts of the self, and guards against the potentially distorting tendencies of the Categorical Imperative.

Critique of Habermas' Justification of (U)

There have been many criticisms levelled at Habermas' discourse ethics, but for our purposes the central concern is his derivation of (U) from the structure of language. Habermas' claims about the presuppositions of argumentation are certainly plausible as an account of the rules embedded in speech acts. It does indeed seem to be the case that when we engage in discourse we implicitly accept a number of rules that have normative implications for our behaviour and intentions, the sorts of arguments that are acceptable, and the consideration we should give to other arguments. However, these norms should be understood as norms constitutive of the practice of discourse, rather than moral norms.

Now it may be true, as Habermas points out, that argumentation is indeed so inescapable a feature of human interaction that this practice is not something we can choose whether or not to engage in. Since language is an all-pervasive, indeed constitutive element of social interaction, we cannot opt in or out of commitment to the rules embedded in language depending on whether we choose to speak. There is simply no alternative mode of rational interaction. In this sense, the commitment to the presuppositions of argumentation is inescapable not only to those who have decided to engage in argumentation, but is inescapable for any rational agent interacting with others. Nonetheless, the point is that these rules are not in themselves moral. They may prescribe norms for discourse, but there is no in-built relation between these rules of discourse and moral obligation. If I violate these norms of speech, then I am perhaps being irrational but I am not behaving in an immoral fashion. I could indeed be accused of acting immorally if I preclude black people from participating in discussion on rules of justice. But the immoral nature of my act derives from my disrespect of black people, not from my failure to act in accordance with rules of argumentation. While there may, in cases like these, be a coincidence between violation of rules of argumentation and moral norms, the coincidence is contingent.

We can clarify this gap between norms of discourse and moral norms through considering the way in which they diverge in their prescriptions. The gap is especially evident as concerns the relation between moral validity and the requirements of equal respect for participants of discourse. We saw that the aim of discourse as presupposed in any serious discussion was to find true, or universally valid norms. Now it does not follow from this objective of discourse that we should be committed to a rule of argumentation that guarantees equal rights of participation. What *does* seem to follow from the objective of truth is that we should subject our convictions to scrutiny from all possible viewpoints and arguments. But this does not imply a requirement to engage in argumentation with all potential participants. As Wellmer writes, 'the obligation to enter into genuine discourse can therefore only stretch as far as the obligation to achieve a genuine and universal rational consensus, and it is therefore also not identical in meaning with universally conceived obligations to cooperation'.[32] In other words, the presuppositions of argumentation are not sufficient to produce moral norms of equal participation. The aim of finding true norms may commit us to consider all possible rational objections, but it does not generate any commitments about with whom, or when, or on what subjects, I ought to engage in discourse. Again, it is worth quoting Wellmer, who argues that norms of rationality do not in themselves have any moral content.

> Obligations to rationality refer to the acknowledgement of arguments, moral obligations to the acknowledgement of persons … Overstating the point a little, we might say that obligations to rationality are concerned with arguments regardless of who voices them, whereas moral obligations are concerned with people regardless of their arguments.[33]

Now the only way Habermas can bridge this gap between presuppositions of argumentation and equal participation is through a rather unusual conception of moral validity. We saw that if the goal of truth is a presupposition of argumentation, then it generates a requirement to consider all rational objections, but not necessarily to accord an equal right of participation in discourse. Habermas can, however, claim to derive such a moral norm from the goal of truth if he defines truth as consensus. In other words, if the truth of moral norms is grounded in their being the object of rational consensus, then he can claim that the search for truth generates a requirement to ensure the agreement of all participants. Truth, then, would be established through a process that necessitated the participation of all rational beings, hence the search for truth would generate rules of equal participation.

It should be noted that this line of argument involves shifting the level of justification form the claim that (U) is presupposed in argumentation, to the rather different claim that valid norms are those agreed on under conditions set out in (U). To understand this shift, we should recall the distinction made towards the beginning of this section between two senses in which discourse is related to claims of validity. First, (U) was valid as a meta-principle, presupposed in the structure of communication. As we have seen, Habermas cannot directly derive (U) from these presuppositions, except on the assumption of a rather unusual theory of truth as rational consensus. Second, substantive moral norms agreed to in conditions stipulated in (U) were defined as universally valid. It is this second grounding of validity in the fact of rational agreement that concerns us here. Given that Habermas' justification of (U) relies on a consensus theory of truth its defence must now rest on the plausibility of the second claims. He must justify the validity of substantive norms through the fact that they generate rational consensus, i.e. a consensus theory of truth.

Further examination of the consensus theory of truth, however, unearths more problems. The consensus theory claims that the truth of moral norms is dependent on their securing the rational agreement of all affected by their implementation. The role of rational consensus is not simply to prevent coercive imposition of norms or guarantee the compliance of subjects. If this were the case, then (U) would simply be a principle of legitimation, guaranteeing the agreement and cooperation of participants in discourse. Negotiated agreements or compromise would be acceptable forms of consensus. In Habermas' theory, consensus plays a more fundamental role, grounding the universal validity or truth of norms. It cannot be based on compromise, because that would imply that participants were accepting a judgement or norm that they did not believe to be valid, but was simply the best available basis for reaching consensus. The consensus theory of truth therefore has to imply the possibility of real consensus on validity claims.

Part of the attraction of the consensus theory of truth seems to be based on an apparent parallel between the role of rational consensus in scientific knowledge and in moral norms. Habermas argues that consensus plays a similar justificatory role in moral questions as rational agreement does in science. There is, however, a problem with this supposed symmetry between truth claims in scientific knowledge and moral norms. Rational agreement plays a far more significant role in grounding truth claims in science than it does in the moral domain. In the scientific community, we may suppose that consensus on truth claims is based on common acceptance of detailed criteria for what constitutes knowledge. A large part of these criteria will be rules of rationality, such as consistency, coherence and the provision of relevant evidence. As Bubner writes, 'rationality is one of the inalienable defining characteristics of knowledge', indeed knowledge is not conceivable 'without certain elements of rationality which must be guaranteed in the structure of all knowledge'.[34] But the same does not hold of moral judgements. In the moral domain, there is far less agreement on the criteria for what constitutes a valid judgement. Reason does play a role in ironing out inconsistencies, clarifying reasons for beliefs and ensuring general coherence. But these functions of reason will in many cases not affect the fundamental moral commitments of individuals or communities. And they will certainly not guarantee consensus on moral norms. Discourse may influence the individual's moral beliefs by forcing her to justify and render coherent her judgements, through exposing them to rational criticism. Engaging in discourse with others with different interests and beliefs may also convince her to modify some of her judgements. But the outcome may well be a clarification of differences in moral judgement, rather than a consensus. There is no good reason – apart from a gut preference for simplicity in moral theory – to suppose that normatively neutral rules of reason will produce a consensus of convictions. In other words, discourse will not necessarily eliminate or even diminish moral conflict.

Now if one accepts the possibility of perennial pluralism in moral norms, then the consensus theory of truth must be rejected in favour of one of two alternatives. Firstly, one could hold that there are universal moral truths regardless of whether they generate consensus or not. For example, one could hold that universal moral truth exists independently of rational convictions, for example as divine law. This route is clearly unacceptable to Habermas. The second alternative would be to abandon the claim to the universal validity of moral judgements derived from rational consensus (although not necessarily the validity of (U)). In this case, one could still defend the value of rational consensus, but as a principle of legitimation rather than as a ground for truth claims. This is the route adopted by Rawls when he characterises agreement on his conception of justice as 'political, not metaphysical'.[35] But Habermas refuses to take this route, defending a conception of moral validity grounded in the fact of rational consensus. On this account, the persistence of conflict between different moral convictions must indicate a failure of rational argument, or else imply that the issues under discussion are not truly moral questions. Lack of consensus on questions of justice must be attributed to the non-ideal conditions of speech or the subject matter of speech, rather than to a divergence of moral judgements.

The problem for Habermas seems to stem from his attempt to combine a principle of legitimation with a principle of universal validity. He seems to be basing his notion of consensus on a characteristically liberal intuition that only rationally agreed principles are morally legitimate. But the notion of the moral value of consensus in the liberal tradition, as we have seen, is firmly rooted in a conception of individuals as free and equal. It is this substantive commitment to freedom that grounds the validity of rational consensus. Rationally agreed norms are not valid in the sense of expressing true or universally valid judgements; but they are valid in the sense of guaranteeing the individual's right to rational scrutiny and uncoerced consent to the principles governing social interaction. This notion of consensus grounded in a commitment to individual liberty allows for the possibility of conflict over substantive moral principles – indeed many liberal theories of justice are seen as a response to the problem of conflict between different moral judgements. But failure to reach consensus on basic moral convictions does not undermine the value of agreement achieved through negotiated compromise. The point about agreement on the liberal account is not that it grounds truth but that it ensures uncoerced compliance, and hence political legitimacy.

Habermas' mistake in conflating this principle of legitimacy with a theory of universal moral validity can perhaps be understood if we consider his justification of the second order principle (U). This principle claims universal validity in virtue of the fact that it is presupposed in argumentation. But the validity of (U) – if it is to be accepted – should not be confused with the validity of norms generated through (U). As we have seen, these latter are best understood as valid in the sense of legitimate, rather than in the sense of being expressive of moral truth. Yet if we reject the consensus theory of truth, then there is no longer any good reason to accept (U) as universally valid. For if (U) cannot be justified on the grounds that norms agreed through the procedure specified in (U) are universally valid, then it must be justified on the grounds that it follows from the rules of argumentation, including the goal of truth. As we saw, the justification of this derivation was dependent on a conception of truth as rational consensus. Only on this understanding of truth could the goal of seeking true norms be achieved through the rule of equal participation in speech. And once we reject the consensus theory of truth, (U) cannot be derived from the presuppositions of argumentation.

Neither language, nor rational consensus, can in themselves guarantee the derivation of universally valid moral norms. In both justifications of validity – for the second order principle (U) and for the first order norms generating rational consensus – Habermas' argument rests on a commitment to the value of persons as free and equal.

Conclusion

This chapter began with a critic of the rationalist theory of motivation underpinning most liberal universalist accounts. The criticisms centred on the question of how reason could motivate action without the presence of a desire. Kantian and neo-Kantian accounts all faced a version of this problem, leading us to consider the traditional Humean alternative. This too was found wanting, and the argument defended instead a theory of the interdependence of beliefs, reason and desire in motivation. The rejection of rationalism in principle left open the question of the role of reason in defining morality. A proponent of the interdependence thesis could either adopt a cognitivist account, or she could deny that moral duty is defined through reason. This necessitated a discussion of cognitivist claims about the role of reason in defining morality. The chapter considered two main cognitivist theories, one constructed along Kantian lines, the second the discourse ethics of Habermas. Neither could offer a convincing cognitivist account. I opted instead for a conception of morality as shaped through intersubjcive conceptions of the good.

It should be stressed that the rejection of moral cognitivism does not imply that there is no role for reason in moral motivation. As we saw, rational deliberation can modify desires and beliefs, thus helping shape conceptions of duty and indirectly influencing motivation. But it does have substantial implications for our view of the foundations of ethics. Specifically, it implies that our commitment to refugee rights cannot be grounded in any universally valid claims. Rather, it is derived from intersubjective values. The next chapter will consider what this implies for our ethical theory of duties to refugees.

Notes

[1]   Rationalism in ethical theory has also often been used to denote the claim that there can be *a priori* intuitions of moral truths, which are derived from reason (rather than from experience, or sentiment). However, I employ the narrower definition of rationalism as referring to a certain sort of theory of motivation. This is so I can distinguish between

rationalist theories of motivation, and the claim that morality is derived from reason – a theory often termed cognitivism.

2   Thomas Nagel, *The Possibility of Altruism* (Princeton, 1978), p. 12.

3   Ibid., pp. 13–14.

4   G.E.M. Anscombe, 'On Practical Reasoning', in Joseph Raz (ed.), *Practical Reasoning* (Oxford, 1978), p. 45.

5   For his discussion of abstraction and moral motivation, see Nagel, *The Possibility of Altruism*, pp. 99–115; and *Equality and Partiality* (Oxford, 1991), pp. 10–20.

6   Immanuel Kant, *The Moral Law: Kant's Groundwork of the Metaphysic of Morals*, ed. Alan Paton (London, 1989), p. 68.

7   Ibid., p. 84.

8   Ibid., p. 67.

9   Ibid., p. 88.

10 David Hume, *Enquiries Concerning Human Understanding and Concerning the Principles of Moral*, ed. L.A. Selby-Bigge (Oxford, 1975), p. 294.

11 G.E.M. Anscombe, *Intention* (Oxford, 1957), pp. 75–6.

12 John Charvet, *The Idea of an Ethical Community* (Ithaca, 1995), p. 28.

13 See Barry Stroud, *Hume* (London, 1988), pp. 180–4; and Annette Baier, *A Progress of Sentiments: Reflections on Hume's Treatise* (London, 1991), pp. 180–1 – although both defend Hume against the accusation of emotivism.

14 Charvet, *The Idea of an Ethical Community*, p. 22.

15 Ibid., p. 29.

16 Ibid.

17 Ibid., pp. 29–30.

18 Nagel refers to these as 'motivated desires'. See *The Possibility of Altruism*, pp. 29–30.

19 I am terming this disposition a 'desire', although it might more accurately be defined as an 'affective state'. The point is that it is an affective state that usually involves a desire to bring about some sort of change in the external world, and is thus equivalent to a desire in its motivational force.

20 This follows a Kleinian account, as elaborated, for example, in the work of Richard Wollheim, *The Thread of Life* (Cambridge, 1986).

21 Ibid., p. 217.

22 Axel Honneth, *The Struggle for Recognition: The Moral Grammar of Social Conflicts*, trans. Joel Anderson (Cambridge, 1995), p. 77.

23 Williams points out that this version is simpler than Kant's account, avoiding many of the difficulties specific to Kant's account. He suggests that it is more akin to contemporary Kantian accounts – particularly Alan Gewirth's account in *Reason and Morality* (Chicago, 1978). See Bernard Williams, *Ethics and the Limits of Philosophy* (London, 1985), p. 55. But it also highlights the basic problem with the claim of Kantian accounts to derive moral norms from reason.

24 Williams, *Ethics and the Limits of Philosophy*, p. 64.

25 See Jürgen Habermas, 'Discourse Ethics: Notes on a Program of Philosophical Justification', in Habermas (ed.), *Moral Consciousness adn Communicative Action* (Cambridge, 1990), pp. 87–9.

26 Ibid., p. 87.

27 Ibid., p. 65.

28 Ibid., p. 86.

29 On this point, see Thomas MacCarthy, *The Critical Theory of Jürgen Habermas* (Cambridge, 1984), p. 309.

30 Ibid., pp. 324–5.

31 Habermas, 'Discourse Ethics', pp. 66–7.

32 Albrecht Wellmer, *The Persistence of Modernity: Essays on Aesthetics, Ethics, and Postmodernism*, trans. David Midgley (Cambridge, 1991), p. 187.

33 Ibid., p. 185.

34 Rüdiger Bubner, 'Habermas' Concept of Critical Theory', in John B. Thompson and David Held (eds), *Habermas: Critical Debates* (London, 1982), p. 55.

35 John Rawls, 'Justice as Fairness: Political not Metaphysical', *Philosophy and Public Affairs*, 14:3 (1985): 223-51.

Chapter Six

Community and Universal Duties

I ended the last chapter with a rejection of an ethics that claimed to be derived from some universally shared concept of reason. This implies the need for some alternative way of grounding ethics. If one rejects the type of cognitivist account offered by most liberal universalists, the most obvious rival candidate is what can be loosely described as a 'intersubjective' account of the source of morality. On this account, our ethical commitments to the value of autonomy, or refugee rights, must be understood as historically and culturally contingent. They are derived from a set of shared values particular to specific societies, although the commitment to these values may be very deeply rooted in the culture and practice of particular groups. This type of account of morality as grounded in shared values (rather than universally valid norms) is often associated with communitarian political philosophy, and indeed one of the richest articulations of the idea can be found in the communitarian and neo-Hegelian writer Charles Taylor. In this chapter I shall examine the claims of communitarian political philosophy and in particular the work of Taylor, and consider how such accounts could help construct a non-rationalist grounding for a commitment to refugee rights.

The Communitarian Thesis

Ontological Communitarianism

The term 'communitarian' has been applied to the work of a number of contemporary political philosophers who have criticised individualist theories of justice, notably for their conception of the individual as in some sense methodologically or morally prior to her community. They have argued that liberals are committed to a conception of the individual as 'radically disembodied',[1] whose interests and identity are defined pre-socially, and who autonomously chooses her own values and ends.[2] Communitarian theories stress the relevance of community in shaping the individual's identity and conception of the good. For many theorists, this ontological account is used to justify normative claims about the moral relevance of community, and its contribution to human flourishing.[3] This may in turn generate more specific prescriptions about the political and social institutions required to protect or promote community.

It should, however, be stressed that ontological accounts of the individual's relationship to society are in principle distinct from moral and political theories of community. While the debate between liberals and communitarians is often couched in terms of opposing normative theories, those who embrace a communitarian ontology have divergent views on the prescriptive implications of the communitarian critique of liberalism.[4] In the course of the discussion, we shall therefore distinguish between two sorts of communitarianism. The ontological thesis is essentially a theory of the factors that shape the individual's identity and ends, and will have implications for questions of methodology, as well as the foundations of moral and political philosophy. Prescriptive communitarianism, on the other hand, refers to more normative communitarian theories about the moral significance of community. Prescriptive communitarianism may also refer to political theories of the social institutions necessary to achieve these moral goals.

The writers most famously associated with ontological communitarianism include Michael Sandel, Alasdair MacIntyre, Michael Walzer and Charles Taylor. In the work of Sandel, the self is not prior to her values and goals, but instead constituted by the intersubjective values of her community, an account which he terms 'the constitutive conception of community'.[5] Charles Taylor adopts a Hegelian account of the individual's identity as constituted through interaction with others. Similar conceptions of the communitarian sources of values are defended by Alasdair MacIntyre and Michael Walzer.[6] Despite variations, we can summarise the central claims as a conception of the self as 'encumbered', or constituted by a set of intersubjective values and goals, which are shaped and perpetuated through the shared goods and practices of a community of people. For the sake of simplicity we shall refer to the individual as constituted by her 'social matrix'.

This account of the encumbered individual is similar to the account of moral agency outlined in the previous chapter. While my account defended a conception of the unconscious self as in some sense separate from society, it acknowledged that the individual's self-conscious identity, goals, values and beliefs are constituted by the social matrix. And the account of moral development emphasised the fundamental role of intersubjective values in shaping the individual's conception of morality. This account of the sources of moral motivation can therefore be classified as a communitarian conception of the self.

But as mentioned above, many communitarian accounts take a step beyond this descriptive claim about the individual as constituted by her social matrix, arguing that this ontological account is a basis for attributing special moral relevance to the community. Since the individual is constituted by her community's language, values and conception of rationality, it is argued, these relationships and institutions should be accorded an ethical status denied by individualistic theories of moral agency. In terms of political theory, the normative implication is that since our social context is constitutive of our identity and well-being, the practices and ties which comprise this social matrix should be maintained and even strengthened. Given the commitment of this thesis to ontological communitarianism, we need to consider whether the account of the last two chapters also commits us to prescriptive communitarianism.

Ontological Communitarianism and the Politics of Recognition

One way of establishing a link between ontological and prescriptive theses is to argue that the conception of the self as constituted by a particular culture provides grounds for protecting the practices of this culture. On this account, the communitarian ontology justifies political and legal arrangements to preserve a particular community and its way of life. This type of argument takes as its starting point a Hegelian notion of recognition similar to that discussed in the last chapter. The individual's self-conscious identity is defined through interaction with others, and thus recognition by others is essential for positive individual development and self-realisation. The need for this type of recognition is not limited to the formative stages of development, but continues throughout our life. The sphere of recognition also extends from an initial dependence on the family and what Mead refers to as 'significant others', to the need for forms of social and legal recognition. As the individual begins to interact with wider social spheres, her self-conscious identity is constituted by the intersubjective ethical values of her community. She becomes dependent on legal and social recognition from this wider sphere in order to achieve self-respect and affirmation.

Now I argued in the last chapter that there is an important link between individual psychology and socially defined forms of recognition, and thus strong grounds for linking a person's well-being with the need for social recognition. In his essay on the 'Politics of Recognition',[7] Charles Taylor elaborates the concept and role of recognition, arguing that the need for recognition justifies policies to protect the distinct cultures of different groups. He claims that communities with distinct practices require a form of collective recognition that goes beyond the legal and social recognition owed to their individual members. The justification of group recognition is not grounded in the needs of its current members, but seems to be based on a non-individualist conception of the value of particular traditions and practices. This point is emphasised in Taylor's argument for the preservation of cultures that are struggling for survival. Taylor argues that there is a justification for over-riding certain individual rights in order to ensure the survival and reproduction of a culture that is in danger of extinction. Drawing on the debate about the cultural rights of French-speaking Canadians, he argues that the Quebecois were justified in introducing legislation to restrict freedom of choice regarding language. Since the French language was in danger of extinction, it was right, for example, that French-speaking Quebecois be legally obliged to educate their children in French. Linking this point back to his communitarian ontology, Taylor's argument can be formulated as follows. Certain practices – in this case the speaking of French – are constitutive of the identity of Quebecois people. The recognition of the practice of speaking French is therefore a necessary condition for the self-realisation (positive self-relation) of French Quebecois people. Since the only means of ensuring the continued recognition of the practice is through legal provisions obliging French Quebecois to attend French speaking schools, then such legislation is a precondition for self-realisation.

Before examining the coherence of this argument, it is worth considering the practical consequences of this form of 'politics of recognition'. The claim that community practices constitutive of people's identity should be preserved has a number of implications not just for group rights but also for the rights of non-members. If recognition is really dependent on the preservation of existing practices, then this would presumably justify protecting such practices from erosion or dilution by values and practices external to that community. This would imply the need to defend the community from the outside influence of other communities, and also to restrict the entry of groups that might jeopardise the survival of these practices. The need for recognition would thus justify special duties to preserve the community's way of life, and by extension, undermine the moral relevance of universal duties to those outside of the community. If one accepts Taylor's argument about the link between ontological and prescriptive communitarianism, the communitarian account of the individual could commit us to a potentially restrictionist refugee policy. Taylor does not argue that the need for preservation should necessarily override individual rights, in fact in a subsequent piece he asserts that preservation of a culture may conflict with more important shared values. Nonetheless, if such group rights to preservation do necessarily follow from a commitment to ontological communitarianism, this could justify a more restrictionist refugee policy.[8]

Fortunately, the communitarian account of the individual commits one to no such conclusion. Taylor's argument for deriving a collective right to preserve practices from the need for recognition is problematic on two fronts, one theoretical, the other empirical. First, it is not clear that the individual's need for recognition does justify group rights on any other than individualist grounds. Presumably even Taylor would agree that the value of a community's practices is contingent on the contribution of such practices to the flourishing of its members. There can be no transcending value attached to a particular culture, over and beyond the value derived from the people who make up the community. While the recognition of group rights may be instrumental for securing the recognition of its members, this does not ground a right to maintain these practices regardless of the wishes of members of the community. Thus although current members of the community may be concerned to pass down their practices to future generations, it is not clear that this over-rides the wishes of future generations, who may be critics of existing practices. The notion of intersubjectively defined identities does not preclude the possibility of change, and where such change occurs the members of a group may feel that recognition requires modifying or rejecting past practices. As Habermas writes, 'the protection of forms of life and traditions in which identities are formed is supposed to serve the recognition of their members; it does not represent a kind of perservation of species by administrative means'.[9]

The problem can be expressed in terms of the possibility of conflict between the preservation of existing group practices, and the forms of recognition required by members. Honneth's concept of recognition is useful here.[10] Honneth argues that the individual is dependent on recognition of her achievements and accomplishments for the development of basic self-esteem and confidence. Where this need is not met in the personal, social and/or legal spheres, the gap is likely to be filled by a sense of shame or grievance. A sense of grievance can motivate a struggle for recognition which generates social conflict and change. Examples of this form of conflict include historical struggles for the rights of social classes, racial minorities, religious groups or women. In these cases, the need for recognition may be best met through social change, rather than preserving existing practices. Recognition will require conflict and change, rather than a preservation of existing values and norms.

This brings us back to the point that group practices are not intrinsically valuable, but derive their worth from their contribution to the well-being of their members. If one accepts the instrumental value of group rights, and also accepts the possibility of critique of existing practices, then it seems wrong to suggest that the need for recognition implies a commitment to the preservation of community practices. There is certainly a case for recognising and promoting certain community practices that are constitutive of individual well-being, and for making such practices available for future generations. But this recognition of the group will not necessarily over-ride the changing forms of struggle for recognition of its members. Indeed, Honneth argues that his communitarian ontology implies an ongoing struggle for new forms of social and legal recognition that involve rejecting existing practices. Whether or not we accept this account, the point is that Taylor and Honneth derive different prescriptions from a similar ontology. A commitment to protect existing communities does not necessarily follow from accepting communitarian ontology.

The second point concerns not so much the coherence of Taylor's argument, as its empirical premises. Even if the protection of community practices can in principle be justified on these instrumental grounds, such protectionism would only be possible if there were in fact clearly definable communities. Yet the practices and values that constitute the individual are likely to be diverse and often conflicting, and derived from a number of different (possibly overlapping) communities. Any one individual is likely to be constituted by a unique configuration of values and practices, for example through religion, her family's moral and political values, exposure to other cultures through travel or education, as well as the more obvious influences of language, national and local political and administrative structures, and a shared interpretation of her community's history and culture. There is rarely a single, dominant community, which can be said to be the sole source of the individual's values. Still less plausible is the claim that a community is bounded, and cut off from the influence of other communities. In reality, different communities are constantly influencing one another through media, culture, migration, trade, and so on. In short, there is often no easily definable salient or ultimate community, let alone one exclusive group from which individuals can be said to derive their values. And even assuming there were, in all but the most extreme cases this community will not be bounded but fluid and partly shaped by the values and actions of other communities. The need for group recognition will in many cases fail to provide clear grounds for privileging certain sources over others.

There are evidently exceptions to this pluralist conception of the sources of identity. Some groups (or their leaders) claim that certain distinctive shared traits of their members – usually a distinct history or beliefs or physical characteristics – generate special moral or political claims. Such claims about group identity are often made in order to mobilise support for political goals – secession, imperialism or the restriction of immigration. As with the argument for preserving cultural practices, it is not clear why the communitarian ontology would commit one to recognising the claims of such groups, especially if such claims would conflict with the recognition of their individual members or the well-being of non-members. A second type of claim for group recognition, which often overlaps with the first variety, occurs where a group becomes politically relevant because they are perceived to have been the victims of unfair treatment in the past. In the case of minority groups with special needs, groups that have suffered discrimination or who are economically disadvantaged, there may be a clear case for singling out particular social groups for special treatment. Minority rights or affirmative action for selected groups may be justified on the grounds that such policies will redress a historical imbalance of treatment. Singling out particular social groups as the subject of collective rights is considered to be the best means of realising *de facto* equality. This would provide a justification, for example, for according certain group rights to Quebecois. But accepting the legitimacy of this form of group right does not mean one has to accept a communitarian argument that accords intrinsic value to the group's culture. A liberal could also quite happily endorse collective rights designed to ensure the equal rights of all individuals.[11] If these are the only sorts of collective rights implied by the communitarian ontology, there is no reason to suppose that it could not be compatible with first order liberalism.

To summarise, communitarian ontology does not seem to commit us to recognising the intrinsic values of existing community practices. The need for recognition does not justify prioritising recognition of groups over individuals. And even if recognition of groups were justified, given the fact of pluralism, there would often be no empirical grounds for privileging certain groups over others.

Communitarian Ontology and Participation

The second type of argument for prescriptive communitarianism emphasises the *processes* through which the individual is constituted, rather than the specific practices that are constitutive of its members. What is important on this account is not so much the preservation of the values of a given group of people, but rather the relations between an individual and the processes through which her values are formed and revised. This would imply according special moral weight to the processes through which the individual is constituted by the social matrix. On this account, the communitarian ontology would be used to justify political arrangements to promote certain forms of interaction between members of the community. It might provide grounds for encouraging participation in social and political practices, or playing a more active role in community life.[12]

As with the first type of communitarianism, this could be used as an argument for justifying the moral relevance of special ties. The importance of cultivating special bonds and participating in shared practices would, on this account, give rise to duties to fellow participants, which would outweigh the importance of ties with those not participating in the said practices. However, the argument for participation could also justify ties with new members of the community, or even be a basis for encouraging interaction with different kinds of community. If it is again based on a Hegelian conception of recognition, then it could be argued that recognition would be better achieved through interaction with a wider set of individuals or groups. There is nothing in the concept of recognition as shaping identity that implies there should be limits on the scope of interaction. If interaction is valued independently of the substance of shared norms – which on the participatory account it is – then there seem to be no good grounds for restricting the participation of newcomers. Perhaps the claim would be that a history of interaction with certain groups creates a special pattern of interaction that would be disrupted by outsiders. But then this is already claiming something more for the significance of interaction, namely that it generates group practices that should be preserved. And this of course takes us back to the first argument for protecting existing practices, and we have seen that a justification for this form of group recognition cannot be derived from the ontological account of the individual as constituted by intersubjective recognition.

More generally, if the account of the self as constituted by the social matrix is a fact about human beings, then these processes will carry on occurring regardless of whether we make a point of nurturing them or not. In order to defend the claim that we should actively promote such ties, we would need an account of how the acknowledgement or strengthening of these ties would contribute to personal well-being. It is not enough to say that because certain values and practices define the person, these values or the processes through which they define the person should therefore be protected or extended. What is missing is a defence of the contribution of this constituting process for human well-being. Thus a community that was committed to a substantive first order conception of the value of community life would have grounds for defending a political theory of communitarianism. But an individualist liberal society in which people did not attach value to community life would not be able to justify such a prescriptive communitarianism, even though the sources of their commitment to individualist liberal values could be explained through an ontological communitarian account. Prescriptive communitarian claims do not follow directly from the communitarian ontology, but need to be justified as first order moral goods.

To conclude, it is not clear how a prescriptive communitarian thesis can be established on the basis of a description of the self as encumbered or situated in an inescapable framework. The conception of the self as constituted by the social matrix does not in itself provide a moral justification for strengthening or protecting either the substance of the relevant values and practices, or the processes through which they are shaped and absorbed.

The Status of Universal Duties

Although my ontological account does not necessarily commit me to prescriptive communitarianism, it does nonetheless delimit the range of possible moral theories I can embrace. Most importantly for this discussion, it undermines the claim of justice to foundational supremacy.

Questioning the Foundational and Political Primacy of Justice

One consequence of defending a communitarian ontology will be a rejection of the universalist and cognitivist claims of procedural liberalism. If we accept an account of the individual as constituted, justice can have no *a priori* claim to primacy over competing conceptions of the good. It is worth examining why this should be the case.

The liberal conception of the individual is closely linked to the liberal claim about the primacy of justice. As Michael Sandel argues, on the liberal deontological account, the individual is conceived of as prior to her own ends, as the autonomous chooser of her values and goals.[13] Thus political institutions must be so structured as to allow individuals the maximum possible freedom in choosing their own ends. This freedom of choice is guaranteed through the deontological conception of justice, which views justice as a neutral, regulating principle that ensures all individuals have the freedom to choose their own goals and values. On this account, justice has primacy over particular conceptions of the good. By maintaining a neutral stance between different goods, the claim is that justice respects people's capacity to choose their own goals and values. Unlike in teleological theories where the right is determined by the good, on this liberal account the right should be conceived of as prior to the good. Moreover, on the deontological liberal account, justice is not only accorded moral primacy: it also has a privileged form of justification. Unlike conceptions of the good that are contingent on particular historical and social factors, justice has a special foundational claim to universal validity. As we saw in Chapter Five, cognitivist theories hold that it is a universal regulating principle applicable to all societies, grounded in the shared capacity of human beings for reason (or in Habermas' case in their participation in discourse). The priority of justice thus follows from a particular conception of the individual as a rational agent, or as a participant in discourse; and it is accorded primacy over the good, reflecting a conception of the individual as capable of choosing her own ends.

It should be clear why this account of justice as primary is not compatible with a communitarian ontology. On the communitarian account, the individual is not a chooser of ends, but is constituted by her social matrix. And far from representing a neutral principle of right, the liberal notion of justice is shaped through shared conceptions of human flourishing and the good. On this communitarian ontological account, justice has no privileged foundational status, and no *a priori* claim to primacy.

If justice is denied this ontological primacy, are there alternative grounds for according it the status of regulating principle? After all, denying the foundational primacy of justice may not imply rejecting its *moral* primacy. Two possible routes could be pursued in order to defend the moral primacy of justice, without embracing its ontological primacy. These correspond to the two strands of Rawls' political conceptions of justice as fairness. As we saw in Chapter Four, Rawls argues that his conception of justice is political in the sense of being:

1. a response to empirical conditions of conflict between individuals of roughly equal strength for moderately scarce goods; and
2. worked up from the shared values of members of a liberal democratic society.

The first, empirical proposition might provide grounds for attributing political primacy to justice; the second could justify the moral primacy of justice amongst other goods. Both of these possible justifications will be examined in turn.

The political case for according primacy to justice was based on a characterisation of society as a competition between individuals of roughly equal strength for moderately scarce resources. These 'circumstances of justice' necessitated a regulating principle to avoid conflict. In order to justify the primacy of this regulating principle over conflicting claims, justice would have to be accorded supreme status over all other goods. A political justification of the primacy of justice would therefore involve the claim that the circumstances of justice are the salient problem confronting society, and that addressing this problem must take priority over other goals. Such a defence would need to show that solving this problem of conflict was a prerequisite for realising other rights or goals, such as stability, or freedom.

There are two main obstacles to grounding the primacy of justice in the political necessities created by the circumstances of justice. First, if justice is to be accorded primacy on the basis of the 'circumstances of justice', its primary status will clearly be contingent on empirical conditions. That is to say, the right is prior to the good insofar as there is an actual or potential conflict between different conceptions of the good and regulation of this conflict is the most urgent political task confronting us. As Hume, the original 'circumstances of justice' theorist, observes: 'Encrease to a sufficient degree the benevolence of men, or the bounty of nature, and you render justice useless'.[14] Now we saw in the discussion of social contract theories that the circumstances of justice assumed three conditions: egoistically motivated individuals, of roughly equal strength, competing for scarce resources. These conditions may indeed be said to be characteristic of distributional problems in some societies. In war-torn societies or failed states, conflict and instability may generate a struggle for scarce resources, rendering the need for some regulating principle the salient and most urgent political goal. Even in more stable societies, the need to regulate conflict may be the most important task for a great many political institutions. For example, institutions to deal with criminal justice or taxation must all provide criteria necessary for deciding between competing claims. Regulating the conflicts of interests between criminals and victims, or between tax-payers and the recipients of government services, requires mutually acceptable principles for deciding on how to distribute benefits and burdens.

But this type of trade-off situation is not always the dominant feature of social interaction. Nor can it be characterised as the sole problem confronting political theorists. For a start, many goods are not subject to the sort of competition between individuals assumed by theories of regulative justice. What Raz terms 'collective goods', for example, goods like clean air, public galleries or the benefits of living in a tolerant society, are not subject to this form of zero-sum distribution between individuals. Making these goods available to all is not a question of regulating competing claims, but of ensuring that they are preserved and remain accessible to those who benefit from them. The political questions raised by the need for such goods have little to do with distributional problems.

More fundamentally, it is simply wrong to characterise all members of society as egoistic individuals cooperating for self-interested reasons. Rationalist theories ignore the role of shared values in shaping interests, as well as the possibility of being motivated through concern at the plight of others. Rather than encouraging the development of such social virtues, theories of regulative justice dismiss them as largely irrelevant to the problem of guaranteeing cooperation. The favoured notion of egoistic cooperation is not only descriptively untrue, it also has negative practical implications. By encouraging people to conceive themselves as self-interests individuals, it actively endorses and perpetuates selfish behaviour. As Bernstein writes, 'the idea of morality as a system of rules of cooperation draws its image of morality from what is a defective case, and then idealizes that case as composing the whole'.[15]

The second problem, as we saw in Chapter Five, is that consideration of the circumstances of justice alone will not provide sufficient grounds for deriving a conception of justice as fairness. The need to regulate conflict between individuals of roughly equal strength competing for scarce resources is more likely to produce a conception of justice as mutual advantage than justice as fairness. For Rawls, what swung the choice in favour of a more morally palatable theory of justice was the shared values of the contractors. When we talk about the primacy of justice, or justice as regulating all other goods, we are surely referring to this notion of justice as fairness rather than the establishment of a mutually beneficial *modus vivendi*. The circumstances of justice does not describe a necessary or permanent empirical condition, let alone one that provides an exhaustive inventory of the problems confronting political theory. Even assuming for the sake of argument that it did, it would not produce a justification of the primacy of justice as fairness.

This brings us to the second Rawlsian ground for according justice a primary status: its morally privileged position in the value system of the relevant society.

Here the argument is less clear-cut. As we saw, in his later work Rawls argues that the precise terms of justice are worked up from the shared values of contractors, who are the inheritors of liberal values and democratic political institutions. These citizens of liberal societies will select principles of justice that conceive of individuals as morally equal and as autonomous choosers of their own ends. Now according to the communitarian ontological thesis, subjects embracing this conception of human autonomy must be understood as constituted by the social matrix. They have acquired this conception – indeed their whole moral outlook has been shaped – by the intersubjective values and practices of their society. If they endorse the moral primacy of justice, it is as a product of the value system and moral framework through which they are constituted. The moral primacy of justice in this sense may be reconcilable with ontological communitarianism. On this account, justice is not valued because it has an independent source of justification, as is claimed by deontological theories. Nor does this account imply accepting a characterisation of society as a conflict for scarce resources. Rather, justice may be qualitatively distinguished from other goods as conveying a conception of humans as autonomous and equal, a conception that is integral to our self-understanding.

The Diversity of Goods

Yet while the moral primacy of justice in this sense may be compatible with the ontological communitarian account, its status as trump over other goods is challenged by the empirical fact of diverse goods in liberal societies. Once we start examining the range of goods that define what is of value in our lives, it becomes more and more difficult to define any single and permanent ordering of goods. Recognising the diversity of values therefore delivers yet another blow to the primacy of justice. To understand why this should be the case, we shall look at Charles Taylor's account of the sources of western liberal values.

In his *Sources of the Self*, Taylor provides an account of the individual as situated in intersubjectively defined structures of beliefs and values, or 'inescapable frameworks'. It is with reference to these frameworks that individuals can understand and articulate their beliefs about the good, their moral convictions and values. These frameworks also enable the individual to make a series of what Taylor calls 'qualitative distinctions'.[16] We employ these distinctions to differentiate between the value of actions or virtues or forms of life, some of which we mark out as morally higher or more worthwhile. These morally worthwhile virtues or actions are what Taylor terms 'goods'. It is only through recognising qualitative distinctions of these kinds that we will be able to understand and thus realise the goods embedded in our frameworks. A full understanding of what sorts of actions, goals, virtues and ways of life are morally worthwhile will require articulating these various qualitative distinctions. This articulation, Taylor argues, is only possible through tracing the historical evolution of our shared understanding of goods. Such an historical enterprise is necessary because one can only define and articulate goods through understanding how they have evolved.

Tracing the historical evolution of articulations of goods is also the only means of retrieving those goods that have been suppressed by modern moral philosophy.[17] Taylor's conception of the self as constituted by an inescapable framework therefore implies the need to articulate the components of this framework, in order to achieve self-understanding and moral enrichment. Articulation is vital to human well-being, because it is only through reflection and examination of our qualitative distinctions that our moral convictions can make sense. It can also help to motivate us to realise the goods we have articulated.[18]

Given the need for articulation, Taylor is critical of deontological liberalism for attempting to abstract from our frameworks and thus suppressing an understanding of the goods they affirm. Procedural liberal theories of the kind espoused by Kant, Nagel, Rawls, Scanlon and Habermas are all guilty of this type of suppression. According to Taylor, these 'strange, cramped theories' have the 'paradoxical effect of making us inarticulate on some of the most important issues of morality'.[19] They attempt to cover up the more messy and troublesome reality of a diversity of goods that often prescribe conflicting courses of action or ways of life. The attempt of procedural liberalism to divorce the individual from her constitutive frameworks is not only doomed to failure, it is also profoundly damaging to the moral life of the individual. It thwarts her moral awareness and understanding of what is worthwhile in life, 'making us inarticulate on some of the most important issues of morality'.[20] Taylor calls instead for an articulation of the goods embedded in our frameworks, in order for us to understand and thus realise the goods concerned.

This stress on the need for articulation is of interest to the current argument for two reasons. First, his account of the diversity of goods and how they might be ordered may help us understand the relationship between universal and special duties. It will not provide us with clear-cut formulae of the kind promised by deontological theory, but it can point us in the direction of a more sophisticated conception of duties to non-nationals. Secondly, Taylor argues that articulating the goods underlying our commitment to procedural liberalism can help motivate respect for the requirements of universal rights. I shall return to this second point later. For now, I shall elaborate the first point.

Taylor identifies commitment to liberal universalism as a substantive first order conception of morality reflecting a particular conception of human flourishing. The form of modern liberalism that we have inherited gives central weight to the values of freedom, reason and avoidance of suffering. We saw in the critique of cognitivist theories in Chapter Five that the norms of rights and justice based on these values cannot be derived solely from reason, but reflect commitment to certain conceptions of the good. These ideas about the good can be traced back to the early modern period and have evolved through Deist and Enlightenment forms to the contemporary conceptions of universal justice and human rights with which we are familiar.[21] But liberal conceptions coexist in modern western culture with other, potentially conflicting strands of moral thought, including those that accord moral weight to particular ties or community life. As we uncover the 'layers of suppression', Taylor argues, we will begin to discover a wide range of different goods.[22] The central conflict in western culture over the past two centuries has been between the goods associated with Enlightenment ideals of universal rights or duties of benevolence, and goods associated with the Romantic strand of western thought. As Taylor writes: 'A series of disputes of this form runs through modern culture, between what appear to be the demands of disengaged freedom, and equality and universality, on the one hand, and the demands of nature, or fulfilment, or expressive integrity, or intimacy, or particularity, on the other'.[23]

Taylor argues that it is simplistic and misguided to assume we should have to choose between different goods. In the case of justice, 'The fact that the theory designating one [of these conceptions] is valid need not mean that designating the other is confused and invalid'.[24] Different conceptions of justice may be appropriate for different contexts, and likewise we may prioritise different goods or values over justice for certain moral questions.

Taylor is certainly not the first to locate the contemporary conflict between universal and special duties in the debate between rationalist liberalism and romanticism. What is distinctive about his account of the history of ideas is his conception of the source of these values, and his acceptance of the phenomenon of value conflict. Taylor conceives of shared values as intersubjectively defined and so particular to different groups and historical eras. So both the rationalist liberal and the romanticist or nationalist strands in western thought were shaped by the historically contingent evolution of political and moral thought in western culture. He also recognises the moral relevance of both strands of thought, which are constitutive of the identities of members of western societies.

In descriptive terms, this clears up a number of confusions. It explains why members of liberal democracies have a strong commitment to national ties, and why these could be felt to have special moral significance even where they conflict with universal rights claims. And by understanding our commitment to liberal rights as shaped by shared values, it becomes clearer how people could be motivated via the desire for affirmation to internalise these norms. So this account of the sources of liberal values can avoid the rationalist's problematic dichotomy between the individual's contingent will and the requirements of reason. Yet characterising liberal universalism as historically contingent does seem to create a new set of problems. It might imply demoting the status of universal duties. If impartial justice is denied foundational and absolute moral primacy, surely there is no guarantee that it will feature on the top of the list of valued goods.

What Taylor provides, however, is some indication as to how one might evaluate and order these different goods. While he refuses to attribute any foundational or overarching moral primacy to universal justice, Taylor does suggest that liberal values could have the status of higher order goods. Such goods are singled out from the plurality of goods in virtue of their importance in giving direction to our lives, determining action or helping us to order other goods. As Taylor writes, they are 'goods which not only are incomparably more important than others but provide the standpoint from which these must be weighed, judged, decided about'.[25] These higher order, or 'hyper'-goods may be seen as having moral primacy in many situations, although their primacy is not an *a priori* or foundational as in the case of procedural liberalism. Hyper-goods are not derived and justified independently of other goods. Rather, they have the status of one good amongst many, which may often – but do not necessarily – trump other goods. So while higher order goods would usually be considered to trump other situations, there may be situations in which an individual does not consider a hyper-good to be primary. He may, for example, be a committed universalist for many issues, but nonetheless decide on reflection to give a donation to the local hospital rather than to help victims of famine in another country, because of a commitment to helping his community. This notion of higher order goods is worth unpacking in the context of liberal universalism and duties to non-nationals.

Liberal Universalism as a Higher Order Good

There are a number of senses in which liberal universalism could be said to have the status as a higher order good in liberal cultures, depending on which type of liberal theory one embraces. For the precise status of liberty as a higher order good will vary according to the specific conception of how liberty contributes to human well-being or flourishing. A teleological liberal theory, for example, might hold that human beings are distinguished from other species by their capacity for reflection, and from this justify a system of rights that guarantees the maximum scope for exercising this capacity.[26] Liberal theories based on conceptions of interests or needs would ground rights in the shared interests of all human beings in security, subsistence and liberty, or some equivalent list.[27] The needs-based account may also be combined with a theory of basic or preconditional rights that are instrumental for realising all other goods and rights. Each of these accounts provides a moral justification for marking out liberal universalism as a higher order good, a good that is uniquely important to human flourishing. According to these theories, given its vital function in contributing to the good life, liberty should take precedence over other goods in most or even all circumstances. These types of justification for liberalism are likely to be familiar and intuitively persuasive for those bought up in liberal cultures. Conceptions of human interests and flourishing similar to these have shaped our beliefs about the value and goals of human life.

The special status of liberal values as higher order goods thus reflects their central role in shaping the identities, values and goals of those brought up in liberal cultures. While we are deeply committed to these conceptions, this commitment does not reflect the objective superiority or validity of liberalism. Rather, it is a product of the trajectory of political and moral thought over the past two millennia, a trajectory which was both historically contingent and, at least initially, particular to European culture. There was no inevitability about liberalism emerging as the salient good in contemporary western culture: perhaps the emphasis could equally have been on some alternative good, such as universal benevolence and the avoidance of suffering; or a teleology with more specific content, such as a form of virtue ethics or communism; or alternatively a welfare based conception of well-being that accorded a lesser status to individual rights. But whatever the reasons for the current configuration of values and beliefs in western liberal societies, these goods are not something we can now opt in or out of. The commitment to liberal values may be historically contingent, but this does not render it any less constitutive of the identities of members of liberal societies. This is surely the case with conceptions of liberal rights, whose persistence and extension of scope seems to point to a special sort of appeal. The extension of rights in liberal political theory from their initial application to wealthy white males, to universal coverage of all human beings (plus or minus unborn children, the mentally handicapped and insane, and so on), is not something that is easily revocable. Whatever the reasons for their extension (and it is beyond the scope of this discussion to examine these) once extended they are difficult to retract.

One reason for this lies in the moral grounding of such rights in a first order commitment to a conception of human interests or flourishing. Once the relevant characteristics – be they reason, material needs or interest in happiness – are attributed to all human beings, it becomes logically inconsistent to limit the application of rights. Indeed, a genuine and consistent denial of the moral claims of liberal rights theories would be extremely difficult for those with minimal intelligence and mental health who have been socialised in liberal democracies. While these societies clearly value a range of other goods – such as those associated with particular ties and community life, protecting the environment or promoting the arts, and so on – the liberal conception of the individual nonetheless shapes discourse and practice in the economic, social and political spheres of liberal democracies. It is a deep-seated (although often unarticulated) conviction that does not necessarily take precedence in all political questions, but is one which members of liberal societies automatically factor in to political decisions, and at least take into account even where other goods seem to over-ride these considerations. For those who have successfully internalised liberal values, the denial of their universal ascription would be logically incoherent. Nowadays western liberals cannot consistently defend a conception of individuals as free and equal whilst denying the right to freedom of the subjects of colonial rule, or illiterate rural communities, or refugees.

Of course there are a number of possible justifications for limiting the duties generated by universal rights. One could argue that rights would be more effectively realised through a division of responsibility into national units, or that intervention to ensure the rights of other peoples may be counterproductive in the longer-run. Or it could be claimed that realising universal rights would conflict with other goods, such as ensuring a good standard of living for fellow nationals, or encouraging a greater sense of responsibility for members of one's own community. Yet the point remains that in contemporary liberal thought, the moral grounds for the ascription of rights is based on a conception of relevant human characteristics that does not include race, nationality or religion. Once people are committed to such a conception of rights as grounded in shared characteristics – and the vast majority of those within liberal democracies will find resonance in such a conception – then there is a strong moral case to be made for recognising universal duties. The types of considerations used to justify women's rights or impartial justice at the national level would equally imply commitment to universal rights. The consistent application of rights theories, then, logically commits one to a universal conception, at least in principle.

The universalist implications of rights theories are reinforced by a second characteristic of liberal rights. The extension of rights is difficult to retract not only on grounds of moral consistency, but also because of the effect of the actual ascription of rights in mobilising people to protect these rights. Once rights have been ascribed, rights holders tend to be extremely resistant to attempts to have them rescinded. Those who have acquired and exercised certain types of individual freedom seem to become rather rapidly accustomed to a conception of themselves as autonomous choosers, or as the instigators of social change. Once mobilised in this way, right-holders are likely to be more critical than before of attempts to limit their freedoms.[28] This characteristic of rights, what one might term their tendency to be self-reinforcing, makes it difficult to obtain consent for pursuing goals that may involve restricting individual rights. In liberal democracies, the restriction of rights usually only secures widespread consent where vital goods are under immediate threat.

These considerations, while far from conclusive, help to explain why liberal universalism may be expected to continue to have the status of a higher order good for many or most members of liberal democratic societies. Recognising the historical contingency of liberal universalism need not imply that it is easily swept aside. Liberal rights have universalist implications that are difficult consistently to deny, and those exercising such rights tend to be tenacious in their defence.

Moral Alienation and Internal Critique of Liberal Universalism

Despite the robust nature of rights discourse in liberal cultures, there are clearly a number of circumstances under which individual or groups in liberal societies may fail to be moved by, or positively reject, liberal rights. In cases where members of liberal democracies do appear to have abandoned liberal rights theories altogether, it may be attributed to a failure to internalise intersubjective norms. Those who have been socialised in liberal societies and who nonetheless reject liberal values in favour of religious fundamentalism, extreme nationalism or generalised violence may be said to lack the psychological predisposition to empathy or the desire for affirmation that motivate individuals to internalise shared values (see Chapter Five). Where whole groups of society reject these shared liberal values, this form of alienation may be attributed to a lack of social recognition of the group in question, again linked to the psychological need for affirmation. It may also be linked to a failure to develop a capacity for empathy, which may result in an incapacity to engage in the sort of sympathetic identification with other individuals or groups that is encouraged by liberal universalist norms.

Quite apart from these psychological sources of a failure to internalise liberal values, there are also a number of material conditions that could constrain the process of internalising liberal norms. For example, those affected by acute poverty or violence may not feel particularly motivated to prioritise liberal values. This is an interesting possibility, but one that I am assuming that these conditions do not characterise most members of western liberal democracies.

The case of outright rejection of liberal values needs to be distinguished from the rather different question of internal critique of existing values. It was suggested in the Introduction that members of a particular culture may challenge existing norms and values through highlighting tensions between different goals, or through demonstrating the inadequacy of existing norms and values in the face of changing conditions. The first type of internal critique is most likely to be generated by tensions in the practical demands of different goals. The classic example of this form of tension within the liberal tradition is between the values of freedom from constraint and equality, and there have been recurrent debates on the correct balancing of the two values. Commitment to an extreme prioritisation of one of these values over the other may justify, respectively, right-wing libertarianism, or radical redistribution of wealth. Other examples might include conflicting views on the preconditions for ensuring liberty, or conflict between liberty and other goods. The second type of critique may be triggered by the inadequacy of existing norms to respond to new challenges. For example, an environmental crisis or economic decline may call for the re-evaluation of previously accepted goals.

These examples illustrate how the values of a particular society may allow significant scope for rational critique and social struggle. Where such forms of internal critique gain sufficient credence, they may in turn generate social change. Demands for equal treatment of women, or judicial reform, or the alleviation of poverty are likely to be viewed as legitimate by many citizens because they invoke a conception of the equal worth of all individuals, the right to impartial treatment, or the value of enabling people to fulfil their potential. These forms of critique are not external to the sorts of goods that are valued in liberal societies, but gain resonance precisely because they draw on shared beliefs. There may be disagreements on how these goods are prioritised, and even different grounds for holding these beliefs (e.g. religious or secular). But most of us can intuitively understand the appeal of the goods in question, even if on reflection we do not accord them priority over others.

Conclusion: Motivating Universal Duties

This chapter has covered a range of rather different issues, in order to tie up some of the loose ends of the non-rationalist account embraced in Chapter Five, and to draw out the implications of this account for political theory. It has considered the question of whether the non-rationalist account could be combined with a commitment to liberal universalist values; the status of liberal rights in relation to other values and norms; and the possibility of critique and outright rejection of norms within liberal societies. The first two of these three issues are especially important to the argument of this book, and it is worth recapitulating the claims I made.

In the first part of the chapter, I located the non-rationalist account in the context of communitarian political thought. The discussion rejected the notion that the ontological account of moral agency outlined in the previous two chapters committed one to prescriptive communitariansim. Those socialised in liberal democratic societies would be likely to retain a strong commitment to the notion of universal rights. Nonetheless, I did concede that on this ontological account, liberal universalist values would lose their foundational and political primacy. The account of liberalism as historically contingent and culturally specific implied denying it any privileged form of justification or absolute moral supremacy over other goods. Even according liberal universalism the status of higher order good will not provide a basis anywhere near as firm as the claims to universal validity and moral primacy made by cognitivist theories. So in what sense has the account of the last three chapters advanced the goal of motivating duties to refugees?

We need at this point to return to Taylor's claims about the need for articulation. Taylor argues that there has been a tendency in liberal theory to suppress the goods that underly notions of universal rights, and that this has made us lose sight of the sources of our commitment to such values. The demands of these universalist values are difficult to sustain, for their sources are suppressed by 'the dominance of proceduralist meta-ethics, which makes us see these commitments through the prism of moral obligation, thereby making their negative face all the more dominant and obtrusive and pushing the moral sources further out of sight'.[29] Taylor stresses the need for better articulation of these sources of liberal values, in order to help sustain our commitment to these ambitious moral norms and goals. He argues that articulating the goods embedded in our frameworks will help motivate respect for them: 'articulation can bring us closer to the good as a moral source, can give it power'.[30]

This claim needs more detailed substantiation, which can be provided by returning to the non-rationalist theory of motivation. The first point to stress is that articulating the goods underlying commitment to universal rights might help to motivate duties to those in distress. If duties to refugees can be understood as an extension of sympathy, then the empathic disposition may generate increased commitment to refugee rights. More extensive public discussion of the types of values that shape our commitment to universal rights would help people to clarify the grounds for their moral beliefs, hopefully triggering sympathy-based motivation.

Secondly, by emphasising that this conception of duties is a shared value, articulation may help link respect for these duties to the desire for affirmation. If respecting norms is seen as a means of securing affirmation, it will encourage a more thorough internalisation of such norms. In a sense this point is rather trite – most people could readily accept the influence of respected figures and prevalent social norms in motivating ethical behaviour. But my account of the desire for affirmation provides a fuller psychological explanation for this. It also helps explain how articulation could assist moral motivation. Articulating a shared commitment to the ethical goal of helping those in distress could encourage people to internalise this standard as a means of securing affirmation.

If we further accept a linkage between the need for individual and group recognition – or at least group recognition as a means of ensuring individual recognition – then there may also be a strong case for articulating shared values to those outside one's community of values. External recognition of these shared characteristics may strengthen the commitment of members to the goods in question. In this sense, it might be possible to build a conception of duties to refugees as constitutive of a nation's identity, and thus an integral component of national interest. I shall consider this possibility in the final chapter.[31]

Notes

[1] Michael Sandel, *Liberalism and the Limits of Justice* (Cambridge, 1982), p. 54.

[2] Sandel; Alasdair MacIntyre, *After Virtue: A Study in Moral Theory* (London, 1981), pp. 232–3; Charles Taylor, *Sources of the Self: The Making of Modern Identity* (Harvard, 1989), p. 514.

[3] For examples of this kind of prescriptive communitarianism, see Charles Taylor, 'The Politics of Recognition', in Charles Taylor and Amy Gutman (eds), *Multiculturalism: Examining the Politics of Recognition* (Princeton, 1994), pp. 25–73; and Michael Walzer, *Spheres of Justice: A Defence of Pluralism and Equality* (New York, 1983).

[4] The distinction between ontological and prescriptive communitarianism has been clarified by Charles Taylor, in 'Cross-Purposes: The Liberal–Communitarian Debate', in Nancy Rosenblum (ed.), *Liberalism and the Moral Life* (Cambridge, 1989), pp. 159–82; and by Axel Honneth in 'The limits of Liberalism: On the Political–Ethical Discussion Concerning Communitarianism', in Axel Honneth (ed.), *The Fragmented World of the Social* (New York, 1985), pp. 231–46.

[5] Sandel, p. 150.

[6] MacIntyre, *After Virtue*, especially Chapter 15; and Walzer, *Spheres of Justice*, as well as his *Interpretation and Social Criticism* (Cambridge, MA and London: Harvard University press, 1987).

[7] Taylor, 'The Politics of Recognition'.

[8] Walzer appears to take this route when he defends restricting the entry of large numbers of refugees who do not have ethnic or ideological affinities with the receiving community. See Walzer, *Spheres of Justice,* pp. 49–50.

[9] Jürgen Habermas, 'Struggles for Recognition in the Democratic Constitutional State', in Charles Taylor and Amy Gutman (eds), *Multiculturalism: Examining the Politics of Recognition* (Princeton, 1994), p. 130.

[10] Axel Honneth, *The Struggle for Recognition* (Cambridge, 1995).

[11] K. Anthony Appiah, 'Identity, Authenticity, Survival', in Charles Taylor and Amy Gutman (eds), *Multiculturalism: Examining the Politics of Recognition* (Princeton, NJ, 1994), p. 161.

[12] Henry Tam, *Communitarianism* (London, 1988), pp. 196–218.

[13] Sandel, *Liberalism and the Limits of Justice*, p. 9.

[14] David Hume, *A Treatise of Human Nature*, ed. Ernest C. Mossner (London, 1969 [1739]) p. 548.

[15] J.M. Bernstein, 'Moral Norms and Ethical Identities: On the Linguistification of the Sacred', in J.M. Bernstein (ed.), *Recovering Ethical Life: Jürgen Habermas and the Future of Critical Theory* (London, 1995), pp. 88–135.

[16] Charles Taylor, 'The Diversity of Goods', in Charles Taylor (ed.), *Philosophy and the Human Sciences* (Cambridge, 1985), pp. 234–8; and *Sources of the Self*, pp. 53–98. The account that follows is primarily drawn from Taylor's discussion in Part One of *Sources of the Self*.

[17] Taylor, *Sources of the Self*, p. 103.

[18] Ibid., p. 92.

[19] Ibid., p. 89.

[20] Ibid.

[21] Ibid., p. 495.

[22] The diversity and frequent incompatibility of different goods is likely to be characteristic of all cultures, although Taylor is not concerned with (and would probably view himself as unqualified to speak for) cultures other than his own. Instead, he traces the evolution of the articulation of different moral goods for 'modern, Western people'. *Sources of the Self*, p. 111.

[23] Ibid.

[24] Charles Taylor, 'Justice After Virtue', in John Horton and Susan Mendus (eds), *After MacIntyre: Critical Perspectives on the Work of Alasdair MacIntyre* (Cambridge, 1994), p. 38.

[25] Taylor, *Sources of the Self*, p. 63.

[26] One can finds this type of approach in the work of Axel Honneth. See 'The Limits of Liberalism'; and *Struggle for Recognition*. Daniel M. Weinstock's also argues that this should be the normative implications of Taylor's conception of the self. See 'The Political Theory of Strong Evaluation', in James Tully (ed.), *Philosophy in an Age of Pluralism: The Philosophy of Charles Taylor in Question* (Cambridge, 1994), pp. 171–93.

[27] See, for example, Alan Gewirth, 'The Basis and Content of Human Rights', and *Human Rights: Essays on Justification and Applications* (Chicago, 1982).

[28] This may be one reason why the language of individual rights seems to have more widespread appeal than related goals such as development or full employment. The struggle for freedom seems to be especially strong where liberty is defined in terms of individual rights, perhaps because the immediate benefits of such rights are more tangible to individuals.

[29] Taylor, *Sources of the Self*, p. 518.

[30] Taylor, *Sources of the Self*, p. 92.

Chapter Seven

Mobilising Commitment to Refugee Rights

The last six chapters have examined a range of political and philosophical theories, in the search for an adequate conception of duties to refugees. This final chapter attempts to pull together these insights, and consider what they imply for practical measures to counter restrictive refugee and asylum policies in Europe. What conclusions can we draw on best approaches for mobilising commitment to refugee rights in European host countries? And, importantly, what are the limitations of this sort of ethical approach?

The chapter will recapitulate the main argument of the book, and then go on to consider implications for lobby groups and individuals keen to expand refugee rights. In the final section, I will place this discussion in a political context, and consider the limits to a purely ethics-based approach to motivating commitment to refugee rights.

The Case for a Non-Metaphysical Account

Revisiting the Criteria for an Adequate Conception

The initial review of liberal universalist theories in the first part of the thesis revealed theoretical problems that necessitated a more extensive exploration of conceptions of moral agency and motivation. So although its starting point was an essentially practical problem – the goal of promoting a more generous refugee policy – the thesis developed a more general critique of rationalist and cognitivist assumptions in liberal political theory. Chapter Five laid the foundations for an alternative non-rationalist account, which was then substantiated by a discussion of communitarian theories in Chapter Six.

The need for this critique of moral agency becomes clear if one considers the failure of liberal universalism to meet the criteria for an adequate account of duties to refugees. It is worth briefly summarising the main steps in the argument in relation to these criteria. In the Introduction I set out three main criteria for assessing the adequacy of a conception of duties to non-nationals: normative desirability, practical feasibility, and internal coherence. I then proceeded to evaluate a range of contemporary liberal universalist accounts of duties to non-nationals on these three criteria. First, in Chapter Two I argued that utilitarian accounts failed to meet the criterion of normative desirability. Meanwhile, pure right-based universalist accounts met this criterion, but failed the test of practical feasibility. Chapter Three considered whether thin universalist accounts could retain a right-based universalist account whilst addressing the problem of feasibility. I argued that such accounts either failed to address the problem of feasibility, or else produced conceptually incoherent accounts. The third set of universalist theories to be considered were social contract accounts, which claimed to address the problem of motivation. Social contract theories failed either on the grounds of normative desirability, or alternatively on the criterion of feasibility.

The book attempted to elucidate the underlying weakness in liberal political theory that generated these tensions. In particular, it focused on the theoretical sources of the problem of practical feasibility, defined more specifically as the problem of moral motivation. Chapter Five examined the adequacy of the rationalist and cognitivist philosophical assumptions underlying liberal conceptions of moral motivation and agency. I argued that both the rationalist account of moral motivation and the cognitivist theory of morality were untenable. In Chapter Six I located this non-rationalist account in relation to communitarian political theories, and showed how this second order theory of moral agency and motivation was compatible with a substantive commitment to refugee rights.

In this way, the argument came full circle back to the practical question of duties to refugees. The non-rationalist account, I argued, was better equipped to fulfil the three practical criteria of an adequate account. It should certainly meet the requirement of internal coherence, which I hope has been demonstrated through the discussion of the last three chapters. The criteria of normative desirability and practical feasibility require more consideration, and I shall deal with each in turn.

Normative Desirability

First, on the question of normative desirability, I suggested in Chapter Six that embracing a non-rationalist account did not commit one to prescriptive communitarianism. Although rejecting the cognitivist premises of liberal universalism, the non-rationalist account could be combined with a commitment to a substantive conception of universal duties. As I argued in the last chapter, recognising the historical and cultural contingency of liberal values does not imply that such commitments are easily cast aside. Rather, these liberal beliefs are constitutive of the identities of those socialised in liberal democratic cultures, and pervade political and moral discourse in these societies. Acknowledging how these ideas have shaped and continue to shape our values and beliefs will not undermine their influence on conceptions of moral duty, but should instead help strengthen our commitment to them. Thus the rejection of a cognitivist derivation of universal duties does not imply abandoning notions of refugee rights, but would hopefully help us to articulate and realise our shared values.

Of course, the compatibility of the non-rationalist account with a substantive commitment to universal duties is contingent on the existence of the relevant beliefs and values in the society in question. Societies that are not committed to liberal universalist values may reject the right-based conception of duties to refugees, and in such cases there will be no Archimedean point from which to criticise non-liberal practices.[1] This does create a tension between the first order beliefs of those from liberal societies, and the second order non-rationalist account of moral agency. On the one hand, the depth of our commitment to liberal universalist conceptions of human flourishing makes it practically impossible to see non-liberal practices as anything other than morally aberrant. Yet at the same time, we should recognise at a more abstract level that these liberal beliefs are particular to our historical cultural context. While we would be in some sense denying our identity to reject these deep-seated beliefs, we should acknowledge that our commitment to them is not derived from some essential characteristic of human beings or the structure of language, but from a particular tradition of moral and political thought.

This claim about the historically contingent sources of moral beliefs may suggest a retreat into some form of cultural relativism. Cultural relativism is the view that the validity of moral beliefs depends on the value system of a particular group, and that there is no universal standpoint from which to evaluate the worth of different value systems. But the relativist thesis only holds on the empirical assumption that the world is split into separate, bounded communities. In fact, cultures have influenced one another in a multitude of ways, spreading values and beliefs through migration, conquest, trade and more recently through various forms of media and communications. So although values and beliefs may be derived from particular communities rather than from the essential characteristics of human beings, this does not mean there can be no evaluation between cultures. Where there is an overlap of values, or where a set of beliefs is shared by more than one society, some form of evaluation will be possible.

A second reason not to be too worried about a retreat into relativism is that concepts of human rights have proved to be particularly tenacious. As we saw in Chapter Six, once people are mobilised to defend individual or group rights, and especially once these rights have been socially and legally recognised, it is extremely difficult to roll back these claims. Individual rights-based political-legal systems have also proved to be the most compatible with capitalist economic systems – another reason for questioning the notion that they are fragile. Both of these factors suggest that commitment to liberal rights is likely to be particularly robust, following an expansive logic. We should not be overly anxious about an erosion in the strength of commitment to this tradition of liberal theory. Although it is not applied consistently in refugee policy, the theoretical and conceptual bases for the liberal universalist approach is deeply embedded in liberal democracies. Denying it a metaphysical grounding will not reduce its tenacity and appeal.

Practical Feasibility

If one were to choose between the liberal universalist and the non-rationalist accounts solely on the grounds of normative desirability, then it would not be evident why one should prefer the non-rationalist account. After all, this first order criterion was not the only reason for rejecting liberal universalist accounts. Rather, the problem with liberal universalism that emerged in the course of the first part of the thesis was that of feasibility: liberal universalist theories defined moral duties that seemed overly stringent, and insisted that the individual must respect these duties from an impartial perspective. It also claimed that this impartial perspective was in conflict with and should serve to constrain the personal, particular perspective.

Now at one level, the non-rationalist account could be accused of a similar problem of feasibility. For insofar as it retains the same first order conception of universal duties, its moral requirements must surely be just as demanding as those of the universalist. The difference between the two accounts is not so much in terms of the moral duties it has defined, but in the way it relates these duties to moral agency and motivation. On the rationalist account, the moral perspective was defined as an impartial, rational viewpoint, in which the individual is abstracted from her personal and social characteristics and ties. This assumed dichotomy created difficulties explaining how a person would be motivated to respect the requirements of morality. The non-rationalist account, by contrast, asserted that the individual is motivated to respect liberal norms precisely by virtue of her personal characteristics and shared beliefs. The individual's empathic disposition and her desire for affirmation motivate her to extend sympathy to others, and to internalise the intersubjective values of her community. Her psychological disposition to act morally is mediated through her cognitive capacities and the shared beliefs and norms that she acquires through socialisation. In liberal societies, these beliefs and norms are likely to include a liberal conception of autonomy and human flourishing, generating a moral commitment to respect individual human rights.

The non-rationalist account of motivation is not simply a better description of moral agency, but also helps address the problem of practical feasibility. It rejects the notion of a necessary split between self-interest and moral duty, instead positing the existence of two types of affective dispositions that motivate moral action. The first was the psychological desire for affirmation, which implies that the individual has an interest in being moral and in respecting the norms of one's community. Internalising shared values and acting in a way that is recognised and approved by the relevant community is important for the well-being and self-confidence of the individual. And second, the empathic disposition is generated by a form of anxiety that is alleviated through extending sympathy and assistance to others. Showing concern for the plight of others does not run counter to self-interest, but is a way of overcoming feelings of concern at the suffering of others. This account of the sources of moral motivation thus rejects any necessary dichotomy between self-interest and moral duty, helping to explain why and how people could be motivated to respect universal duties.

The rejection of a split between interest and duty is not only relevant to the question of individual motivation, but is also applicable to conceptions of national interest and refugee rights. In the Introduction I suggested that it was simplistic to assume that there was a conflict between national interests and refugee rights. Rather, shared values and beliefs play an important role in shaping conceptions of individual and collective interest. Such values can not only shape conceptions of what is in the self-interest of the nation, for example by influencing national policy objectives to achieve social stability or full employment. But more importantly for the issue of refugee rights, the intersubjective values of a community can generate an interest in extending moral duties to non-nationals. In other words, there can be a national interest in recognising the rights of refugees, even if this does not contribute to narrowly defined economic or political interests.

While this point about national interest and universal duties was rather tentatively made earlier in the book, I can now substantiate the claim through drawing on the discussion of the sources of individual moral motivation. First, we should consider how the empathic disposition could be relevant to the question of national interests and duties to non-nationals. The empathic disposition was characterised as a tendency to feel concern and sympathy, generated by anxiety about the suffering of others. Clearly this psychological disposition is characteristic of individuals rather than groups, and it would be methodologically unsound to attribute such a disposition to a *group* of people, over and beyond the psychology of its individual members. Nonetheless, individual members of a society are likely to be motivated by this form of anxiety, and may channel the anxiety into trying to influence national policies towards refugees. Insofar as members of a society can be said to have an interest in extending sympathy to refugees, an interest generated by the need to alleviate distress at the suffering of others, then this empathic disposition could be said to influence conceptions of national interest.

Far more significant for the question of conceptions of national interest, however, is the role of the desire for affirmation. I argued that the desire for affirmation motivates people to adhere to shared values and norms as a means of gaining positive recognition, love and respect. Now individuals seek affirmation not only for their individual characteristics and actions, but can also have an interest in ensuring the positive recognition of *shared* characteristics and actions. Where individuals have a strong sense of membership of a particular group, where they are conscious of a shared history and values, then the positive recognition of these characteristics by others can be an important source of affirmation. By articulating and acting on common values and beliefs the group both emphasises the characteristics that are common to its members, and seeks the affirmation of these characteristics from those outside of the group. In the case of nations, the desire for group affirmation will not necessarily generate benign behaviour – imperialism and ethnic conflict could both be said to be manifestations of a desire for group affirmation. Yet where the shared values and beliefs of the nation are shaped by a liberal commitment to universal human rights, then the group may be affirmed through securing international recognition of its human rights policy, or its generous treatment of refugees. This positive recognition of the shared liberal values of a nation may be an important source of affirmation for the members of the group. Again, this implies that extending duties to refugees may not conflict with the interests of the nation-state, but may positively contribute towards the well-being of its members. The effectiveness of these factors in motivating a more generous refugee policy is of course contingent on a range of other factors, and it would be naïve to be overly optimistic about the possibilities for changing current conceptions. Nonetheless, the analysis of moral motivation does suggest a number of practical approaches that could encourage more generous treatment of refugees. In this final chapter, I shall outline some of the practical implications of the non-rationalist account of moral motivation.

Implications for Refugee Policy

What, then, are the implications of this account of moral motivation for refugee policy? It was observed in the Introduction that the prevalent conception of the refugee problem was that of a conflict between national interests and refugee rights. Given that granting asylum to refugees was considered to run directly counter to the national interest, liberal universalist notions of duties to refugees seemed utopian and were at risk of being perceived as irrelevant to the policy debate. The task of the theoretical analysis was to salvage liberal universalist values from this fate, through re-working liberal assumptions about motivation and the relationship between self-interest and duty.

On the basis of this analysis, it is possible to suggest ways in which we might begin to reconceptualise the problem and thereby avoid this perceived conflict between duties to refugees and duties to compatriots. Most of the critique of this assumed dichotomy was levelled against liberal universalism's attachment to a similar dichotomy at the level of individual moral agency. Yet the two levels of individual moral agency on the one hand, and the ethics of national policy on the other, are closely inter-linked. What follows, then, are some general suggestions about ways in which citizens of liberal democracies could be encouraged to reconceptualise the refugee question, and adopt a more liberal approach to refugee rights.

Refugee Rights and Individual or Group Affirmation

The first way of transcending the assumed conflict between refugee rights and national interests is to encourage the development of group identities that incorporate a commitment to liberal universalist values. In other words, the point would be to promote ways of linking the desire for recognition with generous treatment of refugees.

There are two main ways in which groups may play a role in encouraging a more generous approach to the rights of non-nationals. First, where liberal universalist norms are seen as constitutive of a group's identity, then the realisation of these values should be a source of affirmation for members of the group. It should strengthen the group's explicit attachment to these values, reinforcing the sense of common purpose and thereby providing positive affirmation to group members. In this sense, the group's commitment to refugee rights and its achievement of these goals could be perceived as a source of fulfilment, rather than as running counter to the interests of its members.

Second, individual members of a group can also derive affirmation from their personal actions in promoting liberal universalist goals. If such actions are commended by other group members, there should be an incentive for individuals to engage in activities to promote refugee rights. This source of affirmation is not so much linked to the sort of fulfilment derived from a sense of common purpose: rather, it relates to the desire for affirmation of one's personal characteristics or behaviour, and the influence of this desire on an individual's acts.

I have chosen to refer to 'groups' instead of states, since in liberal democracies there are likely to be a number of different, mainly sub-national spheres that could provide a source of affirmation for individuals. Religious communities provide perhaps the most obvious example of this. For example, in the past (and to some extent still today) the Christian Church has played an important role in encouraging sympathy to those in need, and affirming members for their good deeds (or chastising them for bad ones). The Church provides a good example of the two types of affirmation mentioned above. Its commitment to duties of universal benevolence and the alleviation of suffering constitute shared norms and a set of collective goals that help shape the values and interests of its members, and its positive achievements in this sphere are a source of pride and affirmation for its members. It also encourages its individual members to act in a morally commendable way, providing spiritual or social affirmation to those who extend duties to those in need.

There are other important spheres or groups that can provide a source of affirmation for the ethical behaviour of members. Political parties, pressure groups and other associations with normative goals may all be partly defined by a commitment to liberal universalist goals. Again, they may provide a source of moral motivation to members through engendering a sense of collective purpose, and through affirming the actions of individual members. Institutions such as schools, professional or social groups may also endorse these types of goals, again shaping the values and interests of members and motivating action to respect the rights of refugees. Other relevant groups may include social classes, neighbours, groups of friends or ethnic associations. In a more loose sense, those who watch a particular soap opera or support a particular pop group may be influenced by the values conveyed through these media. They may also be defined as members of a group that is committed to particular values.

This account of the influence of communities on moral motivation is still somewhat vague. We need to consider how these kinds of group influence can be translated into practical action to promote a more generous refugee policy, and also what sort of measures could be taken to increase this form of influence. On the first question, sub-national groups may have an impact on refugee policy either through their direct actions, or through influencing policy makers to adopt more liberal policies. In the first case of direct action, groups or their individual members could be engaged in charity work, or give donations to assist refugees. In the second case, groups and their members could influence policy through voting and various forms of political activity and lobbying. One would also expect policy makers themselves to be influenced and affirmed by the groups of which they are members – be they the person's political party, professional association, church or constituency –, some of which may be committed to liberal universalist values.

On the second question of how to increase this form of influence, the most obvious routes would be through education and media. Campaigners for refugee rights should encourage schools to educate children on refugee issues and to develop a sense of responsibility for guaranteeing refugee rights. In particular, through the teaching of history, religious or citizenship studies, children should be encouraged to develop a sense of collective identity that incorporates a conception of duties to refugees. This type of identity formation could also be influenced by the media, for example through news reporting and popular entertainment. It is clearly also important to involve popular and respected public figures who may influence public perceptions of these issues. Finally, there is a need to explore ways of affirming individuals and groups that extend duties to refugees. In the case of individuals and groups there are a range of possible means of openly affirming action to promote refugee rights, including awards, media coverage, and positive encouragement from popular role models.

These suggestions for encouraging the extension of duties to refugees may seem familiar, and indeed one can find examples of all of these approaches in liberal democratic societies. But the psychological and philosophical analysis provided in this thesis can help explain why such techniques, many of which intuitively seem to be appropriate, can indeed have an impact on moral motivation. These forms of positive recognition of individuals and groups respond to a psychological need for affirmation, a need that many campaigners have instinctively understood, but which is not explained by rationalist theories of moral motivation.

National Identity and Liberal Universalist Values

In addition to the sorts of influence exerted by these communities, there may be scope for political leaders to help develop a sense of national identity that includes a liberal attitude towards refugees. Where a nation defines itself partly through adherence to certain values, then the realisation of these ethical goals can constitute a source of national pride. This seems to have been one of the ideas behind the British Foreign Secretary Robin Cook's much derided attempt to introduce an 'ethical dimension' to British foreign policy in the second half of the 1990s. The notion of linking national pride to respect for human rights is also evident in the rhetoric of United States foreign policy, and seems to influence some of the policies of smaller states that are keen to promote an image of themselves as more neutral and humanitarian members of the international community. Canada, Sweden and Norway are good examples of this latter tendency, and are all reputed for their relatively generous provisions for refugees. Whether or not these states live up to their liberal reputation is of course another question. But the point is that once the national identity is partly defined by a commitment to these values, then the sharp line between national interest and moral duty becomes blurred. Moreover, such rhetoric can serve to strengthen the commitment of the public to liberal values and goals. By articulating shared liberal universalist values and encouraging pride in these aspirations, politicians and public figures can mobilise support for more generous treatment of non-nationals.[2]

Some refugee lobby groups in the UK have begun to use these sorts of arguments in their campaigns to mobilise public support for refugee rights. A 2004 paper produced by eleven refugee, human rights and legal organisations suggested that the country's 'credibility is undermined when it is seen as shirking its internatinoal obligations by preventing refugees from reaching the UK'.[3] In similar vein, the Refugee Council has stressed the idea that '[t]he UK has long prided itself on its commitment to international law and human rights' – again, as an attempt to motivate commitment to refugee rights through emphasising universalism as part of the UK's tradition.[4] The predominant lobbying strategy, however, remains to castigate governments for not living up to international standards of refugee and human rights.

There are also indications that this sort of 'shared values' approach is emerging in European Union (EU) asylum and refugee policy. The EU has been developing a common policy on immigration and asylum since the early 1990s, under the rubric of 'cooperation in justice and home affairs'. However, from the outset it was heavily criticised by human rights and refugee groups as pursuing an overly restrictive approach. It has been castigated for its 'lowest common denominator' approach to legislative convergence of the EU countries' asylum policies; and for encouraging the development of a 'fortress Europe', keen to restrict migration and refugee flows into its member states. At the same time, the EU has been criticised for its persistent focus on control measures: efforts to step up border controls, common EU visa policies, readmission agreements to facilitate the return of irregular migrants, or police cooperation to combat irregular migration and trafficking. This 'security agenda' has become more pronounced since 11 September 2001, and the Madrid bombings of 11 March 2004. Yet EU countries and officials in the European Commission are clearly not insensitive to these criticisms. In 2004, there was a noticeable attempt to improve the image of the Union as a group of rights-respecting, liberal democratic countries. This was manifested as an attempt to reassert the 'normative' dimension of the EU's policies on immigration and asylum, including a restatement of commitment to.... The General Secretary of the European Council for Refugees and Exiles (ECRE) reflected this idea when he urged that: 'For the sake of Europe's values, its future communities and its credibility to the world, it is time to put refugee protection at the heart of Europe's asylum system'.[5] This is a good example of the importance for a community of being recognised as committed to particular norms and values – in this case, those of human rights and liberal democratic principles.

It should be acknowledged that this rhetoric is not always backed up with action. But it can create a self-reinforcing dynamic. Once ethical goals are explicitly articulated, they provide a standard against which to evaluate and criticise the state in question. This can provide a good lever for exerting pressure on the government. The success of this type of approach is of course contingent on the existence of the relevant shared values in a society, and the willingness of political leaders to be influenced by these values. Under these circumstances, a human rights-oriented policy and an intelligent public relations campaign might be able to generate a virtuous circle of public pressure and government action.

British Foreign Secretary Robin Cook's calls for an ethical dimension to foreign policy in the late 1990s could be said to have had this type of positive effect on British foreign policy. While British foreign policy priorities were to change after 11 September 2001, the first years of the Labour Party government offer an interesting example of how a government's stated commitment to certain norms and values can create pressure to meet expectations. Once Robin Cook had publicly stated his commitment to the ethical dimension of foreign policy, the government's actions on human rights were continuously evaluated and criticised by pressure groups according to whether they meet his own criteria; this in turn gave Cook an additional motive for ensuring that they did; and when he had taken measures to this end, he made a point of publicising them, again articulating and reinforcing the government's commitment to these values. The resulting changes in the government's human rights policy may not have been radical, but certainly represented an improvement on previous practice.

Finally, at the international level there is also scope for exerting influence on national policies, through affirmation from those outside the state. Liberal democratic states are especially sensitive to international criticism of their treatment of refugees, and refugee rights activists often use this form of critique as a means of applying pressure on states to respect refugee law. The discussion of the role of affirmation in moral motivation suggests the need for a shift in emphasis in this respect. Rather than adopting an exclusively critical approach, it may be more effective to explicitly affirm states where they are displaying generosity in their treatment of refugees. Where their policies fall short of the relevant standards, refugee rights activists should express concern about the state's failure to meet its own ethical and historical standards, rather than failure to conform to a set of externally imposed, 'universal' criteria.

Sympathy and Duties to Refugees

The notion of appealing to sympathy in order to motivate action to assist those in need is certainly not new – charities and pressure groups often adopt this type of approach in publicity and fund-raising campaigns. For example, pictures of starving children or victims of land mines can play an important role in mobilising public support for these causes.

But while these methods are widely used by many human rights and development campaigners and non-governmental organisations, they could be more effectively employed to encourage the extension of duties to refugees. For although there is often substantial media coverage and charity appeals for the victims of human rights abuses or conflict, there are relatively few attempts to link these cases to the question of granting asylum to refugees. Indeed, there seems to be a sharp distinction between media treatment of conflict and persecution on the one hand, and the question of how refugees should be treated once they reach countries of asylum on the other. Debate on the treatment of asylum seekers and refugees tends to revolve around the financial costs of processing claims, social security benefits for asylum seekers, and social tensions arising from the presence of large numbers of refugees in receiving communities. These are certainly important issues, and the problem of 'abusive' asylum seekers needs to be addressed. But any discussion of the refugee question should also be placed firmly in the context of the causes of flight, and the sorts of persecution or violence from which many asylum seekers seek refuge. As a *Guardian* editorial observed, 'The connection has to be drawn in the public mind between horrific atrocities we see on our television screens, and the frightened families who end up in the bed and breakfast at the end of our street'.[6] In principle there is scope for encouraging reporting on such stories. The type of sympathy incited by media coverage of famines or ethnic conflict should also be harnessed to encourage the extension of sympathy to asylum seekers and refugees.

Clearly, encouraging the media to report on refugee issues in this way, and to make a linkage to asylum seekers in the UK, is no easy task. The popular mass media has tended to adopt a hostile approach to asylum. Stories which are anti-immigrant are more likely to provoke the sort of strong, emotional reactions from readers that populist reporting aims at. As Baringhorst puts it, 'the features emphasized [in the mass media] are those such as the prominence of the actors, the novelty and sensationalism of the events, the emotionality of the content, conflict orientation, and the personalization and simplification of complex structures'.[7] Moreover, given the pressures and opportunities for restrictive populist mobilisation, there will simply be more political actors willing to draw on negative, often distorted information, than those seeking to motivate sympathy for the plight of asylum seekers.

There may be more scope for drawing these linkages between the causes of flight and the treatment of refugees in countries of asylum through school education. One example of this type of approach is the British Refugee Council's efforts to promote better education on refugee issues in schools, placing more emphasis on the personal experiences and accounts of refugees.[8]

Conflicts between Duties to Refugees and Other Values

I have argued that where liberal universal values are constitutive of a person's identity, respecting their claims and being recognised for so doing can be a source of personal affirmation. Moreover, most people have a psychological disposition to extend some form of sympathy to others, which can be channelled into a recognition of the duties defined by liberal universalism. As I hope to have shown, this implies reconceiving the relationship between interest and morality, specifically a rejection of the notion of any necessary conflict between moral duty and self-interest.

But clearly, even if this conception is able to mobilise increased commitment to refugees, there will be limits to the numbers of refugees that European countries are prepared to receive. Where do these limits lie? In fact, there are a number of different ways of defining them. In public discourse and the popular media, the impact of asylum and refugee flows is often defined in terms of tangible 'costs'. The implication is that once these costs reach a certain level, it is necessary to restrict further inflows. One such cost is the financial expenditure made through welfare and social assistance, or the costs of reception and processing cases. Another is the social cost of consumption of finite goods, such as accommodation in densely populated areas, or use of health, education or social services. A third tangible cost is often defined as the problem of the supposedly higher criminality rate of asylum seekers or refugees, or the threat they are considered to pose to domestic security. One can also discern a number of indirect costs that can be assumed to be imposed by the presence of large numbers of refugees refugees. Writers such as Bruce Ackerman or Matthew Gibney, for example, argue that restriction is justified where accepting more refugees would undermine public adherence to the norms of liberal welfare democratic states.[9] Newcomers may not be socialised in, or committed to, the values underpinning the reproduction of redistributive welfare systems, or liberal and democratic norms. Others have argued that restiction is justified in cases where public hostility towards refugees and asylum seekers threatens to produce a backlash in the form of anti-immigrant sentiment, racism, or inter-ethnic violence. If we accept that asylum seekers and refugees do, or potentially could, impose these sorts of costs, then it would seem logical to conclude that there must be some definable threshold beyond which restriction can be justified.

However, there are strong reasons why we should pull back from defining any hard and fast limit to the absorption capacities of European host countries. Most importantly, it is important to understand that conceptions of the costs of refugees and asylum seekers are to a large degree constructed. In other words, they are significantly shaped by shared beliefs about the impact of these groups, beliefs which are often ill-founded or exaggerated. This is clearly to some extent a function of the popular media's negative portrayal of refugee and asylum seekers, as well as attempts by political parties to mobilise support through restrictive asylum policies. But the tendency to over-state the impact of refugees and asylum seekers is also a function of the often emotive and symbolic functions served by these issues in political debates. As Ulrich Beck has pointed out, immigration and refugee problems act as a 'lightning rod' for channelling diffuse concerns about other sorts of social and economic anxieties.[10] There are many theories of why people in late modern societies are prey to these forms of anxieties: changing categories of collective identification, the declining role of the state in guaranteeing socio-economic security, and globalisation can all trigger concerns about identity and access to finite resources. These are often channelled into concerns about immigration and asylum, with refugees and immigrants in part blamed for declining welfare resources, unemployment, poor standards in schools, criminality, or declining solidarity. While these concerns clearly need to be taken seriously, they should encourage us to be cautious about taking current conceptions of the costs of asylum, or notions of 'absorption capacity', as immutable facts. Rather, this way of looking at notions of 'costs' suggests the need to better understand the sources of public concerns, and to attempt to reverse the tendency to channel these into asylum and refugee issues. This is not to deny that there are real costs linked to receiving asylum seekers and refugees: simply that these costs are commonly considered to be far greater than they probably are, because they are linked with a series of other socio-economic concerns and problems that have little to do with refugees and asylum as such.

This book, however, has focused on a rather different avenue for expanding duties to refugees. Rather than seeking to challenge beliefs about the impact of refugees, it has explored the possibility of encouraging more generous treatment of refugees based on a reconception of ethical conceptions of duties to refugees. The emphasis is not so much on chastising failure to live up to the ideal of univresal rights or absolute impartiality. Rather, I have argued that imposing stringent demands on the nationals of receiving countries may be counter-productive – it makes the liberal universalist case appear unsympathetic to the interests and concerns of people, as well as unrealistic. My suggested modification of the ontological and psychological claims of liberal universalism implies adopting a different approach.

Where duties to refugees seem to conflict with other goals, we should not present ourselves with a stark choice between a 'moral' and a 'self-interested' course of action. This is the traditional liberal universalist approach, which posits a conflict between the two, and castigates any failure to realise universals duties as unethical. This black and white approach to moral duty is precisely what makes the liberal universalist position appear so harsh and uncompromising where it is perceived as conflicting with other goals. My suggested alternative is to conceive of these conflicts as a normal and predictable feature of the diversity of values – values which were shaped through the evolution of particular traditions of political and moral thought. In so doing, we give ourselves a better basis for attempting to realise both sets of values. We do not necessarily have to choose between self-interest and moral duty, but can explore ways of realising both sets of claims. So that even where other claims seem to over-ride universal duties to refugees, and we fail to meet the standards of liberal universalism, this does not imply resignation to a self-interested or non-ethical course of action. Rather, we should seek other, 'second best' solutions to refugee problems. I mentioned some of these in the Introduction and Chapter One – the protection of refugees in regions of origin, forms of temporary protection in industrialised states, or internationally monitored repatriation.[11] While the liberal universalist would be likely to reject such measures as failing to meet ideal standards, the advantage of the communitarian ontological account of the sources of moral values is that it can recognise the existence of diverse and often conflicting values. Rather than presenting us with a trade-off calculation, it provides scope for seeking to maximise a range of different values.

Liberal universalism leaves us with a dual choice: either act consistently with moral norms, or accept that your behaviour is unethical and self-interested. It is little wonder that the ethical arguments for recognising duties to non-nationals appear unappealing and utopian. The revised, non-rationalist account of duties to refugees offers a superior set of options: aim to realise the higher order goods of liberal universalism, as these have a special place in our society's values and beliefs; respecting these duties does not conflict with self interest, but can be a source of affirmation and a means of channelling an empathic disposition; and if these higher order values do conflict with other goals and ties, explore ways of realising both sets of values. I hope to have shown why this second account avoids the descriptive and practical limits of liberal universalism, and why it would provide a better conceptual framework for encouraging a more generous policy towards refugees.

Notes

[1]   Although of course, non-liberal societies may have an equally or even more generous conception of duties to refugees. See, for example, Gaim Kibreab, *African Refugees: Reflections on the African Refugee Problem* (Trenton, NJ, 1985), p. 68 – although Kibreab doubts if such generosity is sustainable under conditions of poverty.

[2]   Scanlan and Kent make this point in their discussion of United States immigration policy. See john A. Scanlan and O.T. Kent, 'The Force of Moral Arguments for a Just Immigration Policy in a Hobbesian Universe', in Mark Gibney (ed.), *Open Borders' Closed Societies? The Ethical and Political Issues* (New York, 1989), p. 63.

[3]   Refugee Council, *Refugees: Renewing the Vision* (London: 2004).

[4]   Refugee Council, *Press Release*, 29 March 2004.

[5]   European Council for Refugees and Exiles, *News Release*, 22 October 2004.

[6]   *The Guardian*, 10 February 1999.

[7]   Sigrid Baringhorst, 'Symbolic Politics of Multiculturalism: How German Cities Campaign against Racism', in Sophie Body–Gendrot and Marco Martiniello (eds), *Minorities in European Cities: The Dynamics of Social Integration and Social Exclusion at the Neighbourhood Level* (London, 2000), pp. 75–87.

[8]   Jill Rutter, *Refugees: We Left Because We Had To: Citizenship Teaching for 11–18 Year Olds* (London, 2004).

[9]   Bruce A. Ackerman, *Social Justice in the Liberal State* (New Have, Conn., 1980); Matthew Gibney, *The Ethics and Politics of Asylum* (Cambridge, 2004).

[10] Ulrich Beck, *Risk Society: Towards a New Modernity* (London, 1996).

[11] These policies were discussed in Chapter One. They include measures to address the causes of flight (conflict prevention, development, intervention); mechanisms for ensuring that refugees are protected in their regions of origin (protection of internally displaced persons, safe havens or measures to protect and assist returning refugees); or alternative forms of protection that fall short of the provisions of the Geneva Convention

– for example the temporary protection regimes adopted in Europe and North America to protect refugees from the former Yugoslavia.

Bibliography

Ackerman, Bruce A. (1980), *Social Justice in the Liberal State* (New Haven, Conn: Yale University Press).

Anscombe, G.E.M. (1958), 'Modern Moral Philosophy', *Philosophy*, 13:124, pp. 1–19.

———— (1978), 'On Practical Reasoning', in Joseph Raz (ed.), *Practical Reasoning* (Oxford and New York: Oxford University Press), pp. 33–45.

Appiah, K. Anthony (1994), 'Identity, Authenticity, Survival: Multicultural Societies and Social Reproduction', in Charles Taylor and Amy Gutman (eds), *Multiculturalism: Examining the Politics of Recognition* (Princeton, NJ: Princeton University Press), pp. 149–63.

Baier, Annette (1991), *A Progress of Sentiments: Reflections on Hume's Treatise* (Cambridge, Mass and London: Harvard University Press).

Baringhorst, Sigrid (2000), 'Symbolic Politics of Multiculturalism: How German Cities Campaign against Racism', in Sophie Body–Gendrot and Marco Martiniello (eds), *Minorities in European Cities: The Dynamics of Social Integration and Social Exclusion at the Neighbourhood Level* (London and Basingstoke: Macmillan), pp. 75–87.

Barry, Brian (1975), *The Liberal Theory of Justice* (Oxford: Clarendon Press).

———— (1982), 'Humanity and Justice in Global Perspective', in J. Roland Pennock and John W. Chapman (eds), *Ethics, Economic, and the Law* (New York: New York University Press), pp. 219–52.

———— (1987), 'Can States be Moral? International Morality and the Compliance Problem', in Robert J. Myers (ed.), *International Ethics in the Nuclear Age* (Lanhan and London: University Press of America), pp. 85–110.

———— (1989), *Theories of Justice* (Berkeley, CA: University of California Press).

———— (1991), 'Justice as Reciprocity', in Brian Barry (ed.), *Liberty and Justice: Essays in Political Theory* (Oxford: Clarendon Press), pp. 211–41.

———— (1995), *Justice As Impartiality* (Oxford: Clarendon Press).

Barry, Brian and Robert E. Goodin (1988), 'Symposium on Duties Beyond Borders', *Ethics*, 98, pp. 647–756.

———— (eds) (1992), *Free Movement: Ethical Issues in the Transnational Migration of People and of Money* (Hemel Hempstead: Harvester Wheatsheaf).

Baxter, Brian (1986), 'The Self, Morality and the Nation–State', in Anthony Ellis (ed.), *Ethics and International Relations* (Manchester: Manchester University Press), pp. 114–26.

Beck, Ulrich (1996), *Risk Society: Towards a New Modernity* (London: Sage).

Beitz, Charles R. (1979), *Political Theory and International Relations* (Princeton, NJ: Princeton University Press).

———— (1985), 'Justice and International Relations', in Charles Beitz, Marshall
    Cohen, A. John Simmons and Thomas Scanlon (eds), *International Ethics*
    (Princeton, NJ: Princeton University Press), pp. 282–311.
———— (1989), 'Sovereignty and Morality in International Affairs', in David Held
    (ed.), *Political Theory Today* (Cambridge: Polity), pp. 236–54.
Bellamy, Richard (1992), *Liberalism and Modern Society: A Historical Argument*
    (University Park, PA: The Pennsylvania State University Press).
Belsey, Andrew (1992), 'World Poverty, Justice and Equality', in Robin Attfield
    and Barry Wilkins (eds), *International Justice and the Third World* (London
    and New York: Routledge), pp. 35–49.
Bentham, Jeremy (1970), 'Anarchical Fallacies', in A.I. Melden (ed.), *Human
    Rights* (Belmont: Wadsworth), pp. 28–39.
Bernstein, J.M. (1995), 'Moral Norms and Ethical Identities: On the
    Linguistification of the Sacred', in J.M. Bernstein (ed.), *Recovering Ethical
    Life: Jürgen Habermas and the Future of Critical Theory* (London and New
    York: Routledge), pp. 88–135.
Boswell, Christina (1999), 'The Conflict between Refugee Rights and national
    Interests', *Refugee Survey Quarterly*, 18:2, pp. 64–84.
———— (2000), 'European Values and the Asylum Crisis', *International Affairs*,
    76:3, pp. 537–57.
———— (2003), 'The "External Dimension" of EU Immigration and Asylum
    Policy', *International Affairs*, 79:3, pp. 619–38.
———— (2003), *European Migration Policies in Flux. Changing Patterns of
    Inclusion and Exclusion* (Oxford: Blackwell's and Chatham House).
Boucher, David and Paul Kelly (eds) (1994), *The Social Contract from Hobbes to
    Rawls* (London and New York: Routledge).
Brown, Chris (1999), 'Universal Human Rights: A Critique', in Tim Dunne and
    Nicholas J. Wheeler (eds), *Human Rights in Global Politics* (Cambridge:
    Cambridge University Press), pp. 103–27.
Brown, S.M. (1993), 'Hobbes: The Taylor Thesis', in Preston King (ed.), *Thomas
    Hobbes: Critical Assessments* (2 vols, London: Routledge), vol. 2, pp. 99–115.
Brubaker, Rogers (1992), *Citizenship and Nationhood in France and Germany*
    (Cambridge, Mass: Harvard University Press).
Bubner, Rüdiger (1982), 'Habermas' Concept of Critical Theory', in John B.
    Thompson and David Held (eds), *Habermas: Critical Debates* (London and
    Basingstoke: Macmillan Press), pp. 42–56.
———— (1988), 'The Possibilities of Practical Reason', in Rudiger Bübner, *Essays
    in Hermeneutics and Critical Theory* (New York: Columbia University Press,
    trans. Eric Matthews), pp. 147–94.
Burke, Edmund (1986), *Reflections on the Revolution in France* [1970] (ed.)
    Connor Cruise O'Brien (London: Penguin).
Burton, John W. (1972), *World Society* (Cambridge: Cambridge University Press).
Carens, Joseph H. (1987), 'Aliens and Citizens: The Case for Open Borders', *The
    Review of Politics*, 49:2, pp. 251–73.

——— (2003), 'Who Should Get In? The Ethics of Immigration Admissions', *Ethics and International Affairs*, 17:1, pp. 95–110.

Charvet, John (1995), *The Idea of an Ethical Community* (Ithaca: Cornell University Press).

——— (1998), 'The Possibility of a Cosmopolitan Ethical Order Based on the Idea of Universal Human Rights', *Millenium*, 27:3; 523–41.

Coles, Gervaise (1990), 'Approaching the Refugee Problem Today', in Gil Loescher and Laila Monahan (eds), *Refugees and International Relations* (Oxford: Clarendon Press), pp. 373–410.

Collinson, Sarah (1994), *Europe and International Migration* (London and New York: Pinter Publishers for the Royal Institute of International Affairs).

Defoe, Daniel (1709), *A Brief History of the Poor Palatine Refugees, Lately Arriv'd in England* (London).

Donnelly, Jack (1989), *Universal Human Rights in Theory and Practice* (Ithaca: Cornell University Press).

Dummett, Ann (1992), 'The Transnational Migration of People Seen From Within a Natural Law Tradition', in Brian Barry and Robert E. Goodin (eds), *Free Movement: Ethical Issues in the Transnational Migration of People and of Money* (Hemel Hempstead: Harvester Wheatsheaf), pp. 169–81.

Dworkin, Ronald (1996), *Taking Rights Seriously* (Guildford: Duckworth).

Ellis, Anthony (1992), 'Utilitarianism and International Ethics', in Terry Nardin and David R. Mapel (eds), *Traditions of International Ethics* (Cambridge: Cambridge University Press), pp. 158–79.

Elster, John and John E. Roemer (eds) (1991), *Interpersonal Comparisons of Well–Being* (Cambridge: Cambridge University Press).

European Council for Refugees and Exiles (2004), *News Release*, 22 October.

Fishkin, James (1982), *The Limits of Obligation* (New Haven: Yale University Press).

Fishkin, James (1986), 'Theories of Justice and International Relations: The Limits of Liberal Theory', in Anthony Ellis (ed.), *Ethics and International Relations* (Manchester: Manchester University Press), pp. 1–12.

Frost, Mervyn (1996), *Ethics in International Relations: A Constitutive Theory* (Cambridge: Cambridge University Press).

Garward, John A. (1971), *The English and Immigration, 1880–1910* (Oxford: Oxford University Press).

Gauthier, David P. (1969), *The Logic of Leviathan: The Moral and Political Theory of Thomas Hobbes* (Oxford: Clarendon Press).

——— (1970), *Morality and Rational Self–Interest* (Englewood Cliffs, NJ: Prentice–Hall).

——— (1986), *Morals By Agreement* (Oxford: Clarendon Press).

Gewirth, Alan (1978), *Reason and Morality* (Chicago: University of Chicago Press).

——— (1982), *Human Rights: Essays on Justification and Applications* (Chicago: University of Chicago Press).

Gibney, Mark (ed.) (1989), *Open Borders? Closed Societies?: The Ethical and Political Issues* (New York and London: Greenwood).

Gibney, Matthew (2004), *The Ethics and Politics of Asylum: Liberal Democracy and the Response to Refugees* (Cambridge: Cambridge University Press).

Goodin, Robert E. (1985), *Protecting the Vulnerable: A Reanalysis of our Social Responsibilities* (Chicago: University of Chicago Press).

——— (1988), 'What Is So Special About Our Fellow Countrymen?', *Ethics*, 98:4, pp. 663–86.

Goodwin–Gill, Guy S. (1996), *The Refugee in International Law* (Oxford: Clarendon).

Gordenker, Leon (1987), *Refugees in International Politics* (London: Croom Helm).

Gough, J.W. (1936), *The Social Contract: A Critical Study of its Development* (Oxford: Clarendon Press).

Grotius, Hugo (1953), *Grotius on the Rights of War and Peace*, trans. William Whewell (Cambridge: Cambridge University Press).

Habermas, Jürgen (1992), 'Citizenship and National Identity: Some Reflections on the Future of Europe', *Praxis International*, 12:1, pp. 1–19.

——— (1990), 'Discourse Ethics: Notes on a Program of Philosophical Justification', in Jürgen Habermas (ed.), *Moral Consciousness and Communicative Action* (Cambridge: Polity Press), pp. 116–94.

——— (1994), 'Struggles for Recognition in the Democratic Constitutional State', in Charles Taylor and Amy Gutman (eds), *Multiculturalism: Examining the Politics of Recognition* (Princeton: Princeton University Press), pp. 107–48.

Hansen, Jens Vedsted (1999), 'Non–Admission Policies and the Right to Protection: Refugees' Choice versus States' Exclusion', in Frances Nicholson and Patrick Twomey (eds), *Refugee Rights and Realities* (Cambridge: Cambridge University Press), pp. 269–88.

Hart, H.L.A. (1967), 'Are There Any Natural Rights?', in A. Quinto (ed.), *Political Philosophy* (Oxford: Oxford University Press), pp. 53–66.

Hathaway, James C. (1991), *The Law of Refugee Status* (Toronto and Vancouver: Butterworths).

Held, David (1980), *Introduction to Critical Theory: Horkheimer to Habermas* (London: Hutchinson).

Helton, Arthur C. (1990), 'What is Refugee Protection?', *International Journal of Refugee Law*, Special Issue, pp. 119–29.

Hobbes, Thomas (1957), *Leviathan* [1651] (London: J.M. Dent and Sons).

Hoffmann, Stanley (1981), *Duties Beyond Borders: On the Limits and Possibilities of Ethical International Politics* (Syracuse, NY: Syracuse University Press).

Honneth, Axel (ed.) (1992), *Philosophical Interventions in the Unfinished Project of Enlightenment: Studies in contemporary German Social thought* (Cambridge, Mass: MIT Press).

—— (1992), 'Moral Development and Social Struggle', in Axel Honneth et al. (eds), *Cultural–Political Interventions in the Unfinished Project of Enlightenment* (Cambridge, Mass: MIT Press).

—— (1995), 'The Limits of Liberalism: On the Political–Ethical Discussion Concerning Communitarianism', in Axel Honneth (ed.), *The Fragmented World of the Social: Essays in Social and Political Philosophy* (New York: State of New York Press), pp. 231–46.

—— (1995), *The Fragmented World of the Social: Essays in Social and Political Philosophy* (New York: State University of New York Press).

—— (1995), *The Struggle for Recognition: The Moral Grammar of Social Conflicts*, trans. Joel Anderson (Cambridge: Polity Press).

Honneth, Axel and Hans Joas (eds) (1991), *Communicative action: Essays on Jürgen Habermas's The Theory of communicative action* (Cambridge: Polity).

Hume, David (1969), *A Treatise of Human Nature* [1739] (ed.) Ernest C. Mossner (London: Penguin Books).

—— (1975), *Enquiries Concerning Human Understanding and Concerning the Principles of Moral* [1777] (ed.) L.A. Selby–Bigge (Oxford: Oxford University Press).

Kagan, Shelly (1989), *The Limits of Morality* (Oxford: Clarendon Press).

Kagan, Jerome and Sharon Lamb (eds) (1987), *The Emergence of Morality in Young Children* (Chicago: University of Chicago Press).

Kant, Immanuel (1977), *Kant's Political Writings, Cambridge Studies in the History and Theory of Politics* (ed.) Hans Reiss (Cambridge: Cambridge University Press).

—— (1989), *The Moral Law: Kant's Groundwork of the Metaphysic of Morals* (ed.) and trans. Herbert James Paton (London and New York: Routledge).

Keohane, Robert O. (ed.) (1986), *Neorealism and its Critics* (New York: Columbia University Press).

—— (1984), *After Hegemony: Cooperation and Discord in the World Political Economy* (Princeton, N.J: Princeton University Press).

Keohane, Robert O. and Joseph S. Nye (1977), *Power and interdependence: World Politics in Transition* (Boston: Little, Brown).

Kibreab, Gaim (1985), *African Refugees: Reflections on the African Refugee Problem* (Trenton, NJ: Africa World Press).

Krasner, Stephen D. (1978), *Defending the National Interest: Raw Materials Investment and U.S. Foreign Policy* (Princeton: Princeton University Press).

Kratochwil, Friedrich (1982), 'On the Notion of "Interest" in International Relations', *International Organization*, 36:1, pp. 1–30.

Kymlicka, Will (1990), *Contemporary Political Philosophy* (Oxford and New York: Clarendon Press).

Kymlicka, Will (1995), *Multicultural Citizenship: A Liberal Theory of Minority Rights* (Oxford and New York: Clarendon University Press).

Linklater, Andrew (1998), *The Transformation of Political Community: Ethical Foundations of the Post–Westphalian Era* (Columbia: University of South Carolina Press).

Luard, Evan (ed.) (1967), *International Protection of Human Rights* (London: Thames and Hudson).

Lukes, Steven (1982), 'Of Gods and Demons: Habermas and Practical Reason', in John B. Thompson and David Held (eds), *Habermas: Critical Debates* (London and Basingstoke: Macmillan Press), pp. 134–48.

MacIntyre, Alasdair (1981), *After Virtue: A Study in Moral Theory* (London: Duckworth).

Mackie, David (1985), *Ethics: Inventing Right and Wrong* (London: Penguin).

MacPherson, C.B. (1962), *The Political Theory of Possessive Individualism: Hobbes to Locke* (Oxford: Oxford University Press).

Mann, Michael (1999), 'The Dark Side of Democracy: The Modern Tradition of Ethnic and Political Cleansing', *New Left Review*, 235, pp. 18–45.

——— (1995), 'A Political Theory of Nationalism and its Excesses', in Sukumar Perival (ed.), *Notions of Nationalism* (Budapest: Central European University press), pp. 44–64.

Mapel, David R. (1992), 'The Contractarian Tradition and International Ethics', in Terry Nardin and David R. Mapel (eds), *Traditions of International Ethics* (Cambridge: Cambridge University Press), pp. 180–200.

Marrus, Michael (1985), *The Unwanted: European Refugees in the 20th Century* (Oxford and New York: Oxford University Press).

——— (1990), 'The Uprooted: An Historical Perspective', in Goran Rystad (ed.), *The Uprooted: Forced Migration as an International Problem in the Post–War Era* (Lund: Lund University Press), pp. 47–58.

Marx, Reinhard (1995), 'Non–Refoulement, Access to Procedures, and Responsibility for Determining Refugee Claims', *International Journal of Refugee Law*, 7:3, pp. 383–406.

McCarthy, Thomas (1984), *The Critical Theory of Jürgen Habermas* (Cambridge: Polity Press).

Mead, George Herbert (1934), *Mind, Self, and Society* (Chicago: University of Chicago Press).

Medina, Vicente (1990), *Social Contract Theories: Political Obligation or Anarchy?* (Maryland: Rowman and Littlefield Publishers).

Mill, John Stuart (1991), *On Liberty and Other Essays* [1859] (ed.) John Gray (Oxford: Oxford University Press).

Miller, David (1988), 'The Ethical Significance of Nationality', *Ethics*, 98:4, pp. 647–62.

——— (1995), *On Nationality* (Oxford: Oxford University Press).

Morgenthau, Hans Joachim (1954), *Politics among Nations: The Struggle for Power and Peace* (New York: Alfred Knopf).

Nagel, Thomas (1978), *The Possibility of Altruism* (Princeton, NJ: Princeton University Press).

———— (1991), *Equality and Partiality* (Oxford and New York: Oxford University Press).

Nardin, Terry (1992), 'Alternative Ethical Perspectives on Transnational Migration', in Brian Barry and Robert E. Goodin (eds), *Free Movement: Essays in the Transnational Migration of People and of Money* (Hemel Hempstead: Harvester Wheatsheaf), pp. 267–78.

Nozick, Robert (1974), *Anarchy, State, and Utopia* (Oxford: Basil Blackwell).

O'Neill, Onora (1996), *Towards Justice and Virtue: A Constructive Account of Practical Reasoning* (Cambridge: Cambridge University Press).

Pogge, Thomas W. (1989), *Realizing Rawls* (Ithaca and London: Cornell University Press).

Rawls, John (1972), *A Theory of Justice* (Oxford and New York: Oxford University Press).

———— (1985), 'Justice as Fairness: Political not Metaphysical', *Philosophy and Public Affairs*, 14:3, pp. 223–51.

———— (1987), 'The Idea of an Overlapping Consensus', *Oxford Journal of Legal Studies*, 7:1, pp. 1–25.

———— (1993), *Political Liberalism* (New York: Columbia University Press).

———— (1993), 'The Law of Peoples', in Stephen Shute and Susan Hurley (eds), *On Human Rights* (New York: Basic Books), pp. 41–82.

———— (1999), *The Law of Peoples* (Cambridge, MA and London: Harvard University Press).

Raz, Joseph (1982), 'The Claims of Reflective Equilibrium', *Inquiry*, 25, pp. 307–30.

———— (1988), *The Morality of Freedom* (Oxford: Clarendon Press).

Refugee Council (2004), *Refugees: Renewing the Vision* (London: Refugee Council).

———— (2004), *Press Release*, 29 March.

Ruggie, John Gerard (1983), 'Human Rights and the Future International Community', *Daedalus*, 112:4, pp. 93–110.

Runstom–Ruin, Cecilia (1993), *Beyond Europe: The Globalization of Refugee Aid* (Lund: Lund University Press).

Rutter, Jill (2004), *Refugees: We Left Because We Had To*: *Citizenship Teaching for 11–18 Year Olds* (Refugee Council: London).

Salomon, Kim (1991), *Refugees in the Cold War: Toward a New International Refugee Regime in the Early Post–War Era* (Lund: Lund University Press).

Sandel, Michael (1982), *Liberalism and the Limits of Justice* (Cambridge: Cambidge University Press).

Scanlan, John A. and O.T. Kent (1989), 'The Force of Moral Arguments for a Just Immigration Policy in a Hobbesian Universe: The Contemporary American Example', in Mark Gibney (ed.), *Open Borders? Closed Societies?: The Ethical and Political Issues* (New York and London: Greenwood), pp. 61–107.

Scanlon, Thomas M. (1982), 'Contractualism and Utilitarianism', in Amartya Sen and Bernard Willliams (eds), *Utilitarianism and Beyond* (Cambridge: Cambridge University Press), pp. 103–28.

Schlesinger, Arthur M. (1987), 'National Interests and Moral Absolutes', in Robert J. Myers (ed.), *International Ethics in the Nuclear Age* (Lanham and London: University Press of America), pp. 15–37.

Schochet, Gordon J. (1990), 'Intending (Political) Obligation: Hobbes and the Voluntary Basis of Society', in Mary G. Dietz (ed.), *Thomas Hobbes and Political Theory* (Kansas: University Press of Kansas), pp. 55–73.

Schulze, Hagen (1996), *States, Nations and Nationalism: From the Middle Ages to the Present*, trans. Willian E. Yuill (Oxford: Blackwell).

Sen, Amartya (1990), 'Plural Utility', in Jonathan Glober (ed.), *Utilitarianism and its Critics* (New York: Macmillan), pp. 78–88.

———(1997), *Choice, Welfare and Measurement* (Cambridge, MA: Harvard University Press).

Sen, Amartya and Bernard Wiliams (eds) (1981), *Utilitarianism and Beyond* (Cambridge: Cambridge University Press).

Shapiro, Ian (1986), *The Evolution of Rights in Liberal Theory* (Cambridge: Cambridge University Press).

Shue, Henry (1980), *Basic Rights: Subsistence, Affluence and U.S. Foreign Policy* (Princeton, NJ: Princeton University Press).

——— (1988), 'Mediating Duties', *Ethics*, 98, pp. 687–704.

Simpson, Sir John Hope (1939), *Refugees: A Review of the Situation Since September 1938* (Oxford: Oxford University Press).

Singer, Peter (1979), *Practical Ethics* (Cambridge and New York: Cambridge University Press).

——— (1985), 'Famine, Affluence and Morality', in Charles R. Beitz, Marshall Cohen, Thomas Scanlon and A. John Simmons (eds), *International Ethics* (Princeton, NJ: Princeton University Press), pp. 247–61.

Singer, Peter and Renata Singer (1989), 'The Ethics of Refugee Policy', in Mark Gibney (ed.), *Open Borders? Closed Societies? The Ethical and Political Issues* (New York and London: Greenwood), pp. 111–30.

Statt, Daniel (1995), *Foreigners and Englishmen: The Controversy over Immigration and Population, 1660–1760* (Newark: University of Delaware Press).

Stoessinger, John George (1956), *The Refugee and the World Community* (Minneapolis: University of Minneapolis Press).

Stroud, Barry (1988), *Hume* (London and New York: Routledge).

Tam, Henry (1988), *Communitarianism: A New Agenda for Politics and Citizenship* (London: Macmillan).

Taylor, Charles (1985), 'The Diversity of Goods', in Charles Taylor (ed.), *Philosophy and the Human Sciences: Philosophical Papers 2* (Cambridge: Cambridge University Press), pp. 230–47.

——— (1985), *Philosophy and the Human Sciences: Philosophical Papers 2* (Cambridge: Cambridge University Press).

——— (1989), *Sources of the Self: The Making of Modern Identity* (Harvard: Harvard University Press).

————— (1989), 'Cross–Purposes: the Liberal–Communitarian Debate', in Nancy Rosenblum (ed.), *Liberalism and the Moral Life* (Cambridge, MA and London: Harvard University Press), pp. 159–182.

————— (1994), 'The Politics of Recognition', in Charles Taylor and Amy Gutman (eds), *Multiculturalism: Examining the Politics of Recognition* (Princeton, NJ: Princeton University Press), pp. 25–73.

————— (1994), 'Justice After Virtue', in John Horton and Susan Mendus (eds), *After MacIntyre: Critical Perspectives on the Work of Alasdair MacIntyre* (Cambridge: Polity), pp. 16–43.

Thompson, John B. and David Held (eds) (1982), *Habermas: Critical debates*, *Contemporary Social Theory* (London: Macmillan).

Tilly, Charles (1975), *The Formation of National States in Western Europe* (Princeton, NJ: Princeton University Press).

Tuck, Richard (1979), *Natural Rights Theories: Their Origin and Development* (Cambridge: Cambridge University Press).

Tully, James (ed.) (1994), *Philosophy in an Age of Pluralism: The Philosophy of Charles Taylor in Question* (Cambridge: Cambridge University Press).

United Nations High Commissioner for Refugees (1997), *The State of the World's Refugees: A Humanitarian Agenda* (Oxford and New York: Oxford University Press).

Vernant, Jacques (1953), *The Refugee in the Post–War World* (London: George Allen and Unwin).

Vincent, John R. (1986), *Human rights and International Relations* (Cambridge: Cambridge University Press and Chatham House).

Vitoria, F. de, Vitoria (1991), Political Writings (ed.), A. Pagden (Cambridge: Cambridge University Press).

Waldron, Jeremy (ed.) (1987), *Nonsense upon Stilts: Bentham, Burke and Marx in the Rights of Man* (London: Methuen).

Walvin, James (1984), *Passage to Britain: Immigration in British History and Politics* (Harmondsworth: Penguin).

Walzer, Michael (1983), *Spheres of Justice: A Defence of Pluralism and Equality* (New York: Basic Books).

————— (1990), 'The Communitarian Critique of Liberalism', *Political Theory*, 18:1, pp. 6–23.

————— (1994), *Thick and Thin: Moral Argument at Home and Abroad* (Notre Dame: University of Notre Dame Press).

————— (1987), *Interpretation and Social Criticism* (Cambridge, MA and London: Harvard University Press).

Weinstock, Daniel M. (1994), 'The Political Theory of Strong Evaluation', in James Tully (ed.), *Philosophy in an Age of Pluralism: The Philosophy of Charles Taylor in Question* (Cambridge: Cambridge University Press), pp. 171–193.

Weis, Paul (1994), *The Refugee Convention, 1951: The Travaux Preparatoires Analysed* (Cambridge: Cambridge University Press).

Wellmer, Albrecht (1991), *The Persistence of Modernity: Essays on Aesthetics, Ethics, and Postmodernism*, trans. David Midgley (Cambridge, MA: MIT Press).

Wicclair, Mark R. (1980), 'Rawls and the Principle of Noninternvention', in H. Gene Blocker and Elizabeth H. Smith (eds), *John Rawls's Theory of Social Justice: An Introduction* (Athens, Ohio: Ohio University Press), pp. 289–308.

Williams, Bernard (1971), 'Morality and the Emotions', in John Casey (ed.), *Morality and Moral Reasoning: Five Essays in Ethics* (London: Methuen), pp. 1–24.

——— (1976), *Problems of the Self: Philosophical Papers 1956–1972* (Cambridge: Cambridge University Press).

——— (1981), *Moral Luck: Philosophical Papers 1973–1980* (Cambridge: Cambridge University Press).

——— (1993), 'A Critique of Utilitarianism', in J.J.C. Smart and Bernard Williams (eds), *Utilitarianism: For and Against* (Cambridge: Cambridge University Press), pp. 77–150.

——— (1985), *Ethics and the Limits of Philosophy* (London: Fontana).

Wollheim, Richard (1986), *The Thread of Life* (Cambridge: Cambridge University Press).

Zolberg, Aristide (1987), 'Keeping Them Out: Ethical Dilemmas of Immigration Policy', in Robert J. Myers (ed.), *International Ethics in the Nuclear Age* (Lanham and London: University Press of America), pp. 261–97.

Index